MW00571530

IN TUNE

IN TUNE

CHARLEY PATTON
JIMMIE RODGERS

AND THE

ROOTS OF AMERICAN MUSIC

BEN WYNNE

LOUISIANA STATE UNIVERSITY PRESS

BATON ROUGE

Published by Louisiana State University Press
Copyright © 2014 by Louisiana State University Press
All rights reserved
Manufactured in the United States of America
Second printing

DESIGNER: Michelle A. Neustrom
TYPEFACE: Whitman
PRINTER AND BINDER: Maple Press

LIBRARY OF CONGRESS CATALOGING-IN-PUBLICATION DATA

Wynne, Ben, 1961–
    In tune : Charley Patton, Jimmie Rodgers, and the roots of American music / Ben
Wynne.
      pages cm
    Includes bibliographical references and index.
    ISBN 978-0-8071-5780-0 (cloth : alk. paper) — ISBN 978-0-8071-5781-7 (pdf) —
ISBN 978-0-8071-5782-4 (epub) — ISBN 978-0-8071-5783-1 (mobi) 1. Popular music—
United States—1921–1930—History and criticism. 2. Blues (Music)—To 1931—History
and criticism. 3. Old time music—History and criticism. 4. Patton, Charley, 1891–1934.
5. Rodgers, Jimmie, 1897–1933. I. Title.
    ML3477.W96 2014
    781.6430973—dc23

                                                                        2014011363

For Lily

CONTENTS

Illustrations follow page 115

ACKNOWLEDGMENTS

This book would not exist without the help and encouragement of many people to whom I will always be grateful. I would like to thank Rand Dotson, Lee Sioles, Jennifer T. Keegan, as well as the entire staff at LSU Press for being willing to take a chance on my manuscript. They have been a pleasure to work with. I would also like to express my gratitude to Stan Ivester for his outstanding editing skills. This book is the culmination of a five-year effort during which time I met and corresponded with staff members at many libraries and archives. I would like to thank the always friendly and helpful staff at the Mississippi Department of Archives and History as well as the staffs at the Eudora Welty Public Library in Jackson, Mississippi; the Tennessee State Library and Archives; the Alabama Department of Archives and History; the Department of Archives and Special Collections at the J. D. Williams Library at the University of Mississippi; the Southern Historical Collection at the University of North Carolina; the Hal Leonard Corporation; Special Collections at the Mississippi State University Library; the Millsaps-Wilson Library at Millsaps College; Special Collections at the University of Southern Mississippi Library; the University of Georgia Library; the John Harrison Hosch Library on the Gainesville campus at the University of North Georgia; the Roberts-LaForge Library at Delta State University; the Country Music Hall of Fame in Nashville; the Rock and Roll Hall of Fame in Cleveland; and the Delta Blues Museum in Clarksdale, Mississippi. Although readers will find their names in the book's notes and bibliography, I would like to recognize Nolan Porterfield, David Evans, Barry Mazor, Gayle Dean Wardlow, Stephen Calt, and Jocelyn Neal, whose past work on Jimmie Rodgers and Charley Patton provided insights and biographical details that were helpful as I tried to weave together the stories of the two artists.

I owe a debt of gratitude to many individuals who were willing to take the time to help me with photographs and illustrations. Paramount among these were Greg Johnson, curator of the outstanding Blues Archive at the University of Mississippi, Neil Lerner from the Music Department at Davidson College, John Tefteller of Blues Images, Betty Lou Jones, president of the Jimmie Rodgers Foundation in Meridian, Mississippi, and cartographer Mary L. Eggart. I would also be remiss if I did not thank Tom Rushing for his correspondence about his family as it related to the Charley Patton song "Tom Rushen Blues," and Robin Rushing, noted daughter of the Delta and good friend whose input and opinions on the southern existence are always highly valued. Though I have never met him personally, I would like to thank Keith Richards of the Rolling Stones who, many years ago, shocked me by answering my simple fan letter with a handwritten note paying homage to Jimmie Rodgers. In its own way that note was inspirational, and I still have it in a frame on my wall.

I owe an intellectual debt to a number of people who have helped and inspired me through the twists and turns of academia. Among those are Robert Haws, Charles Reagan Wilson, Ted Ownby, Nancy Bercaw, Sheila Skemp, Michael Namorato, Charles Eagles, and David Sansing, all of whom were at the University of Mississippi while I was in graduate school; Ron Howard and Kirk Ford from Mississippi College in Clinton, Mississippi; Charles Sallis and Robert S. McElvaine from Millsaps College in Jackson, Mississippi; and James C. Cobb from the University of Georgia. I would also like to acknowledge every teacher that I had at St. Andrew's Episcopal School in Jackson, Mississippi, from the first grade in 1967 through my senior year in 1979. They laid the foundation for my life at what I believe is one of the best schools in the nation.

I would like to thanks a number of my colleagues from the University of North Georgia, including Chris Jespersen, dean of the College of Arts and Letters; Ric Kabat, associate dean of the College of Arts and Letters; and Tim May, chair of the History, Anthropology, and Philosophy Department, all of whom helped me locate resources for this effort. I would also like to single out my history and anthropology colleagues from the university's Gainesville and Oconee campuses who, for the last decade, have creating a warm and collegial work atmosphere conducive to academic ventures of all kinds. These fine scholars are Jeff Pardue, our department's associate chair, and in alphabetical order, Martin Blackwell, Lorraine Buchbinder, Dee Gillespie, Phillip Guerty, George Justice, Jonas Kauffeldt, Johanna Luthman, Heather Murray,

Steve Nicklas, Clay Ouzts, Warren Rogers, and Pam Sezgin. It is a pleasure to know them all, and I hope I am worthy of their company. I would also like to thank my former colleague at the University of North Georgia, the formidable political scientist and proud North Carolinian H. Lee Cheek, for his encouragement and counsel.

I have many old friends and family members who are perpetually a great source of comfort. While my friends are numerous, I would like to acknowledge three, Brant Helvenston, John Leggett, and Alan Vestal, who were there during a rough patch while this manuscript was in process. Last but certainly not least, I would like to thank my wonderful family, Carly Wynne, Lily Wynne, Patricia Wynne and Noelle Wynne, who are always there with love and support. Lily, I am proud to dedicate this book to you.

IN TUNE

INTRODUCTION

We never would have had any segregation if people
would've had enough music around.

—B. B. KING

On the afternoon of May 24, 1933, a frail, tubercular shell of a man strained to stand up and lean toward a microphone set to capture his voice. He was a singer and songwriter who had come to the Victor recording studios in New York City to make a record, though his doctors had advised him against making the trip. It was clear to anyone who came in contact with the man that he belonged in bed. His lungs were failing and his body ached, but despite the pain he was still able to sing. Refusing to cut the session short, he recorded four songs that day. At one point he could no longer stand—it took too much energy—and a well-stuffed lounge chair was brought into the studio for him to sit in as he performed. A special cot had already been set up nearby so that he could lie down and rest between takes. Everyone at the session, the engineers and the other musicians, at some point were likely thinking the same thing: How is this man able to perform? How is he still alive? When the session ended, the singer struggled to make his way out of the building, into a taxi, and back to his room at the Taft Hotel. Less than forty-eight hours later the end came. Jimmie Rodgers, the Father of Country Music, was dead at the age of thirty-five.[1]

A little less than a year later and a world away, another doomed musician gave his final performance as he drew some of his last breaths. At the time he was not famous like Jimmie Rodgers, but one day his singing and guitar playing would influence musicians all over the world. He was a bluesman who practiced his craft on the stages of black juke joints and at house parties in places like Robinsonville, Mississippi; Helena, Arkansas; and Bogalusa, Louisiana. Locally renowned, he had a following who admired the way

1

he played, the way he looked and moved onstage, and the dark charisma that manifested itself through his music. He had even managed to have some of his songs captured on disk by a recording company, no small feat considering his race and the place and times in which he lived. In early April of 1934 the man performed publically for the last time in front of a large and boisterous crowd of agricultural laborers and other members of the local African American community at the Strickland plantation near Greenwood, Mississippi. It was a typically raucous Saturday night and, according to later reports, the bluesman was in top form despite recently being in poor health, displaying symptoms of heart disease. While such plantation "frolics" usually lasted into the wee hours, the event was cut short after an angry woman in the crowd went after a man with an ax. She allegedly killed the man and the party with one well-aimed swing. Mayhem ensued, and many of those in attendance fled the scene rather than risk being questioned or detained by local white police. Among those who disappeared into the night was the party's main attraction, the bluesman who, although he did not know it at the time, would never perform in public again. Several days later he began having heart problems serious enough to warrant a rare visit to a doctor. Not long after that, his heart gave out completely and, on April 28, 1934, he died in bed in a ramshackle old house where he sometimes stayed in Indianola, Mississippi. Charley Patton, King of the Delta Blues, was gone at the age of forty-three.[2]

Charley Patton and Jimmie Rodgers are today little more than distant memories, shadowy figures kept alive by true believers who worship the echoes of their performances, or by cultural historians who struggle to explain the complicated origins of American popular music. However, the lives and careers of these two men, one black and one white, paralleled one another in culturally significant ways during a unique era. The individual stories of their lives and careers, fused together, tells a single story of a world segregated by race but filled with black and white individuals who lived lives that were not all that different from one another, a story in which poverty and class-consciousness weakened racial boundaries to allow the release of an important American art form. The story of Patton and Rodgers, contemporaries who never met, is the story of cultural flux in a land where everything was designed to remain the same, where prejudice was written into law and where the word "mixing" had a special connotation fraught with danger. The story is also one of triumph in that the two men represented twin strands of cultural development that could not be separated by human law. They produced not black music or white music, but American music that oppressive racial etiquette ultimately could not soften or mute.

Charley Patton and Jimmie Rodgers were both born a little more than a century ago, and both died not long afterwards. They were not only both from the South, they were both from the same state, Mississippi, and their birthplaces were separated by only a hundred miles or so. At the time that they came into the world, no one knew that they were special. No one knew that somewhere deep inside both men there were sparks that would one day ignite a fire that would help advance American culture. Patton and Rodgers both grew up poor. They came of age in a region and a state suffering from a myriad of social ills. The deck was stacked against them, and the miracle was not that they became notable as musicians, but that their talent was able to rise above the conditions under which they lived. At the turn of the twentieth century the American South was not a region well known for nurturing the formal arts. While there were pockets of sophisticated culture in places like New Orleans, Charleston, or Savannah, much of the South was still the land of cotton, where old times were definitely not forgotten. As a result, it was also the land of poverty, and the land of perilously complex and conflicted social tenets, most of which were tied to race. Still, Patton and Rodgers persevered, creating their own popular art—a form of primitive art or folk art—that would endure and become more potent with each passing decade. In this environment Charley Patton and Jimmie Rodgers did not merely entertain. They expressed themselves in ways that moved people, reflecting both the times in which they lived and a range of human emotions that were timeless.

In the South during the early twentieth century few people had hope. A small number of wealthy and influential white southerners in the states of the old Confederacy controlled most of the money, most of the political offices, and almost all of the good fortune. The masses, both black and white, were poor and uneducated, and they stayed that way generation after generation. In the South an entertainer—be it a singer, a guitar player, a fiddler, or even just a good storyteller—provided a certain type of magic that the common man and woman needed. They provided the escape that most people of the period sought, a few moments of pleasure to temporarily soften a lifetime of struggle. The better the entertainer, of course, the more potent the magic. "Nostalgia, fantasy, romance and pure escapism are of course very much part of that larger

reality through which we define ourselves and learn to cope with life's vaga-
ries," prominent country-music historian Bill C. Malone has asserted. "And
like no other musical form in our culture, country music lays bare the uncer-
tainties that lie at the heart of American life." Likewise, in his definitive study
of blues culture David Evans maintained that "blues singers offer no solutions
for life's problems, but instead dramatize their existence and try to make the
best of them by stating them on social occasions where their universality can
be affirmed."[3] In short, music, regardless of the race of the composers who
make it or the audiences that listen to it, can bring people together in ways
that calm life's rougher moments and temper the harsher realities that many
people grapple with on a daily basis.

Charley Patton and Jimmie Rodgers wrote songs, played the guitar, and
sang in ways that allowed them to stand apart from other performers of their
era and make a name for themselves. Patton would later be recognized as a
central figure in the history of blues music in America while, in Nashville,
Rodgers would be known in country-music circles as "the man who started
it all." With every generation, artists appear on the scene who personify their
times and are able to express those times so thoroughly through their art that
they influence those who follow them. Such was the case with Patton and
Rodgers. When they played and sang, their audiences listened to the music
and were able to absorb its meaning because they related to it completely,
whether it was happy or sad, frivolous or reflective, or whether it evoked the
Lord or the devil. They related to Patton and Rodgers because the two men
were of their time and place. They were a product of the audiences that they
performed in front of. They grew up in a common environment with them.
They were storytellers whose musical musings evoked and chronicled an era
and seemed to speak directly to the lives of those who listened. As John A.
Burrison pointed out in the introduction to his collection of southern folktales, "People have always loved a good story. For thousands of years stories
were narrated strictly orally, the storyteller performing before an audience of
family, neighbors, or patrons. As prime sources of entertainment and knowledge, good stories were too precious a commodity to allow to die on the lips
of the originator. They were carried on within the community."[4] The music
of Patton and Rodgers was original though it also reflected popular tastes of
the period. It mimicked certain things that had come before, but also created
something new, something that would have great influence for years to come.
With regard to their work being heard by larger audiences, the two men were

also at an advantage in that, unlike many of their contemporaries, and those who came before them, they were recorded.

Charley Patton and Jimmie Rodgers came of age in a strictly segregated South where, on the surface at least, they seemed to occupy different social strata codified by southern legislatures and guarded by a specter of violence that manifested itself from time to time as the need arose. However, the Jim Crow system that took root in the states of the former Confederacy following the Civil War and Reconstruction had greater depth, and a great effect on both the black and white communities. The presence of segregation in the South divided the races from a legal perspective, but in practice it created a social system conducive to silencing the poor, both black and white. It was a system that quickly and easily gave way to an oligarchy in the southern states that lasted for a century after the Civil War, and the effects of which are still felt today. On the surface, it would seem that in the segregated South all whites had privilege, or at least a degree of privilege, with the African American population being subjugated as a permanent social and political underclass. This interpretation of the Jim Crow South tells only half the story. The other half of the tale involves a permanent white underclass that segregation also created. Segregation firmly established the color line that powerful whites in the South used to maintain political dominance over their poorer white brethren, but it also blurred that same color line by drawing poor blacks and whites together in a permanent economic underclass. When racial supremacy became the foundation on which the southern political system rested, as was the case in the states of the old Confederacy following Reconstruction, it subordinated most, or maybe every, other pertinent issue of the day. White supremacy became the primary political doctrine of the power structure in the South, overshadowing more practical concerns that affected everyone, such as good roads, good schools, diverse forms of economic development, innovative or progressive political action, and poverty. Chester "Howlin' Wolf" Burnett, the African American bluesman who literally studied at the feet of Charley Patton and listened to Jimmie Rodgers records as a child, summed up the situation perfectly when he told an interviewer, "A lot of poor white folks come out of the South playing good music, you know what I mean. . . . They come along on that same track that I fall on."[5]

While segregation and its consequences created a restricted social universe and stagnant, ultra-conservative political environment in the states of the old Confederacy, it did not cause cultural development in the region to cease. Music in particular could not be confined. It moved freely through the open air from the ear of one musician to another, fostering creative exchange either directly or indirectly. Black and white musicians in the South took in and processed each other's songs while traveling medicine shows and carnivals brought new music in from the outside world. "Like other expressions of American culture in the late nineteenth century," music historian James P. Kraft wrote, "music mirrored the changing times. Musical styles broke with tradition and became more complex in melody, harmony, tonality and form . . . . New styles of music, with greater emphasis on rhythm, freedom and energy characterized the new world of cultural innovation." New songs were created from scratch or reshaped from existing tunes—an old verse here, a new verse there. The end result was a musical melting pot that never stopped percolating, a fluid fusion of sounds that could miraculously sidestep race in a region where race was the litmus test for just about everything. Charley Patton and Jimmie Rodgers came of age in this environment. They were a product of it, as was the music they produced and the audiences who loved to hear them perform.[6]

Charley Patton plied his trade in the Mississippi Delta, and if you were black in the early twentieth century there was probably no place bleaker. The Delta region encompassed the northwestern part of the state of Mississippi along the Mississippi River and contained very rich soil suitable for growing cotton. By the early twentieth century, thousands of black sharecroppers in the Delta worked cotton plantations owned by a handful of wealthy whites, and they usually worked for very little money. In the decades following the Civil War and Reconstruction, those who ran the state of Mississippi promoted the sharecropping system that became widespread throughout the South. The system was designed to do two things: keep landowners supplied with laborers who would keep the land productive at minimum cost, and keep large segments of the African American population economically dependent on the white establishment. At the beginning of the growing season a landowner rented land to a sharecropper and lent the sharecropper money that would allow him to cover expenses and purchase everything he needed to make a crop. The landowner charged interest on this money, and theoretically the sharecropper would pay his rent and the balance of his loans when his cotton crop was gathered and sold. In many cases, however, arrangements were made by which the sharecropper was never able to completely cover his debts at the end of the growing season, leaving him in even further debt at the beginning of the next crop cycle.

In the end, the sharecropper could never quite break even with the landowner, could never quite pay off his obligations, and in the states of the old Confederacy legislators authored laws that made it difficult for a sharecropper to square his debts and move from one place to another to find more lucrative employment. The result for many sharecroppers was dawn-to-dusk labor that never improved their station in life and kept them tied to land they did not own, paying off a perpetual debt that could never be completely retired. By the early twentieth century only about 8 percent of African Americans in the major cotton-producing regions of the South owned their own land. It was a stagnant existence for most black farmers of the period, but anyone who complained too loudly about the arrangement might end up losing what little livelihood he had because the foundation of the system was more than economic. It was a system that kept the black populations subordinate, particularly in areas like the Mississippi Delta where African Americans outnumbered whites by a large majority. It was a means of social control. By the time Charley Patton was born, the Civil War had been over for a generation, and so had slavery, but racial oppression in the Delta was alive and well. The man who would become a great musical legend was born a prisoner of this world, and only his music made its way to freedom.[7]

Jimmie Rodgers was also trapped, but in a different way. In many parts of Mississippi at the turn of the twentieth century, being poor and white was only marginally better than being poor and black. The color line that was so rigidly defined in law was not nearly as rigid with regard to the distribution of economic resources. For both whites and blacks, good jobs were hard to come by, as were profitable farms on which a family could make a good living. Like their black counterparts, many white sharecroppers were mired in an unending cycle of debt that did not discriminate, and most whites who did non-farming work were in equally dire straits. By 1900 only around half of whites in the "Cotton South" were landowners, with much of the farming population working as tenants or sharecroppers on property they did not own. As a white man in the South, Jimmie Rodgers had more freedom of movement than the average African American, but aside from that he never really had anything else for much of his life. He was not subjugated in the same manner as Charley Patton and other people of color, but as a young man he did not flourish, either. In Mississippi, before he started making records, being white was just about all that Jimmie Rodgers had going for him, and in the end that was not really all that much. As a result, he left his home in Meridian, in the eastern part of the state, and for a time rode the rails, hoping to make enough money to feed his family. He traveled around the country as a railroad man, but it was still difficult for him to divest himself of the anguish that he had become accustomed to as a poor southern white. "My pocket is empty, and my heart is full of pain," he sang in one of his most popular songs, "I'm a thousand miles away from home just waiting on a train." Even after he hit it big, he was not destined to enjoy the fruits of his labors for very long.[8]

In large part it was the harsh environment in which they both grew up that made Charley Patton and Jimmie Rodgers extraordinary musicians. Their experiences provided the themes for many of their songs: the struggles of an insecure existence, the hope of escape, lost love, found love, transience, hell-raising, and death. All of these were themes that audiences of the period understood and lived with. These ideas also transcended racial boundaries at a time when so much else did not. Although Charley Patton sang the blues at house parties or in black juke joints, and Jimmie Rodgers sang his country laments in white honky-tonks and later on larger stages, both men sang about similar things. They sang to audiences that were different on the surface, but similar on the inside. While their interpretations of the music may have been different, the music itself was thematically integrated in a land where hard living on many levels was the general rule for individuals of both races. Although music never completely trumped racism and erased the color line, Rodgers and Patton both sang about hard times. They sang about escape as a means of relief from a bad situation, including physical escape through transience. They sang about leaving town on trains, or walking away down long dusty trails or dirt roads. These were themes that poor audiences both black and white could relate to—the idea, many times a fantasy, that one day they would be able to relocate, make a new start, and leave their troubles behind them. For instance, in one verse of "Train Whistle Blues," Rodgers wrote in a rhythmic sequence usually associated with black blues:

> I'm weary now, I want to leave this town
> I'm weary now I want to leave this town
> I can't find a job, I'm tired of hanging around.[9]

Expressing the same sentiment, though with a bit of a harder edge, Patton wrote in "Down the Dirt Road Blues":

> Every day seems like murder here
> Every day seems like murder here
> I'm gonna leave tomorrow, I know you don't bid my care.

Rodgers and Patton also sang about temporary emotional escape through bouts with the bottle or escapades with women. They sang about whiskey and relationships between the sexes, love and hate, cruelty and sentimentality, and the need for redemption, all tenets of the universal human condition. Their music made everyone, regardless of color, tap their foot, jump for joy, yell, scream, or cry. Whereas Rodgers wrote about a "mean mama" that he had come across in his "Jimmie's Mean Mama Blues," Patton complained about a woman he knew who had "a heart like a piece of railroad steel" in his song "Heart Like Railroad Steel." Patton wrote an autobiographical tune, "Tom Rushen Blues," about waking up in jail after a drinking spree, while Rodgers recorded "In the Jailhouse Now," about being incarcerated after "playing cards and shooting dice" with a disreputable friend. Both men recorded versions of "Frankie and Johnny," the traditional folk tune about a woman who shoots the man who was "doing her wrong." In addition, both Rodgers and Patton recorded songs with religious themes, praising the Lord and proselytizing about life and death.

The music of Charley Patton and Jimmie Rodgers would have never become famous without Thomas Edison. During the 1870s, Edison invented what he referred to as his "talking machine" but what everyone else would call the phonograph and later just the plain old record player. The phonograph made Patton and Rodgers immortal. It allowed their music to be passed on to future generations and, as a result, it allowed their influence on other musicians to spread not just geographically, but over time as well. Before the phonograph, an audience could listen to a performance and, if it was a good performance, the experience might linger for a while until the memory of it eventually faded. The echo of any performance did not last long. The music went out into the air and then dissipated in much the same way that a morning fog evaporates in the sunlight. The audience was left always wanting to hear a good performer again, and the phonograph allowed good performers to give millions of performances without physically playing a musical instrument or singing a single note. Recorded music could not completely substitute for a live performance, which by definition was raw and uncensored, but for a listener it was the next best thing. Recordings brought to life the performer to a much greater degree than a piece of formalized sheet music, which at the time was also an effective vehicle for preserving tunes. With a record, listeners could hear an artist's work as many times as they liked. They could memorize the words, the tonal qualities and inflections of the voice that set the artist's work apart, and they could hear the essence of the music's message over and over again. In short, they could take the music's message to heart.

While the recording of music allowed artists to transmit a particular thought, emotion, or idea to a much wider audience, it also very quickly became a business. Charley Patton and Jimmie Rodgers were part of the first generation of American recording artists. Though they did not know it at the time, as they created their music they were also involved in what would become a multi-billion-dollar industry. During the early twentieth century, astute entrepreneurs were quick to recognize that there was money to be made producing music for the masses. The ability to make records gave artists an unlimited audience, and those in that audience who were moved by a certain song or performance were willing to pay to bring the music into their home. They were willing to part with hard-earned money to have the experience of listening to their favorite artist literally at their fingertips. Still, the music had to be good and it had to have its own appeal, which was why Charley Patton and Jimmie Rodgers became such influential figures. Many of those who acquired Patton and Rodgers records in the years before the Second World War were younger artists, singers, and players who idolized the two men and who sang their songs and practiced their chord changes and picking styles. These younger artists, in turn, passed the music on to the next generation. Today the songs of Charley Patton and Jimmie Rodgers are sometimes referred to as "roots music," and for good reason. Together the two men represent a significant part of the taproot of a great family tree of musical artists who for decades have driven American popular culture.

While the music that Patton and Rodgers created drew crowds to their live performances, both men also were popular because they projected a certain image of mystery that future generations of solo entertainers in a variety of genres would also seek to create. Both were American musical prototypes who carried on the tradition of the lone troubadour, the itinerate minstrel who could grab his guitar and move with stealth from place to place, plying his trade before audiences and moving on once again before the applause even died down. They were performers who could adjust to playing with others, but whose music and message came from such a personal place that it was most powerfully delivered to the public in a straightforward manner with limited accompaniment. This tradition of the traveling performer or itinerate minstrel has ancient origins in world culture. For hundreds if not thousands of years performers held a special place in the courts of kings and queens, with nobles and peasants alike, and in the streets of bustling cities and isolated villages. In medieval times the minstrel was a prominent member of European society who the masses both embraced and feared. He generated excitement and joy as well as a sense of mystery wherever he performed. "People flocked to hear him and loved him for his fantastic nature and dexterity," Paul Henry Lang wrote of the medieval minstrel. "Yet they feared him because of his multiple abilities, which seemed sinister not only to the Church, which realized the enticing charm of entertainment, but to the people too, who suspected supernatural powers at play."

Parallel characters in many African cultures were musicians and poets called *griots* (pronounced GREE-ohs, with a silent *t*). While some griots served particular villages as part songster and part oral historian, others traveled from place to place performing for any audience that was willing to be seduced by their talents. "Griots are found in the earliest records of African civilization," Khonsura A. Wilson has pointed out. "The griot was compelled by fame, vocation, and tradition to keep the national record or teach through moral narratives. . . . These poets were both feared and admired for their gifts." All of these descriptions could easily apply to musicians and poets of the more modern world and certainly to Patton and Rodgers, both of whom carried on time-honored traditions of individuality and personal expression. Like the traveling minstrels of England and France or the griots of West Africa, Patton and Rodgers were primarily solo performers, which placed them on a unique cultural plane. Wherever they went and whenever they performed, they had an intensely pure relationship with audiences, an emotionally charged relationship undiluted by the presence of a supporting cast of other musicians. To many they were also the personification of freedom in that they were mobile at a time when many who saw them play or listened to their records were not.

They could ramble from one stage to the next, moving from place to place, from town to town, or even from state to state in a manner that most members of their audience would never experience. Their unsettled existence generated a degree of intrigue. They seemed to have a certain degree of independence that most of their contemporaries could not enjoy. This was particularly true of Patton, who through his ability to perform was able to avoid the difficult dawn-to-dusk experience of a typical African American fieldworker in the South. Although there was certainly a darker side to the life that both men led, on the surface at least it looked glamorous compared to the lives of others, and while the image helped draw crowds, it also helped influence others to take up music as a trade.[10]

As the musical generations passed, the legends of Charley Patton and Jimmie Rodgers grew until they became mythic figures in the history of American popular culture. However, in terms of public recognition their legends evolved differently. Rodgers was a well-known personality during his lifetime, particularly in the South and West, but his influence and career were obscured by the passage of time. He was for years recognized, even revered, in country-music circles, but by the end of the twentieth century his name was not widely remembered. Most country fans of the modern era have never heard of Jimmie Rodgers and certainly have no idea that contemporary country stars are part of an industry that the talent and personality of Jimmie Rodgers helped create. Charley Patton, on the other hand, was a relatively obscure figure during his lifetime, well known in the clubs and in the region where he played but unknown to the rest of the world. He was one of many itinerate musicians who plied their trade in the South's black juke joints during the 1920s and 1930s, desperate to make a living at anything other than hoeing potatoes and picking cotton. Even the circumstances surrounding his somewhat early demise were not viewed as unusual in the environment that Patton occupied. Most who knew him considered it just another tragedy at a time and in an area where tragedy was commonplace and quickly forgotten. While a special train delivered Rodgers's body to his hometown with great fanfare after his death, Patton was buried without much notice in a poorly marked cemetery at Holly Ridge, Mississippi. By the time blues enthusiasts hailed him as a founding father of the Delta blues, Patton had been dead for thirty years. His name became well known only after blues music began to inspire the likes of major rock figures like Eric Clapton, the Rolling Stones, Bob Dylan, and Led Zeppelin during the 1960s and beyond.

Whether they recognize it or not, anyone who listens to blues music today knows Charley Patton just as anyone who tunes their radio to a country station knows Jimmie Rodgers. Rock-and-roll enthusiasts know them both. While black and white music mingled in the South long before Rodgers or Patton picked up his first guitar, the pressures brought on by desegregated music enduring for so long in a segregated land finally reached a point of critical mass during the middle of the twentieth century. During the 1950s a combination of Charley Patton's style of blues and Jimmie Rodgers's country influences helped create a great hybrid, or what some would call a great bastard, that young people loved and their parents hated. It was called rock and roll, and it changed American culture forever. Scholars have attempted to dissect the elements that made rock and roll what it is, but the job is difficult because the music itself was originally made to be felt and not scrutinized. "The history of music is fascinating," Keith Richards of the Rolling Stones once opined. "It's one of those great clichés, which unfortunately are always true, that the more you find out, the less you know."[11] Early rock and roll, with its blues roots, evoked feelings in the young that did not lend themselves to deep discussions about style and substance. The era produced the flash of Elvis Presley and Jerry Lee Lewis, country boys heavily influenced by the blues who also grew up in the shadow of Jimmie Rodgers, as well as the grit and growl of Muddy Waters and Howlin' Wolf, true bluesmen who came out of the Charley Patton tradition but also listened to Rodgers's records when they were young. Into the 1960s and afterwards, songs by Patton and Rodgers influenced cutting-edge artists who were not concerned in the least that the music itself was decades old. It was, and is, a testament to the power of good music, and the enduring human spirits that create it.

By modern standards, Rodgers and Patton lived only one complete life in cumulative years, with Patton dying in his early forties and Rodgers surviving only into his thirties. As a result, while their recordings were masterful, they were also relatively few in number—52 songs for Patton and 110 for Rodgers—compared to what might have been. This naturally gave rise to abstract and sometimes embellished notions of what they could have accomplished had they lived to be old men. How many more songs would they have recorded?

How many more people could they have touched? Such questions are always asked because there is a magic quality surrounding those cut down prematurely, particularly artists. Those who die young do not become enfeebled by age. They do not decline in their creative production or become hopelessly jaded by the ebb and flow of success and failure. Because they do not live long enough to diminish into a weakened state, they leave behind an image of creative vibrancy that is frozen in time and not likely to fade, which is perhaps one reason why their art holds up and transcends the eras in which they lived. With regard to the ghoulish concept of untimely celebrity death in the music community, Charley Patton and Jimmie Rodgers were two of the earliest names on a list of special but doomed musical talents who through their deaths became forever entwined in the fabric of American popular culture. Buddy Holly, Hank Williams, Jimi Hendrix, Otis Redding, Kurt Cobain, and the like followed Patton and Rodgers as cultural heroes whose untimely deaths made them immortal in the minds of many of their fans.

Today, the names Charley Patton and Jimmie Rodgers are rarely uttered outside the confines of documentary films or scholarly publications dealing with American roots music. Most people do not routinely listen to Patton or Rodgers records, and their songs are no longer heard on the radio. Then again, the work of Charley Patton and Jimmie Rodgers is everywhere, in every American generation, because members of every generation listen to music that they like. Every generation listens to music that is influenced by something that came before. Patton and Rodgers were not the first to play their styles of music, and they would certainly not be the last to have great influence. However, they were contemporaries who lived and performed at a unique period in American history during which traditional strains of music were maturing into a commercial product that could be heard by the masses. On the quest to find the origins of American popular music, the trail does not end with them, but it goes through both men at a critical juncture during the early twentieth century.

⸻ 1 ⸻
THE SETTING

Huge swatches of blues and country music do after all come from the
cotton fields in a very real way. Many a seminal song was actually
created there, and even more were spread person to person.
—JOHNNY CASH

T he American South is different from the rest of the United States. It always has been, and probably always will be. Though the southern existence is complex, one singular fact has consistently defined the region. That is, there have always been two Souths, one white and one black. The region has always contained two strains of humanity, each with definitive social and cultural components. They represent two populations with distinct and deeply engrained perceptions of one another, and of the world around them. The two Souths are no longer legally segregated, as they were for generations, but they are still separated somewhat by custom and by a mutual wariness and anxiety that never quite goes away even in the modern era. However, despite this constant tension, it is not the separation of the races that makes the South a different place. On the contrary, it is the indisputable reality that the two Souths are actually just one South after all, and that, despite the presence of two races, a common culture exists among the region's entire population. It is a culture with a long tradition that many times can be heard before it can be visualized, or even recognized, by those immersed in it.

As Darden Asbury Pyron pointed out in his biography of author Margaret Mitchell, "Far into the twentieth century, Southern culture flourished in oral knowledge" and "nurtured word of mouth as a standard means of communication. . . . Southerners instinctively minded assonance and alliteration; their words formed natural rhythms." This was certainly the case with southern music, a vibrant form of oral tradition that excited the senses, be it folksongs, hymns, old-time spirituals, juke-joint blues, or country laments sung *a capella* or accompanied by a guitar, banjo, mandolin, piano, or harmonica. Most southerners preferred singing, playing instruments, and dancing to reading and writing as standard forms of expression. As Edward Ayers wrote in his study of the southern existence, "whether at opera houses or medicine shows, barrelhouses or singing schools, music attracted people of every description." The region's music, the blending of black and white words and rhythms, has helped define the South as one world. "It is a southern culture," James Mc-Bride Dabbs once stated, "born of all our people—the immortal spirituals, the blues, the plaintive mountain ballads, the hoedowns—binding us together." It has always made the South different from a cultural perspective from any other part of the United States. Nowhere else in the country has black and white culture mixed to form such an explosively colorful shade of grey. Country music came out of the South, as did the blues, two powerful forms of musical expression that both have been called quintessentially American. In short, every southerner, regardless of race, can rightly boast that his or her heritage includes a great soundtrack.[1]

Charley Patton and Jimmie Rodgers were born and raised in the American South, a unique land with a turbulent history that actually began twice. The origins of the South, and indeed of the United States, can be traced back to the year 1607 when a group of 144 men boarded three ships, the Discovery, Godspeed, and Susan Constant, and made the treacherous journey from England to the New World to found the Jamestown colony in Virginia. While this was indeed a landmark event, the history of the South also began twelve years later, in 1619, when a Dutch ship brought in the first "cargo" of Africans to Jamestown. They were around twenty in number and had recently been stolen from a Spanish vessel. The Dutch captain, a man named Jope, exchanged the Africans for food, and then sailed away, leaving them in the colony to serve as laborers. More Africans followed, and within a relatively short time Virginia lawmakers began authoring legislation distinguishing between white and black workers in the colony and providing for more oppressive treatment of African laborers. This was one of the first steps in a process that established chattel slavery in America.[2]

As the South's agricultural economy developed, slavery flourished up and down the eastern seaboard. Beginning in the 1620s, Virginians exported tons of tobacco, as did Maryland planters after that colony was founded in 1634. In the 1670s European planters and their slaves relocated from the Caribbean colony of Barbados to South Carolina, creating a rapidly developing plantation economy there grounded in rice and indigo. Georgia's agricultural economy, also based in rice and indigo, began to expand not long after the British established that colony in 1732.[3] Later still, after the American Revolution and the invention of the cotton gin, slavery fueled the South's cotton economy in new states like Mississippi, Alabama, and Louisiana, setting the stage for political rancor between the North and the South and eventually civil war. By the time the war began in 1861, slaves represented more than a third of the Confederacy's total population.

Southern planters of European descent chose to enslave Africans as a people for a number of reasons. Unlike the Native American population, who the Europeans also tried to subordinate, the African population had natural immunities to many of the diseases that the Europeans brought with them to the New World. As a result, they were healthier as a group and therefore more dependable workers. In addition, once they reached America, the Africans were trapped. Unlike the Native Americans on the East Coast, they could not escape into the forests of the American interior and easily blend in with the indigenous population. While these practical considerations were important to the development of slavery in what would become the United States, at the core of the institution was the fact that the Europeans in America were racially biased against Africans, and viewed African culture as inferior. Europeans stereotyped Africans as an uncivilized people with no hope of social redemption. From there it was relatively easy for the ruling classes in places like Virginia, Maryland, and the Carolinas, and later in Mississippi, Alabama, and Louisiana, to pass laws subordinating the African population in a manner that they could never subordinate a person of European descent. The importance of racial identity evolved with the institution of slavery, and a rigid social system based on race became the cornerstone of the southern existence. Early on the large planters, and many white southerners in general, created a web of rationalizations dealing with slavery in what became a long, convoluted struggle to justify the institution.[4]

During the antebellum period no state was more heavily invested in slavery than Mississippi. Congress created the Mississippi Territory in 1798, not long after Eli Whitney invented the cotton gin, and from the time Mississippi entered the Union in 1817 cotton and slavery were central components of the state's economy. At the time of statehood the population stood at 25,000 free whites and 23,000 slaves. Initially, planters along the Mississippi River produced most of the state's cotton, but as more settlers came the cotton kingdom expanded to other areas. By 1840 Mississippi was the South's leading cotton producer, and the state's white population was in the minority. By 1860, the year before the Civil War began, 55 percent of Mississippians were owned by other Mississippians.

The presence of so many slaves in Mississippi created a racially charged atmosphere that radical politicians—those who played on the fears and insecurities of the white population—could easily exploit. In Mississippi, racial awareness was particularly palpable in areas where slaves outnumbered whites in large numbers. For instance, in 1860 cotton-rich Hinds County, which included the state capital at Jackson, had a population of around 9,000 whites and more than 22,000 slaves. These anxieties among the white population eventually gave way to political tensions affecting slaveholding and non-slaveholding whites alike in that they were all intimidated by the sheer number of slaves in their midst coupled with an expanding abolition movement in the North. By the time the Mississippi Secession Convention met in Jackson on the eve of the Civil War, the political leaders in the state were determined to preserve slavery at all costs, even if it meant severing ties with the United States. Poorer, non-slaveholding whites, who represented the majority of the state's population, were willing to follow this course as well as they had become increasingly fearful of a potentially free black population with whom they would compete for jobs and land. "Our position is thoroughly identified with the institution of slavery—the greatest material institution in the world," members of the convention stated emphatically as they voted to leave

Mississippi Population Statistics, 1820–1860 (% total)

YEAR	FREE	SLAVE	TOTAL
1820	42,175 (56%)	32,272 (44%)	75,447
1830	70,433 (52%)	65,659 (48%)	136,092
1840	179,074 (48%)	195,211 (52%)	374,285
1850	295,718 (49%)	309,874 (51%)	605,592
1860	353,899 (45%)	436,631 (55%)	790,530

Source: U.S. Census data.

the Union, "There was no choice left us but submission to the mandates of abolition, or a dissolution of the Union, whose principles have been subverted to work out our ruin." During the war's first year, white Mississippians were not shy in signing up to fight, and over time more than 60,000 white Mississippians took part in the conflict, a third of whom perished. Conversely, around 17,000 former slaves from Mississippi ended up fighting for the Union before the war's end. From the time that federal armies first began moving through the state, slaves flocked to the lines seeking freedom, and many male slaves chose to support the war by signing up for military service. They saw their efforts as a chance to help create a new "southern way of life" in which their people and culture could fully thrive.[5]

While the South changed in some ways after the Civil War, in other ways the region remained the same. Before the Civil War, masters controlled every aspect of their slaves' lives. Even if they could not break their slaves' spirit, they exercised complete control of their physical being. The master literally owned and controlled the bodies that were in the field picking cotton in the same way that he owned and controlled the body of a mule that he used to pull a wagon. The slave owner's place in this one-sided relationship could sometimes be intoxicating. As noted psychologist John Dollard once wrote, "Actually to own the body of another person and to control it completely is probably the most exalting possibility from the standpoint of the owner's self-esteem." In the South the master was not merely a master, he was not just a boss or an owner, and he was much more than just a patriarch in the ruling classes. In the small universe of the plantation he was a god, a man who could alter other men's futures on a whim. He could break up families with the stroke of a pen and routinely issued orders that he expected others to follow immediately and without demur. Southern slave owners, particularly those in the white ruling class, suddenly and dramatically lost this wellspring of self-esteem and sense of power as a result of the Civil War, and after Reconstruction they and their heirs wanted it back. Seeing it as a threat to their own status, the poorer classes of whites were also uncomfortable with any new system that empowered the former slaves. Ultimately this all led to the systematic stripping of civil and political rights from former slaves in an effort to subjugate them and establish their race as inferior in much the same manner that slavery had.[6]

While slavery was eliminated by the war's outcome, the social problems related to the institution did not go away. In fact, they were magnified. During the Reconstruction period the federal government under the control of the Republican Party supported the creation of state governments in the South that offered African Americans the opportunity to participate in the political process. While these governments functioned for a time, they eventually fell prey to northern apathy and massive resistance from a major segment of the South's white population. As the Reconstruction period wore on, many whites in the North lost interest in the process while the white power structure in the South fought to regain control of the southern state governments by any means possible. Through voter fraud and violence promoted by political leaders as well as by the Ku Klux Klan and other domestic terrorist organizations, the conservative Democratic Party emerged during the 1870s as the party of white supremacy in the South. Democratic leaders used racial politics and Confederate imagery to consolidate their power by appealing to white voters on an emotional level. The Democratic Party organization became dominant in what became a one-party political system in the states of the former Confederacy. Once in control, the Democrats took further steps to turn back the clock and recreate the old social system that had existed before the war.[7]

With slavery abolished, citizenship defined, and voting rights protected by the thirteenth, fourteenth, and fifteenth amendments to the U.S. Constitution, the Democratic power structure in the southern states struggled to create oppressive, race-based legislation to lay the foundation for a new system that was meant to replicate the old as closely as possible. In the Old South, master and slave could not occupy the same legal status; hence, the same needed to be the case in the new environment. Just as the old slave system had rested on the premise of African American subordination, the new system of segregation began with clearly defined notions of racial inferiority and superiority. The old system had been based on control—the control of masters over their slaves— so the new system must also rest on the control of one group over another. With slavery outlawed, legal chicanery, usually in the form of laws established and enforced with a wink and nod, became the weapon of choice in the states of the former Confederacy in their fight to reestablish something close to the old order. Prime examples were the so-called "vagrancy" laws that southern legislatures established after the Civil War. Technically, attorneys and legislators wrote the laws in racially neutral terms, but in practical application they were meant to subordinate one race over the other. Many of the laws revolved around labor and labor contracts in the new world that emancipation had created. Any African American who refused to sign a work contract that a white landowner might offer could be jailed as a vagrant, which was defined in Mississippi as a person who was not holding a job at the specific instant that white authorities chose to arrest him. After being charged as a vagrant, the man would then have to remain in jail until he paid a fine, even though he had no job or income. The final part of the equation involved someone else paying the vagrant's fine for him, after which the vagrant was required to work off the debt without wages. The former master was usually given preference in paying the fine of one of his former slaves, thereby completing a cycle that effectively made the former bondsman a slave again. "Vagrancy and enticement laws soon characterized the whole of the former Confederacy," Houston A. Baker Jr. wrote, "Convicted blacks were seldom (if ever) equipped to pay exorbitant fines levied against them. Hence, they were released into the custody of the white person who covered their court cost and fines. Then the true incarceration began." More oppressive legislative followed, such as laws requiring "agricultural laborers" to work from dawn until dusk every day except Sunday, and statutes requiring that workers should remain on the plantation even when they were not working. In some places workers were not allowed visitors unless they received permission from their employer. The end result was a skewed legal system for "white criminalization of black bodies in order to supply labor demands."[8]

Segregation laws, collectively called "Jim Crow" laws, served as the foundation for subordinating the African American population in the South following the Civil War and Reconstruction, and they were well entrenched in the southern states by the turn of the twentieth century. These laws forbade blacks to enter any public accommodation frequented by whites, meaning that the races could not mingle in public parks, could not stay in the same hotels, eat together in the same restaurants, or ride in the same railroad cars. They had to drink from separate water fountains and use separate public restrooms; later laws would be passed that even segregated "black" and "white" vending machines. The states of the old Confederacy also established separate school systems for black and white children, the mere presence of which foreshadowed the segregated world that black and white youngsters would enter as adults. As southern solons established the Jim Crow system of segregation, they were also busy neutralizing the black vote using vehicles such as poll taxes, literacy requirements for voter registration, and grandfather clauses that allowed the descendants of antebellum whites to vote but not the descendants of antebellum slaves. As Jennifer Lynn Ritterhouse stated in her study of the Jim Crow South, the white governing class attempted in the late nineteenth and early twentieth centuries to undo what the war and Reconstruction had wrought through "not only the subjugation of free black labor and the expulsion of blacks from electoral politics, but also the reassertion of a code of domination rooted in slavery—in short, racial etiquette." The result was a social and political system that mirrored the antebellum environment, at least to the extent that disenfranchisement and segregation denied certain rights to large segments of the southern population based on their race. It subordinated the African American population economically and in the field of politics, giving them very little control over their condition. It was, as Neil McMillen stated, "a system of racial segregation, degradation, and repression designed to stifle their initiative, insure their poverty and illiteracy, and isolate them from American democratic values, and render them politically powerless."[9]

Of course the new system, like the old, generated constant social friction. Just as they had been wary of outside influences during slavery, white southerners became acutely aware of anything different that appeared in their community once segregation was in place. They were suspicious of outsiders who might come in with new ideas that might somehow upset a southern "way of life" that was both new and old at the same time. As the rest of the country matured during the early twentieth century, the South continued to lag behind in quasi-isolation. Southern African Americans knew where they could and could not go, as did southern whites, and everyone knew that there were strict limits to every type of interaction that took place between the races. As author Gayle Graham Yates, a white Mississippian who grew up in the Jim Crow South, later reflected, "When we were children, ironclad ancestry was racial and racial identity definitive. People were either black or white. Even if some tanned white people might be darker than some blacks and if some blacks were whiter than whites, we all knew instantly who was which." In this environment, new ideas that came from other places tended to be viewed with suspicion that sometimes gave way to paranoia. People from other regions, some southerners claimed, did not understand the "special problems" caused by the presence of two races living in such close proximity to one another. "As culture, southern segregation made a new collective white identity," Grace Elizabeth Hale observed. "Reconstruction dissolved into a formless recapitulation of the war [where] former Confederates fought the freedpeople's voting, office-holding and land ownership."[10] Meanwhile, most northerners grew tired of the controversy that civil rights issues generated, and for decades the federal government did little to combat the abuses against African Americans in the South.

Just as Mississippi was immersed in the antebellum cotton culture, the home state of Charley Patton and Jimmie Rodgers was at the forefront of implementing and enforcing segregation laws. In 1890 the Mississippi legislature called a convention to create a new state constitution that included Jim Crow statutes and reinforced white political domination by disenfranchising most of the state's black population. "Our chief duty when we meet in convention," Mississippi's U.S. Senator James Z. George declared shortly before the meeting, "is to devise such measures . . . as will enable us to maintain home government, under the control of the white people of the state."[11] Among other things, the new constitution made it illegal for white and black children to attend school together, called for the separation of white and black convicts at the state penitentiary, and outlawed interracial marriage. During the same period Mississippi adopted a new state flag that included in its design the "stars and bars" Confederate battle flag.[12] Hence, by the turn of the twentieth century in Mississippi, most blacks were not allowed to vote, oppressive segregation was the law of the land, and the Confederate flag flew proudly over every public building.

Any African American who dared complain about this emerging system with its severe racial inequalities risked a swift beating or even a death sentence, which usually involved local vigilantes beating the offender to death or hanging him (or occasionally her) from a tree. Soon the worst type of racial demagoguery was at the forefront of state politics, punctuated by extremely harsh rhetoric. Popular Mississippi politician James K. Vardeman, who was elected governor in 1903 and would later serve as a U.S. senator, once stated publicly, and without hesitation, that he was firm in the belief that "the best way to control the nigger is to whip him when he does not obey without it."[13] According to one estimate, between 1880 and the 1930, 3,220 African Americans were lynched in states of the old Confederacy with their primary crime being that they had, in some way or another, "gotten out of line" and forgotten who controlled the South and how that control was maintained. Many of these executions were public, drawing large and enthusiastic crowds who cheered lustily as victims were tortured before they were killed. In addition to hangings, many lynching victims were burned alive. "Lynchings in the American South had three entwined functions," one expert on the subject later explained, "first, to maintain social control over the black population through terrorism; second, to suppress or eliminate black competitors for economic, political, or social rewards; and third, to stabilize the white class structure and preserve the privileged status of the white aristocracy."[14]

In practical application the Jim Crow environment created a multi-layered system of segregation. First and foremost, it segregated the races from one another and gave members of the white race certain rights and privileges that their African American neighbors did not possess. However, while blacks suffered under the system, so did the poorer classes of whites, although in a different manner and for different reasons. If segregation created a restricted social environment that made it impossible for former slaves and their descendants to advance, it also created a system where it was almost impossible for poor whites to make headway. Jim Crow legislation created, in law at least, a clear and distinct line of demarcation based on race. On one side of the line was the African American community, most of whom were poor. On the other side was the white community, many of whom were poor and a small group of which composed the wealthier elite. The system was designed to subordinate the African American population, which it did, but it also created a false impression that all whites in the divided society had privilege. Subordinating the poor black population in this way elevated by definition the status of poor whites, who were seemingly on the more preferable side of the color line with their wealthier brethren. "In the North a man may have a prestige position because he has money, or is learned, or is old," Dollard concluded. "The novelty in the South is that one has prestige solely because one is white." Even the poorest white male under this arrangement could draw strength and self-esteem from the fact that once the color line was established, he would rank higher in the "pecking order" of society than those who were being held below him by law. He would always enjoy rights that a large segment of the population did not have, and he would never be last, never be at the bottom. The color of their skin served poorer whites in two ways. It allowed them to identify with the more prosperous whites in their region, and it set them apart from the African Americans who occupied a subjugated world beneath them. Of course it was all a facade, which was why the color line sometimes blurred among the poorer classes of whites and blacks who had many of the typical daily struggles of life in common. The wealthier class of whites—those who ran things—used the economic insecurities of poorer whites to hold power. As J. Wayne Flynt pointed out, "The entire structure of poor white society groaned beneath the burden. The family structure, already shaken by war, was further disrupted by the threat of equality for blacks. . . . Whites might borrow from black culture in their songs, rhythms, crafts, stories, and superstitions, but they disdained the people from whom they borrowed." The white elite made sure that the poorer classes of whites concentrated more on the racial divide than on the economic inequities within the white community. In effect, the wealthier classes used race to divide the poor blacks and the poor whites, ensuring that they would never unite to change the system. Richard K. Scher described the system: "White elites wanted poor whites to maintain the illusion of higher social position than blacks. . . . If poor whites began to think otherwise, there was always the danger that class consciousness and economic deprivation would overcome racial antagonism to create a potent political alliance."

White supremacy became the foundation on which the dominant Democratic Party rested in the South for a century after the Civil War, and anyone who challenged the Democrats ran the risk of being branded a race traitor in an environment where race was a definitive component. Hence, the Republican Party—the party of Lincoln and the party that promoted civil rights during Reconstruction—never gained traction. As Bradley Bond maintained, "racism, then, assured that freed people would not return to the polls in large numbers and that intraparty and third party challenges to the Democratic Party would be regarded as threats to white domination of politics and society." Likewise, the system took away the political rights of many poor whites by compromising the entire democratic process in the southern states. The disenfranchisement mechanisms—poll taxes, literacy tests, and the like—used against African Americans in the South to neutralize more than 65 percent of the black vote between Reconstruction and 1900 also took the vote away from a significant number of southern whites in the lower classes during the same period, as much as 25 percent according to some estimates. As a result, the white elites in the states of the former Confederacy were able to fend off challenges to their power from grassroots groups or movements that might have benefited poorer whites, such as the Greenback Party or the Populists. Elections were held and outcomes determined based on maintaining white supremacy as a form of the status quo, rather than on issues that would allow more in the poorer classes, both black and white, to make a better living or rise in society. It was a simple divide-and-conquer strategy in which the wealthier class of whites, a small minority of the total population in the southern states, played poor whites and blacks against each other to maintain control of both groups. And it was a system that worked. The political elites routinely held offices indefinitely or rotated offices as they saw fit, making it difficult for any new blood to circulate in the southern body politic. Nowhere was the system more firmly entrenched than in Mississippi, where, for example, during the twenty-year period from 1876 to 1896, only two men held the office of governor. In the end, while the system segregated whites and blacks from one another in the legal sense, it also segregated poor whites from wealthier whites in an economic sense, allowing the rich to keep what they had and get even richer. While the color line never went away completely, it blurred in the case of some whites and blacks in the poorer classes. Poor whites and blacks were on a similar quest to survive their economic condition, and therefore they had shared experiences that drew them together, experiences that did not apply to the wealthier class of white elites. The poor of both races actually had a great deal in common with regard to how their lives progressed on a daily basis, which was why the music that came from blues performers and country performers had so many common elements and themes.[15]

While most southern whites did not realize—or perhaps did not want to realize—that their own racism was holding them back, they were not blind to their economic condition. During the early decades of the twentieth century the onset of modernization began to affect their thought processes. Anxieties related to race remained strong, but change during the period also created new fears. As the Industrial Revolution began firing on all cylinders in the decades after the Civil War, and as industry slowly began creeping into the South, many whites felt an uneasiness that their way of life was somehow under siege from outside forces. The onset of the Great Depression magnified these concerns, giving way to a sense of hopelessness and desperation among many whites in the poorer classes. The agrarian ideal, a staple of the southern existence since colonial times, seemed to be teetering. To an increasing extent wealth was being redefined in terms of capital and commerce rather than in traditional terms related to the amount of acreage a property owner had under cultivation. A farmer was theoretically his own boss who, through hard work, could expand his holding and remain independent. However, farm life seemed to be in decline as a small group of merchants, bankers, and railroad executives began controlling more and more resources. During the first half of the twentieth century, social comment related to perceptions of hard times began to manifest itself in country music just as it did in blues. According to country-music historian Bill C. Malone, "The reaction to hard times of hillbilly musicians and their audiences ranged from outright indifference to passionate activism. The 1930s, after all, were marked by a popular culture of escapism; many Americans sought relief from the Depression." Themes related to nostalgia, hopes for a brighter future, and compassion for the victims of suffering surfaced as hillbilly artists began reflecting the concerns of their audiences. Jimmie Rodgers, for instance, recorded several "hobo songs" filled with the laments of the downtrodden. Other down-on-their-luck characters featured in Rodgers's recordings had problems with "the man" in the form of the local sheriff or maybe just the world in general that were similar in nature to those of troubled characters in blues songs. Later, artists like Woody Guthrie would inject an element of politics into this type of music, creating a template of sorts for the type of protest music that would emerge through the folk movement of the 1940s and 1950s and rock music of the 1960s.[16]

Still, for generations after Reconstruction most of the South's population, white and black, made their living on small farms, and regardless of how hard they worked most farmers remained poor. Cotton was still the region's primary cash crop, but a volatile market provided little long-term security for those who staked their livelihood on the fiber. The poor conditions under which most farmers toiled were aggravated by a new system of agriculture that developed throughout the South in the last quarter of the nineteenth century. During the period, little money circulated in the South and the economy was tightly controlled by conservative politicians and their allies. Many farmers could not acquire land or lost their land due to their inability to pay taxes or retire other debts. Forced to survive on credit, they worked land that they did not own, either as tenants or as sharecroppers. The tenant usually owned his own tools and farm animals and paid a flat rate to the landowner for use of the land. At the end of the growing season he would pay his rent with proceeds from the sale of his crop. The sharecropper was at the bottom of the economic ladder. He too had to pay for the use of the land he cultivated, but he also had to purchase on credit all the tools and other necessities needed to produce a crop. His debt burden was greater, and it was therefore more difficult for him to meet his obligations. One bad growing season or one year of depressed cotton prices could cause the sharecropper to fall hard into a cycle of debt from which he could not recover. Two bad years could be catastrophic. By 1880 sharecroppers, white and black, worked 80 percent of the land in the Deep South cotton-producing states, with many permanently tied to large farms, working off a perpetual debt.[17]

As with every other aspect of the southern existence, there was a sharp racial component associated with the sharecropping system. Sharecropping "evolved out of an economic struggle in which planters were able to prevent most blacks from gaining access to land," according to historian Eric Foner. "But in general, sharecropping became the South's replacement system of labor after the end of slavery." Major white landowners, particularly in areas with large black populations, routinely manipulated the system as a means of exercising control. They controlled local crop prices and adjusted interest rates sometimes as high as 50 percent to make it all but impossible for a black sharecropper to meet his obligations, even during a relatively good year. State legislatures passed laws making it illegal for a farmer to leave a landowner's employ if he owed the landowner money, thus legally restricting sharecroppers to a system that produced little more than generational economic dependence, and in essence recreated in some ways the conditions of slavery for many African Americans. "Contrary to the widely held view," historian John Hope Franklin once wrote, "there was no significant breakup of the plantation system during and after Reconstruction. Day labor, renting, and sharecropping were innovations, to be sure, but those occupying such lowly positions bore a relationship to the planter that, while not slavery, was nevertheless one of subordination." In short, the planter was still a despot who controlled the destiny and determined the social position of everyone who worked on his property, and his word was law. World-renowned blues legend B.B. King, who grew up doing farmwork in the Mississippi Delta, later recalled that the great landlords there were "absolute rulers of their own kingdoms. Sheriffs didn't like to violate their boundaries even if it meant giving up a criminal." According to King, "it gave you a double feeling—you felt protected, but you also felt small, as if you couldn't fend off the world for yourself. I could feel the old link to slavery." By the end of the nineteenth century, around three-quarters of the Deep

South's African American population languished as sharecroppers under this harsh system with little hope of bettering themselves.[18]

Despite their difficult existence both before the Civil War and after, southern slaves and their descendants were able to create their own vibrant culture, which included their own forms of musical expression. Beginning in the early seventeenth century, slaves brought the rhythms and vocal styles of their African homeland to America, where an evolutionary process began that filtered the music through the circumstances under which they lived. According to Gerhard Kubik, the music of African Americans that evolved into the blues maintained its foundational connection with African music through "semantic and grammatical tone, phonetic structure leading to offbeat phrasing and melodic accents, and the concept—widespread in African cultures—that the meaning of the song derives from its lyric rather than from melody, rhythm, or chord sequence."[19] "Although stripped of the vestiges of their homeland," Barbara Wilcots pointed out, throughout the South during the eighteenth and nineteenth centuries, "newly-arrived slaves brought a bounty of African traditions and beliefs to America. . . . Put to work in the cotton, rice, tobacco and indigo fields of the southern plantations, slaves translated the call and response of their African oral tradition into folk cries and field hollers." Among the West African tribes, from which many American slaves descended, music was an integral part of most activities, particularly those involving strenuous labor, and it would be an integral part of the existence of the American slave. According to noted blues authority Robert Palmer, the slaves in the field, "through singing to themselves, hollering at each other across the fields, and singing together while working and worshipping . . . developed a hybridized musical language that distilled the very essence of innumerable African vocal traditions."[20] In 1853 New England journalist Frederick Law Olmsted described the sound made by a group of slaves he encountered during a trip through South Carolina: "One raised such a sound as I had never heard before, a long, loud musical shout, rising and falling, and breaking into falsetto, his voice ringing through the woods in the clear, frosty air, like a bugle call. As he finished, the melody was caught up by another, and then another, and then by several in chorus."[21]

For the slaves, the field holler was far more than a primitive form of musical expression that helped pass the time as they worked. It had a much deeper function. The music of the fields allowed the slaves to exert limited control over their situation. In a world where they were under scrutiny and did not fully control their day-to-day lives, slaves developed subtle ways of influencing their environment through song. They learned that through their music they could sometimes lull the white community into a false sense of security with regard to the collective disposition of the slaves around them. Whites equated singing in the fields with contentment and were therefore less likely to discipline a field full of what they believed to be peaceful laborers. In a way, the music allowed members of the white community—most of whom were constantly nervous about slave uprisings when they were anywhere near a significant population of slaves—to relax. In turn, they might be more relaxed in their treatment of the slaves, might exercise less direct control over a slave population that they believed was docile. At the same time, under less scrutiny, slaves could control the pace of their work by slowing down or speeding up the rhythm of their songs. Because whites mainly heard only the rhythm of the slave music and rarely listened carefully to the words, slaves in the field could also communicate with one another through their music. "Under the power of the planter, slaves had to depend on ingenuity, imagination, and creative use of information," historian James Oliver Horton maintained. "Since slaveholders generally assumed that slaves' singing connoted contentment and passivity, the slaves used music to pass along messages, to control the pace of work, to placate the master, or to subtly comment on a person or a situation."

What many whites dismissed as the primitive utterances of a primitive people could actually be a complex form of communication. "I have often been utterly astonished, since I came to the north," Frederick Douglass wrote in his famous nineteenth-century autobiography, "to find persons who could speak of the singing among slaves as evidence of their contentment and happiness. It is impossible to conceive of a greater mistake." While slaveholders generally linked the slaves' singing with passiveness, the slaves actually used music to communicate with one another, pass messages, or articulate social comment, and in the process they created an art form that would reverberate in one form or another through the passing generations. According to historian John W. Blassingame, "Relying heavily on circumlocution, metaphor, and innuendo, the slaves often referred to fear, infidelity, love, hard times, work, slave coffles, conjuration, food, drinking, sex and freedom, in their songs. When away from whites, however, the slaves frequently dropped the metaphors. Freedom was a major motif." By 1850 southern slaves had created the foundation of a music that would later evolve into and be popularized as the blues. B.B. King in his 1996 autobiography summed up his view of the phenomenon as he remembered stories that his great grandmother, who was born a slave, told him during his childhood in Mississippi. "She'd talk about the beginning of the blues," King remembered. "She said that, sure, singing helped the day go by. Singing about your sadness unburdens your soul. But the blues hollerers shouted about more than being sad. They were also delivering messages in a musical code."[22]

The use of music in this way was all part of a coded language that slaves used to freely express themselves in a way that would not threaten or anger their masters. Through song they could break the monotony of the workday by communicating with one another while committing a minor act of rebellion. Using metaphor, imagery, and double entendre, slaves could sing about things that they were not allowed to talk about. "Through an array of coded language," Sandra L. Beckett wrote, "slaves could sing songs of freedom and tell rebellious folktales in the very presence of their masters, yet escape punishment." The opportunity represented a small triumph in the restrained environment, a psychological victory of sorts that helped reinforce a sense of community. "Enslaved Africans and their descendants," Beckett continued, "were able to create communities that allowed them psychological identities distinct from those provided by the white community." They were able to "craft a language and whole different world that whites did not understand and from which whites were excluded, even though it manifested itself right in front of them." For slaves, this evolution of a coded language in music was also a function of shared experiences that allowed them to communicate in nuances. From the beginning, from the first inspired utterance, music was, according to authors Kellie Jones and Imamu Amiri Baraka, "a coded language, on the surface appearing earnest, sorrowful and pious, yet containing occluded messages of escape, retribution, joy, and strength."

Later, through the blues, this penchant for coded language would survive and thrive. Slavery gave way to segregation following Reconstruction, creating a more modern world of oppression for the children and grandchildren of the bondsmen who were freed by the Civil War and the Thirteenth Amendment. While this new environment was not as restrictive as slavery, it was still cruel and confining, and it still created the need for a form of communication that fooled whites, and particularly whites in positions of authority, on a regular basis. Just as slaves sought to express ideas through song in a way that the master or the overseer could not understand, later generations of African Americans would do the same thing, hoping to fool the landlord or the local sheriff. In his composition "High Sheriff Blues," for instance, Charley Patton sings about the treatment he received at the hands of the sheriff in Belzoni, Mississippi, and during his career the bluesman would name other local whites in his songs and suffer no consequences. According to historian Lawrence W. Levine, this coded language of song allowed African Americans in both the slavery period and after emancipation to "express themselves communally and individually, to derive great aesthetic pleasure, to perpetuate traditions, to keep values from eroding," and, in so doing, created a process through which they maintained their culture under harsh circumstances. In short, it allowed black voices to be heard loudly at a time when they were supposed to be muted.[23]

While slaves certainly developed their own culture in spite of the conditions under which they lived, their cultural development was also in large part a result of their circumstances. The primary components of slave culture in the antebellum South were not short-term reactions to oppression, nor were they reflexive attempts to resist their condition or adapt to harsh surroundings. Instead, the tenets of slave culture were deep expressions of unity, reflections of commonality from a people filled with self-awareness and engaged in a constant struggle to maintain their own individual identity as well as a collective ethos. More than a simple survival mechanism, slave culture was actually a counterculture used as a vehicle to bring some sense of order or normalcy to a disorderly and tumultuous world. Hidden from the white community, this counterculture fostered solidarity, self-esteem, and a sense of higher purpose in that it was something that needed to be maintained and subsequently transmitted to future generations. "Like in any true counterculture," William Freehling wrote, "slaves raised resistance to higher levels of insight, beauty, and awareness." Former slaves clung to this counterculture and even built on it after emancipation as segregation laws in the states of the former Confederacy once again boxed them into a subordinate class. Segregation, along with disenfranchisement and lynch law, gave former slaves and their descendants a permanent suspicion of mainstream southern society, which was dominated by whites. This distrust helped perpetuate the slave counterculture and created the perfect environment for the development of blues music, described by historian R. A. Lawson as "a shared music that preached a message of personal freedom in a cultural environment so repressive that the expression had to be performed behind a veil."[24]

In addition to the work song, religious music was a significant part of the slave world. By the nineteenth century, most slaves had converted to Christianity as either Baptists or Methodists, the South's two largest denominations. Masters imposed Christianity on their slaves in large part as a means of social control, but it did not take long for slaves to create their own special brand of American religion. As historian Eugene Genovese stated, "From the moment they arrived in America and began to toil as slaves, they could not help absorbing the religion of the master class. But, the conditions of their new social life forced them to combine their African inheritance with the dominant power they confronted and to shape a religion of their own." This new religion would help shape mainstream Christianity in the future, yet always maintain its own core identity. Most masters were firm in the belief that the Christian religion promoted stability as opposed to more animated African religious traditions that whites did not understand and therefore feared. The conversion of slaves also allowed slaveholders to make the claim that slavery had a noble purpose. Were the slaves never brought to America, slaveholders argued, they would still be in Africa practicing a heathen religion which most whites in the South considered no religion at all. By keeping slaves in the United States, slaveholders claimed that they were actually doing slaves the ultimate service of saving their souls and ensuring for them a place in heaven. As time wore on, white preachers in the South were quick to praise the benefits of slavery and point out that the institution is mentioned numerous times in the Bible. Ministers in pulpits throughout the South regularly quoted a biblical passage from Ephesians that read: "Slaves, obey your earthly masters with deep respect and fear. Serve them sincerely as you would serve Christ." Slaves could receive their religious instruction in a number of ways, depending on the church and the community in which they lived. Some larger churches had separate seating arrangements for slaves and whites with both groups listening to the same white preacher at the same time. In other churches the white preacher might preach to the whites in the morning and the slaves in the afternoon. Another arrangement involved separate services for white and black congregants with a slave preacher used to instruct the slaves. In such cases the slave preacher could only deliver his sermon if white congregants were present to observe and supervise the situation.[25]

While masters saw religion as a positive force in the slaveholding world, many slaves who embraced Christianity had a different perspective from whites on the Bible and its teachings, though they could not reveal this perspective to members of the white community. Slaves were particularly interested in stories from the Old Testament, with Moses being by far the dominant figure. The story of Moses delivering his people from bondage in Egypt was the story that slaves seized upon to give them hope for a better future. Slaves could relate well to the stories of the Israelites, who faced many trials and tribulations before finally gaining their freedom, and who eventually smote their enemies with the help of God. With the onset of the Civil War many slaves believed they were experiencing their own Exodus story as liberating federal armies moved through the Confederacy. According to one Union Army chaplain of the period, "There is no part of the Bible with which [the slaves] are so familiar as the story of the deliverance of the children of Israel. Moses is their ideal of all that is high, noble, and perfect in man." In the South, the slaves and their white masters saw different "promised lands" even as they listened to identical words from a preacher. For whites, deliverance to the promised land meant saved souls and the prospect of eternal life in heaven. On the other hand, for slaves the promised land reflected their dreams of freedom. As John W. Blassingame pointed out, "The slave's faith in God was deep and abiding. He was no abstraction, but a Being who took an interest in the lowly slave and interceded on his behalf. He was the God of freedom to whom slaves prayed for deliverance from bondage."

As was the case with field music, slaves could also use religious music to express themselves in a way that allowed them brief respite from their situation. When whites heard the slaves singing of Moses and the Israelites, they assumed that the slaves were simply praising God and in so doing passively accepting the type of religion that whites had thrust on them. They failed to realize that, when African Americans sang their spirituals, they saw Pharaoh as a central character in a simple musical narrative. He was the white master who kept his slaves in bondage, threatening them with the lash. Likewise, the River Jordan was not a mystical boundary between earthly life and eternal bliss in heaven. It was the great Ohio River that marked the border between the slave states and free soil. Because whites generally underestimated the complexities of black culture, and the degree to which slaves could think, hope, and imagine, they were content to hear those in bondage sing religious songs because to them it seemed to reflect conformity and a sense that the slaves were accepting their place and condition. In reality, the exact opposite was often true. "Slaves prayed for the future day of deliverance to come," maintains scholar Albert J. Raboteau, "and they kept hope alive by incorporating as part of their mythic past the Old Testament exodus of Israel out of slavery." When the slaves sang of Moses they were singing of earthly deliverance in a way that whites completely misunderstood. When they sang about God's gifts they were not the same gifts that whites sang of, even though many of the words of the songs were the same. The slaves took the spiritual music of the whites, based in large part on hymns and other songs of European origin, and added their own words, phrasings, and rhythms to make the music their own. This music would evolve and later be broadly labeled "black gospel music," and in its own way it would move people unlike any other form of American music. Religious music gave slaves the right to express themselves openly under the guise of worshipping the same God as the white masters that they served, but the musical style of their spirituals remained unique to their community.[26]

One former slave later recalled: "The colored people have a peculiar music of their own, which is largely a process of rhythm, rather than written music. Their music is largely . . . a sort of rhythmical chant. . . . Their stories of the Bible placed into words that would fit the music already used by the colored people. While singing these songs, the singers and the entire congregation kept time to the music by the swaying of their bodies or the patting of the foot or hand. . . . The weird and mysterious music of the religious ceremonies moved old and young alike in a frenzy of religious fervor."[27]

Just as many whites viewed the work song as an expression of passivity, they misjudged the slave religious music as a sign that the slaves accepted the world around them and their place in that world. Slave religious ceremonies could not take place without white supervision, and in situations where slave services were held separately, with a slave preacher leading the proceedings, a small committee of local white congregants were usually charged with attending. Sometimes other whites would attend slave services simply to watch the slaves worship and sing as a form of entertainment. "I heard very wild singing at the church," one white observer wrote in 1865, "and looking in I saw a scene of barbaric frenzy. . . . The men sat around singing in monotonous tones, but the women were shuffling and leaping in a circle, clapping their hands high in the air, their heads thrown back. . . . They really looked wrought up to frenzy. Sweat pouring down their faces and eyes glittering." Ironically, the whites who attended the slave services generally shared the collective southern white ethos of slave inferiority and ignorance, yet they were actually witnessing an emotionally complex expression of the slaves' disdain for their situation. Rather than representing acceptance, the religious music of the slaves was an acute manifestation of their belief that one day God would smile upon them, and deliver them from bondage.[28] Because of the way that southern history unfolded after the Civil War, many foundational elements of African American religion in the South that were vestiges of the slave experience remained the same despite emancipation. While the war's outcome had ended the institution of slavery as it had been defined up to that time, it did not give southern African Americans their universal freedom. For decades members of the black community would continue to dream of true freedom and continue to practice their own brand of Christianity. According to Eric Foner, African Americans also inherited from slavery a distinctive version of the Christian faith "in which Jesus appeared as a personal redeemer offering solace in the face of misfortune, while the Old Testament suggests that they were a chosen people, analogous to the Jews in Egypt, whom God, in the fullness of time, would deliver from bondage."[29]

The major difference between African American religious practices before and after the Civil War was that the black community worshipped after the war in their own churches. Once the war ended, former slaves in the South were quick to abandon white churches and form their own separate congregations. This happened for two very basic reasons. After slavery, African Americans were desperate for self-determination in their personal lives, and the South's white congregations refused to recognize former slaves as full-fledged members. The result was the rapid spread of black churches throughout the South. In these churches, free from white scrutiny and interference, former slaves could pray, sing, shout, and stomp as they looked to the heavens and articulated their dreams of freedom and equality in a society that remained closed to them in so many ways. "Black churches are historic, deeply rooted in a separate black religious tradition," historian Charles Reagan Wilson maintained. "Churches served as crucial institutional centers of black life. Under Jim Crow segregation, they were centers of African-American social life—the shelter from the storm and training ground for leaders."[30] Music remained a mainstay of religious rituals and celebrations in black churches, expressing powerful themes of struggle, perseverance, deliverance, and hope. Little wonder that a hundred years after emancipation civil rights demonstrators would sing these same songs, using the words and rhythms of timeless Africa American spirituals to make their points. As in the white churches, the music was designed as an appeal to God, but it went much further. It was (and is) a manifestation of unity and strength with an unmatched intensity. According to noted theologian James H. Cone: "Black music is unity music. It unites the joy and the sorrow, the love and the hate, the hope and the despair of black people; and it moves the people toward the direction of total liberation. It shapes and defines black being and creates cultural structure for black expression. Black music is unifying because it confronts the individual with the truth of black existence and affirms that black being is possible only in a communal context."[31]

Just as the former slaves made their churches their own after the Civil War, they maintained their own brand of religious music, some spontaneous and some created as reworked and reworded versions of traditional white hymns. Commenting on what he saw and heard while visiting services held by former slaves, Unitarian minister Thomas Wentworth Higginson stated, "As they learned all their songs by ear, they often strayed into wholly new versions, which sometimes became popular and entirely banished the others. . . . they sang, reluctantly, the long and short meters of the hymn books, always gladly yielding to the more potent excitement of their own spirituals." African American spirituals and the religious songs of the white community were similar in some ways, but they also differed a great deal in cadence, structure, and musical pattern. The spirituals had godly themes in common with the white music, but they also reflected the daily conditions under which the singers lived, a compilation of sacred and secular verse that dealt with a range of emotions. "In many ways black and white spirituals of the Old South paralleled one another in essence and in thought," Charles Joiner wrote, "But both white and black spirituals retained distinctive characteristics. . . . The slave spirituals were distinguished by an explicit sorrow over the actual woes of the world, an indignation against oppression . . . that had no counterpart in the white spirituals." According to A. E. Perkins, an early chronicler, these songs, with their roots in slavery, were "composed in the fields, in the kitchen, at the loom, in the cabin at night, and were inspired by some sad or awe-inspiring event."[32]

Beginning in the late nineteenth century, music characterized as "blues" would come in large part from a mixture of work-song traditions and religious traditions among the African American community, stirred by other outside influences as well as by the general human need for self-expression. On the surface, it seemed that blues music, with its earthy themes of sex and vice, would be anathema to God-fearing, churchgoing members of the African American community. In reality, however, just as sin and salvation are forever linked, the dividing line between the Saturday-night juke-joint patrons and the Sunday-morning church crowd sometimes blurred, and many blues artists, Charley Patton included, composed blues music with religious overtones. "Though some churchgoers associate blues with the devil," pioneer blues researcher William Ferris has noted, "blues singers call on the Lord for support in their verses, and audiences encourage performers to 'preach the blues.'" In the South's African American community, the pressures of an outside world based on white supremacy both before and after the Civil War tended to trump perceptions of morality and immorality, particularly those that seemed petty, drawing members of the black community together regardless of their moral proclivities. The hardships experienced by all African Americans in an environment controlled by whites lent itself to a sense of black solidarity. Blues scholar Jeff Todd Titon once wrote that within the black community there were "respectables" and "no-counts" who were "brought together by the same outside pressures of white discrimination." As a result, many individuals in the African American community "moved often, if not easily, between Saturday night parties and Sunday services. . . . Blues songs and the dances at which they provided entertainment served a positive social function, not a guilt-ridden negative one."[33]

The talented bluesman and talented black preacher of the era actually had quite a bit in common. They were both charismatic and inspired intense loyalty among members of their audiences. They both had natural charisma and communication skills, and both helped preserve and spread different elements of African American oral traditions. When they spoke, sang, or celebrated, people listened and responded in an intense and emotional way. According to author Michael Harris, the "preaching of enslavement culture flourished" in both the minister's sermon and the bluesman's song. The solicitation from their audiences of emotional release were comparable if not arguably identical. "Far from being antitypes of one another," Harris argued, "the bluesman and the preacher were joint solicitors of response. . . . Church and blues performances in this culture were common experiences, for religious ecstasy and vicarious emotionalism, but were different means to the same ends." Blues musicians in many ways served as "folk theologians" in that they regularly commented on the nature of good and evil, pointed out society's great hypocrisies, and dissected human relationships. Church became a place for young musicians to learn and hone their skills, which they could later place in the context of sinful adult themes, particularly those of a sexual nature, as the musician grew up and experienced more of the real world.

In addition, the dramatic, visionary nature of religious conversion and blues performance drew from a long and complicated lineage of African folk traditions in which a spiritual presence guided individual lives and moved individuals to act in one way or another. As Paul Harvey argued, while the preacher and the bluesman often found themselves in competition for an audience, and for the nickels and dimes that could be either gambled away on Saturday night or dropped in the collection plate on Sunday morning, they actually "offered two apparently contradictory but ultimately complementary versions of black folk spirituality." The preacher and the bluesman were also more than just weekend figures in the black community. They were fixtures of the community who remained in character even when they were not officially working. As Albert Murray pointed out, "The off duty blues musician tends to remain in character much as does the Minister of the Gospel, and as he makes the rounds he also receives a special deference from the Saturday night revelers equivalent to that given off duty ministers by the Sunday morning worshippers." In his recordings, Charlie Patton would at times personify the fine line that separated the bluesman and the preacher. While his rowdy repertoire included primarily secular songs, many with risqué lyrics, he also recorded a version of the traditional spiritual "I Shall Not Be Moved," which he sang with equal passion. In the end, however, blues always seemed to pay better. Patton found this to be true as would later African American performers from B.B. King to Sam Cook. According to King, substituting "my baby" for "my Lord" was definitely more profitable. "That was my first lesson in marketing," King wrote in his autobiography. "Real-life songs, where you feel the hurt and heat between man and woman, have cash value."[34]

Because good musicians have the ability to move people in ways that others do not, there has always been a sense that there might be something spiritual, or perhaps other-worldly, involved with regard to the source of their talents. Believers sometimes use the term "God given gifts" to describe the phenomenon while others simply credit one muse or another for an artist's abilities. With regard to African traditions, Gerhard Kubik has pointed out that "it is even thought generally that no one can develop extraordinary skills or attain fame without some 'medicine' or secret liaison with the supernatural. The spectrum covers musicians, statesmen and so on." An interesting facet of African musical tradition that was transplanted to America—with some later drawing a loose parallel between it and the emergence of blues culture in the American South—was the tradition of the *griot*. Some West African tribes counted among their number special members with musical talents, called griots, who many believed had supernatural powers. The griot was part musician, part poet, part historian, and part holy man, and he held a special place among his people. The griot was a mysterious character who served as a cultural conduit and human archive, memorizing vast numbers of names, places, and events associated with his tribe, and periodically recalling them through song and story. The griot could be a troubadour of sorts, and his music many times addressed current events through biting social comment on the world around him. Some griots served as advisors to village leaders, where they usually formed their own small but significant social class within a particular tribe. Others served royal courts in an imperial setting while still others were traveling musicians performing for the general population or for specific patrons. While griots usually were respected within the African cultural hierarchy, they were also feared and even hated by many who believed that the griot's talents were the result of some sort of interaction with evil spirits. Most Africans traditionally looked upon the griot with an odd mix of admiration and suspicion. Much later, some would romanticize the connection between the African griot and the American bluesman, drawing a parallel between the two in hopes of establishing some type of direct lineage that spanned both the distance between continents and the passage of time. Such claims were generally unfounded although blues singers in the Mississippi Delta like Charley Patton did serve as oral historians and they were, to some, mysterious characters who seemed to have mysterious abilities, especially on Saturday nights. In addition, it can also be argued that the solitary nature of the blues performance links it to the griot tradition and differentiates it from other African American folk styles, including work songs and spirituals, which are forms of song more collective in nature. One first-person eighteenth-century account of African culture, *Green's Collection of Voyages,* gave a description of the griot from a

European perspective that would certainly hold up if applied to the lone blues player of the early twentieth century. According to an observer, the griots he encountered among the African tribes were "persons of a very singular character, and seem to be their poets as well as their musicians, not unlike the bards among the Irish or the ancient Britons."[35]

The presence of race-based slavery in the South from its earliest history created a unique culture in the region that grew more fluid with the progression of time. Whites and blacks lived in two worlds, one that was free and one that was not, yet both races also occupied the same larger world. They interacted with one another on a regular basis in an atmosphere that lent itself to a great deal of cultural exchange. The two groups occupied separate spheres, but the spheres continually cross-pollinated each other. Masters and slaves lived in a distinct environment that accentuated close contact while slaves and poor whites frequently fraternized on the fringes of plantation society. Any encounter between whites and slaves was always complicated and heavily layered. With regard to the poorer reaches of the white community, slaves and poor whites sometimes worked together and relaxed with one another during leisure time, more often than not in the "profane and the overwhelmingly male subculture of drinking and gambling." Some poor whites at times acted violently or cruelly toward the slaves they encountered, while others acted with compassion or kindness as a matter of routine. Some poor whites gained pleasure by arbitrarily exercising the dominance their white skin afforded them over neighborhood slaves. Conversely, others treated neighborhood slaves as equals, at least in the context of an individual, interpersonal relationship. The interplay between slaves and white masters was equally layered. Because most southern plantations included thirty slaves or less, most masters personally supervised their workers. Personal contact between master and slave was frequent and could range from informal and reasonably friendly to regimented and hostile. Regardless, any interaction was defined by the irreconcilable fact that, by law, slavery denied the humanity of individuals who were obviously human beings. "Bought and sold like cattle," historian Philip D. Morgan stated, "bequeathed and inherited like furniture, won and lost like lottery prizes, slaves never-the-less were flesh and blood human beings with whom working relationships had to be established, negotiations arranged, and accommodations reached."

Masters might sign documents describing slaves as property, but when they communicated with their slaves, owners were unequivocally confronted with their bondsmen's humanity. Such realities could not help but affect the master, the slave, and the common environment they shared. As Eugene Genovese stated, "Cruel, unjust, exploitive, oppressive slavery bound two peoples together in bitter antagonism while creating an organic relationship so complex and ambivalent that neither could express the simplest human feeling without reference to the other." In the legally segregated American South, cultural blending was not uncommon. Words with African origins entered the white vocabulary while slaves of African descent learned to speak their own brand of English. As time wore on, most slaves converted—voluntarily or otherwise—to Christianity, yet they practiced their own brand of religion and interpreted the lessons of the Bible in their own way. Musically, the African banza gave way to the banjo, which later emerged as a popular country-music instrument, and slave musicians became proficient at playing Irish reels on the fiddle. The South was a black and white world in terms of law and custom, but in terms of culture there were definitely grey areas in which individuals of both races could express themselves. This created a unique environment for artistic exchange that the South's divisive social system could not suppress. While postbellum southerners, white and black, also worked hard in the railroad yards, lumber camps, and on the loading docks, most were agricultural laborers whose daily life in the fields sometimes touched them as if it were a muse. "Huge swatches of the blues and country music do after all come out of the cotton fields in a very real way," country-music legend Johnny Cash once said; "many a seminal song was actually created there, and more spread person to person."[36]

While slavery was a foundational element of antebellum southern society, most whites in the pre–Civil War South were not slaveholders but simple farmers who worked their own land and who could not afford to purchase slaves. Many of the earliest southern settlers of European descent were primarily of English stock, but others came from Ireland, Wales, and Scotland. Among the most significant Northern European immigrants of the early and mid-eighteenth century was a group known as the Scots-Irish. As the name implies, they were of Scottish descent, but their families had lived in Northern Ireland for decades, transplanted there by the English in an early attempt to introduce Protestantism to the Emerald Isle. Most Scots Irish who came to America arrived first in Pennsylvania and then moved west and south, populating the backcountry of the southern colonies. They remained a minority in their new country but were still represented in large numbers, and the vast majority tended to migrate to the frontier regions in part as a function of their distrust of English authority.

They were rugged pioneers, trailblazers on the cutting edge of American western expansion during the colonial period and afterwards. They lived on the frontier where they built log cabins, made their own laws, and tended to be very clannish. The iconic frontiersmen Davy Crockett was of Scots-Irish descent, as were many average whites who populated the Appalachian region and later the small farms of western Georgia, Alabama, and Mississippi. James H. Webb refers to them collectively as "the wildest, most contentious people on earth . . . their emotions spattering out in poetry, music and brawls. . . . A people who had a strong love of oratory and music, who invented many types of dancing, and who relished any form of competition." The Scots-Irish in the South worked hard and in the rare event that they had any leisure time, they made the best of it. Their community gatherings were often boisterous occasions involving bonfires, freely flowing whiskey, dancing, laughter, music, and physical contests such as foot races and wrestling. However, though described by some as a rowdy lot, in truth the Scots-Irish were a complex people whose ranks did not maintain a singular moral proclivity. They could be ministers who deplored vice, or backwoods louts to whom drinking and gambling were indispensable facets of life. They could be stern, forthright family men or shiftless drifters; petty criminals or respected politicians; rich, poor, or neither.[37]

Beginning with the colonial period, the South was certainly a section of the country conducive to pioneer settlement. Even in the decade leading up to the Civil War much of the region remained an uninviting "thinly populated area of untouched forests and vast grazing lands." In 1850 the distribution of population in the states of Alabama, Georgia, Louisiana, and Mississippi was less than sixteen individuals per square mile. "Such a region was ideally suited," Grady McWhiney pointed out, "for the clannish, herding, leisure-loving" immigrants from the British Isles who "relished whiskey, gambling and combat." By the time of the America Revolution, pioneer immigrants were concentrated in the backcountry from Pennsylvania to Georgia, and they were constantly on the move, as if they were involved in an ongoing quest for prosperity that they believed lay just out of reach over the western horizon. "Migration was a constant in the lives of many of these antebellum southerners," Mc-Whiney continued. "For some it literally meant a chance to escape. . . . Other people moved because they were restless or programmed to do so by their culture." For some families relocation seemed to be a generational rite of passage. In Mississippi, for example, the family histories of many settlers in the years leading up to the Civil War included parents born in Georgia or Tennessee, grandparents born in Virginia or the Carolinas, and perhaps, among the Scots-Irish especially, great-grandparents born in the Pennsylvania backwoods. One English visitor to the South during the 1840s referred to families he encountered as "resolute pioneers of the wilderness, who, after building a log-house, clearing the forest, and improving some hundred acres of wild ground by years of labor, sells the farm, and migrates again to another part of the uncleared forest, repeating this operation three or four times in the course of his life."[38]

Like the slaves, the immigrants from Europe, regardless of their heritage, brought their music with them into the South. Country music, or "hillbilly music" as it was called during the early years of its commercialization in the twentieth century, descended in large part from the Anglo-Celtic ballad brought to America by immigrants from the British Isles. Most of these ballads were simple songs with simple melodies that were influenced over the years by a variety of other sources, particularly the music of African Americans. Most of the early Anglo-Celtic music was not written down, but came to colonial America stored in the hearts and minds of the immigrants. The songs represented an oral tradition that evolved over time, and the tunes that survived to become widely disseminated usually told a good story that reflected the environment in which the immigrants lived. As time and generations passed, many of the melodies remained the same, but new verses and words were added that were more American in character, reflecting not the rolling hills of Ireland, the British glen and dale, or the noble knight and damsel in distress, but the American countryside and the experiences of Americans and their neighbors. According to Bill C. Malone: "Southerners gradually forgot the ballads of their ancestors, but they did not soon abandon the ballad form. They adopted songs from other regions . . . and they also composed their own. Train wrecks, murders, mountain feuds, fires, mine disasters, labor disputes, bad men, lovers' quarrels, war experiences were only a few of the topics that appealed to ballad makers. . . . No one has ever tried to document the precise percentage of themes and moods favored by the southern folk in their music, but the predilection for mournful would certainly rank very high. In part, this inclination was a legacy of the British tradition, because many of the British songs dealt with somber themes."[39]

The story of country music's origins was much more complicated than immigrants from the British Isles simply coming to America, bringing their music with them, and having their descendants alter the music over time to fit American sensibilities. Once in America, any music brought in from the outside by immigrants underwent a transformation due to the nature of the colonial population. American pioneers moved west very quickly, where they mingled with immigrants of different cultural origins. As the English, Irish, or Welsh immigrants began moving west across the southern frontier, they came in contact with a variety of different cultural groups with whom they traded and worked with, fought with, and even intermarried with, including Germans immigrants in Virginia; backcountry Native Americans; Spanish, French, and multi-heritage elements in the Mississippi Valley; Mexicans in the Southwest; and African Americans throughout the South. Later, according to Norm Cohen, "Musicians who got their first calluses on their pappy's fiddle and banjo learned to play the guitar from black construction workers who were part of railroad road gangs. . . . Older Anglo-American fiddle tunes and dances gave way to ragtime or jazzy numbers. Reels and hornpipes, carried across the Atlantic by Scots and Scots-Irish fiddlers played with double stops and drones, were joined by relaxed and syncopated blues melodies." The result was music with an Anglo-Celtic foundation that was influenced by other ethnic and racial strands of culture. Unlike later stereotypes of the genre, country music was never completely pure. That is to say, it was never completely Anglo-Celtic in origin and never completely white.[40]

While the roots of country music are tangled in the old ballads, the ballad form also offered a parallel between the country and blues traditions. Both genres are forms of oral tradition in cultures with a strong reverence for the spoken word. Many southerners, black and white, had a preference for hearing stories about real events as well as tall tales through a musical delivery rather than by reading a book. This was obviously the case for the many eighteenth- and nineteenth-century southerners of both races who were illiterate. While the ballad style is more generally associated with white country music, the blues ballad was not uncommon in the African American community, though it had its own special traits. There is a general consensus among those who have charged themselves with the tedious task of dissecting the music that, while both blues and country ballads constitute a narrative, blues ballads have "an emphasis upon feeling and response to events rather than on narration proper." Similarly, while country ballads have a tendency to "stick to the story," in a journalistic sense, David Evans has argued that the blues equivalents "are narrative folk songs that tell a story in a very loose, subjective manner and tend to 'celebrate' events rather than relate them chronologically and objectively in the manner of other American folk ballads."[41]

Just as it had great influence on the blues, religious music also had a major influence on what would become country music, with the catalyst for the spread of white gospel tunes being the Great Revival, or so-called "Second Great Awakening," that sent tremors through the South in the early nineteenth century. Named for a similar phenomenon that took place in the United States decades earlier, the Second Great Awakening began in the 1790s as a religious movement that emphasized individual redemption and personal moral codes over the philosophical or theological pontifications of the learned. Leaders of the movement argued that "to be fit for heaven, individuals must be regenerated by the power of the holy spirit and born again." They spoke of the wonders of heaven and the inner peace of the converted, but also "upheld the traditional view of hell, argued that divine justice required it, explained the purpose it served, and emphasized its horrors to stimulate sinners to accept Jesus as their savior." While evangelicals of the period did not dismiss education per se, they did warn against any type of teachings or educational pronouncements that might cloud God's message. They believed in taking the Bible literally, and they dedicated themselves to encouraging others to do the same. Samuel S. Hill pointed out that adherents to this new fiery brand of religion had a relatively simple creed. Every person is lost and must be told the good news in an effort to "rescue the perishing from a desperate, eternal condemnation. They are exhorted to and pleaded with to receive the pardon for their sins, which is realized by accepting God's salvation." In 1801 a group of evangelical ministers held the South's first major camp meeting, a massive gathering in Kentucky that drew a crowd of around twenty-five thousand individuals in search of salvation. Year after year these types of gatherings became more common as evangelical Protestantism swept through the South with great fervor, energizing the Baptists, Methodists, and Presbyterians with each denomination doing its best to spread the word among the masses. This explosive brand of religion spread quickly because converts did not have to be educated to be brought into the fold. All they had to do was believe. The message of evangelical preachers usually included emotional appeals to unconditionally accept God's grace, along with stern warnings that nonbelievers were destined to burn with the devil in hell. There was no middle ground.[42]

In addition to emotional appeals by ministers, music was a fixture at the camp meeting and in evangelical churches around the South. Believers seized upon the biblical passage from Psalms that directed them to "Make a joyful noise unto the Lord."[43] Many hymns were traditional in nature, transplanted from Europe, but as time wore on American composers from both the North and the South began writing religious music that had great appeal among southern evangelicals. The music had simple themes that could be easily understood and celebrated, such as the characterization of God as a shepherd tending his flock, an idealized afterlife in heaven, the suffering of Jesus Christ on the cross, and daily struggles with sin and the devil. One of the most popular hymns of the nineteenth century and beyond, "Onward Christian Soldiers," reflected the missionary zeal upon which much of the evangelical movement rested, and the idea that there could be no compromise between following the Lord and going to the devil. Salvation was an all-or-nothing proposition, and the battle between good and evil was fierce and ongoing. "Onward Christian soldiers," the still-popular hymn directed, "marching as to war."[44]

In addition to offering salvation and an eternity of heavenly bliss to the converted, revivalism spread quickly through the South because it met a general social demand. For those isolated in the rural back country, church was a premier social outlet. Even if a rural church met only sporadically, services represented cherished community events, temporary respites from the monotonous daily exercise in survival that characterized most forms of frontier farm work. The church represented the community bosom, providing comfort and hope to those who desperately needed both. As southern historian J. Wayne Flynt has stated, "Among people who generally tended their own medical needs, where the rate of infant mortality was extremely high, where even simple fevers and maladies often took lives, and where raging epidemics occasionally wiped out total communities, the solace of the Balm of Gilead was no small comfort." The church also provided security. To many frontier settlers who were at the mercy of the elements for most of their lives and had little control over their political or economic existence, the promise of ulti-mate vindication and equality for the saved in the eyes of the Lord was a ve-hicle for psychological survival.[45]

Parallels can also be drawn between the experiences of whites and blacks with regard to how many practiced their religion. "Evangelical religion," Flynt maintained, "like country music, sometimes crossed the color line to appeal to both blacks and whites alike." White evangelicalism of the period could be very emotional in character. While some whites of the antebellum period were taken aback at the dancing and wailing of black church services that they vis-ited, others observed similar traits among white evangelicals. One man who attended tent revivals during the 1830s later remembered, "It was not un-usual to have a large proportion of the congregation prostrate on the floor. . . . No distinct articulation could be heard unless from those immediately by. Screams, cries, groans, songs, shouts and hosannas, notes of grief and notes of joy, all heard at the same time, made a heavenly confusion, a sort of inde-scribably concert." Similarly, Godly themed singing outside the confines of the church in both the white and black communities traditionally blurred the line between secular and sacred music. Hymns of praise inside the church were also sung outside the church, where they represent more of a response to the struggle of life than a direct vehicle for praising the Lord. Components of country-music culture from the outset included religious imagery of the home and hearth, a love for a God who can be understood in intimate, fa-milial terms, and above all, the search for salvation. According to researcher Michael J. Gilmour, "Certain themes appear central to this discursive world, including home, family, religion, love and death. The everyday experiences and emotions of working-class life dominate the scene. Suffering, strife, and the potential for redemption from pain are also central motifs, and humor—in theme or wording—often lightens the more painful accounts." The experience was similar with regard to the music of African Americans during the slavery period or afterward, especially the notion that a downtrodden population may one day be liberated from their earthly suffering. Simple themes with broad contexts that fiercely reflected daily life were the rule in many black songs. As in the white churches, African American hymns were expressions of faith but also words to live by in the broader world on the other side of the stained glass. Similar human emotions of struggle, hope, and redemption were tied to the music.

Peeling back the layers of experiences of the black and white American from the seventeenth century forward reveals some similarities among the obvious differences. They were separated by race but also brought together culturally by common threads of class. Regardless of circumstance, the struggle to simply survive was a great concern for individuals of both races, as was the notion of drawing comfort and temporary peace from interaction with loved ones, or from amorous interaction with members of the opposite sex, or from strong drink, or from the Bible. For both races there was always a reward at the end of the struggle, a great release for the believers who worked so hard for what seemed to be so little return.[46] Two stanzas, one from a song by Charley Patton and one from a Jimmie Rodgers song, bear out the similarities and lend weight to the notion that class and religious concerns can transcend race. In "Lord I'm Discouraged," Patton in 1929 sang of pain in the first person:

> Sometimes I get discouraged. I believe my work is in vain
> But the Holy Spirit whispers revive my mind again
> There'll be glory, what a glory, when we reach that other shore
> There'll be glory, what a glory, praising Jesus evermore.

The same year, Jimmie Rodgers recorded "A Drunkard's Child," an ode to the poor and underprivileged who cling desperately to the hope that they will occupy a better world after death. The Rodgers recording included the following lyrics:

> All thru this world I wander,
> They drive me from their door,
> Some day I'll find a welcome
> On Heaven's golden shore.[47]

The stanzas from these different songs offered common, underlying themes of struggle and for the hope of release in the afterlife. They were both laments for the down-and-out who looked forward to a heavenly reward. Their message was similar, and although they were from different works, they could have both fit cozily in the same song.

The old camp-meeting and revival songs transcended denomination through their simplicity, repetitiveness, and general appeal to the "lowest common theological denominator." According to gospel-music researchers Michael P. Graves and David Fillingim, "Because the music was essential in creating the evangelistic and inspirational atmosphere of the camp-meetings and revivals, it remained an essential element of congregational life in the churches." By the late nineteenth and early twentieth century, religious music was widespread in the South's white community thanks in large part to commercial circulation of the "shape-note" hymnal. In these hymn books different notes were represented by different shapes, making it possible for those who did not read traditional music to sing, play, and in general follow the tunes of the songs. During the 1870s Ephraim Ruebush, a Virginia music teacher, and his brother-in-law, Aldine Sillman Kieffer, a Missouri-born musician and printer, founded the Ruebush-Keiffer publishing company. For decades the company was the South's leading producer of shape-note hymnals, distributing hundreds of thousands of books to churches well into the 1940s. In 1903, Tennessean James Vaughan, who is often called the "Founder of Southern Gospel," started the James D. Vaughan Publishing Company and also began distributing religious songbooks throughout the South. Vaughan was a true entrepreneur with a good head for marketing. He employed traveling singing groups, usually gospel quartets similar to the traditional "barbershop" quartet, that promoted his songbooks by performed throughout the southern states. By the 1920s Vaughan had expanded his commercial empire to include his own recording company and one of the first radio stations in Tennessee. In turn, one of Vaughan's employees, Virgil O. Stamps, and songwriter Jesse R. Baxter Jr. partnered in 1926 to found the Stamps-Baxter Music and Printing Company, headquartered in Dallas. Stamps-Baxter helped blur the lines between traditional gospel music and emerging trends in popular music. The company sponsored quartet performances and all-day singing affairs at churches, schools, and county fairs around the South that sometimes included a mix of gospel and more contemporary popular tunes.

In the end, religious or gospel music became a foundational element of emerging country-music culture during the early twentieth century and helped create some of country music's more enduring themes of sin, temptation, and redemption. The phenomenon also brought together the songs and celebrations of both the Saturday-night beer joint and the Sunday-morning sanctuary to produce popular music in a process similar to that which linked the Saturday-night blues juke joints to the pews and pulpits of black churches.

Even in the modern era the phenomenon continues, and religious music remains a potent, traditional link between black and white culture. As Charles Johnson, one of the most successful African American gospel artists of the second half of the twentieth century, once told an interviewer, "This thing has been called black gospel. They call it white gospel. Gospel don't have no color to it. This is programming from man. . . . Man formats his radio station to play white gospel or man programs his station to play what they call black gospel. . . . Now how am I going to put a label on the gospel of God—God's gospel. It don't have a color.[48]

While gospel music at religious gatherings was a traditional manifestation of southern culture during the nineteenth century, other forms of music in the South provided a non-religious social release for whites and blacks alike. For white southerners of the antebellum period, community socials or other parties might include music of a faster tempo that inspired audiences to dance. The music might be performed by one artist or by a small band. The gathering was usually scheduled to punctuate the workweek and give partygoers a temporary respite from the hard agricultural labor that most performed on a daily basis. On large plantations slave musicians sometimes played for white audiences at structured social events and for their peers in the slave quarters at more informal gatherings. The choice of songs at all these events would depend on the audience but would usually include versions of various standards of the day at which slave or white musicians were proficient. At these gatherings, whether formal or informal, the musicians usually accompanied themselves on instruments including the banjo, the fiddle, and the guitar. The evolution of these three particular instruments crossed racial lines time and again until their association with exclusively African American music or exclusively white music was difficult to determine.

European in origin, the fiddle, a type of violin, was probably the most popular instrument in the rural South from the time of the earliest English colonists. It was a mainstay at local white house parties, barn dances, political gatherings, carnivals, and any other gathering where southerners came together to enjoy one another's company. The only exception was the church meeting, where old English folk tales associating the fiddle with the devil led many among the pious to reject the instrument. Southerners liked the fiddle because they viewed it as an all-purpose vehicle for musical entertainment. A talented fiddler could use his instrument to play soft, sad ballads that might provoke a tear, or upbeat reels and jigs for dancing. Fiddling contests were popular community events in colonial times with contestants usually competing for prizes such as a new fiddle, a horse saddle, or even a horse. Like other string instruments used at parties, the fiddle was popular with musicians because it could be packed into a case and carried anywhere very easily. In the South, settlers of European descent took their fiddles with them through the generations as they moved from the East Coast to the Appalachians and beyond. By the close of the nineteenth century, fiddle music could be heard from the Atlantic coast of Virginia to the Texas plains, and from the banks of the Ohio River in northern Kentucky to the Mississippi and Alabama gulf coast. Fiddlers might play solo for hours at parties or dances, and eventually fiddle music became one of the foundations upon which modern country music rested.

In the antebellum South both free whites and slaves mastered the fiddle. In fact, according to Giles Oakley, musical talent could even enhance the market value of a slave. There were frequent references to musical abilities in the slave-advertisement columns in early American newspapers. According to Oakley, "These adverts were either offering slaves for sale or hire, or frequently they were offering a reward for the capture of runaways. Such and Such, a runaway, 'makes fiddles' or 'plays upon the fiddle'; another might be 'artful and can both read and write and is a good fiddler.'" Plantation owners routinely kept fiddlers on their property to entertain at picnics or parties, and these same musicians were popular in the slave quarters where they entertained their peers in the evening or at social events that the planters sometimes allowed workers to organize during slow periods. The slave fiddler used his talents to receive special privileges and, because he entertained at functions for both races, he was unique in that he could move, at least to an extent, between the black and white spheres in a way that other slaves could not. He also played many of the same songs to both audiences. According to fiddling expert and historian Chris Goertzen, "The African American who fiddled at a picnic may stand for hundreds of slave fiddlers busy at white dances. Such occasions constituted the real beginning of the black-white musical exchange that would be so important to American music in general."[49]

While the fiddle remained popular, beginning in the early twentieth century the banjo began to rival it as one of country music's most important instruments, with banjo strummers and especially banjo pickers becoming some of the South's most beloved country entertainers. As the banjo gained popularity in "hillbilly" circles, many southern whites were unaware that this instrument that produced the music they enjoyed, a music that was viewed as almost exclusively "white," was actually of African origin. The long lineage of the banjo traces back to Africa, where strings stretched across drum-like instruments were strummed and plucked for centuries. These more primitive offerings evolved over time into string instruments made from hollowed-out gourds. Slaves brought these instruments into America during the seventeenth century, where they were called by many names including the banza, banjil, banjar, and banshaw. Soon variants of these instruments were in widespread use. In describing slave music in his own state, Thomas Jefferson wrote in 1781 that "In music they (slaves) are generally more gifted than the whites with accurate ears for tune and time. . . . The instrument proper to them is the banjar, which they brought with them from Africa." Likewise, missionary Jonathan Boucher reflected in 1832 that during his early travels through Virginia and Maryland, "The favorite and almost only instrument in use among the slaves then was the bandore, as they pronounced the word banjar. Its body was a large hollow gourd, with a long handle attached to it, strung with catgut and played on with the fingers." Few whites publically performed with banjos until the 1830s, when a traveling white entertainer named Joel Walker Sweeney popularized the instrument by using it in his act. Born in Virginia, Sweeney is generally credited as the artist who added the shortened fifth string to the instrument to provide a richer sound, and with introducing a more sophisticated banjo design to fellow musicians and the general public.

Following the Civil War, the banjo became more mainstream with commercial interests eventually standardizing and manufacturing modern banjos with more complex designs. By the beginning of the twentieth century, musicians who specialized in strumming the banjo toured extensively and the instrument became an integral part of many touring bands. Eventually, many players concentrated on "picking" the banjo—creating music by plucking individual strings in rapid succession—rather than strumming. This new form of musical expression was later labeled "bluegrass," and it became one of country music's most popular genres. Ironically, as white musicians began picking up the banjo, an instrument with African origins, blacks were abandoning it. As racial attitudes evolved, many African Americans associated the instrument with antebellum slavery and paternalism, and its depiction in various forms of media in the South became associated with negative racial stereotypes. It was depicted in many instances as the instrument of a "simple and childlike race." According to Karen Linn, "The general racist ideas that clung to the image of the black banjo player not only encouraged the abandonment of the instrument by blacks, in the end it discouraged the survival of the instrument as a viable vehicle for music making in American culture." As a result, the banjo acquired an antiquated, decidedly lowbrow image that tainted it and at least for a time relegated the instrument to obscurity outside the venues of medicine and minstrel shows and other less sophisticated forms of theater or entertainment. However, this later changed as the modern era unfolded.[50]

For blues and country musicians of the early twentieth century—men like Charley Patton and Jimmie Rodgers—the instrument of choice was, of course, the guitar. The origins of the modern six-string guitar can be traced back to Europe, and particularly Spain, where classical guitar was popular for centuries. During the 1700s Spanish-style guitars were prized throughout the rest of Europe and classical players toured the continent to great acclaim. Most guitars of the period were constructed by violin makers who were members of a tightly controlled guild, which meant that the actual supply of guitars in Europe was limited and individual guitars usually cost a great deal of money. As a result, the guitar was seen as an instrument of the affluent classes far removed from the unsophisticated general public. This changed as the instrument gained popularity over time and other woodworkers began making guitars to meet the demand. Eventually, serious problems developed in Europe between the violin makers' guild and the new guitar makers, with many of the latter craftsmen immigrating to America, where they could freely produce their instruments.

Among those who brought the guitar to America was Christian Friedrich Martin, the son of a Saxony cabinetmaker who arrived with his family in New York in 1833. Martin was a talented woodworker who held positions in European violin shops before chasing his dream of creating a successful guitar-manufacturing business in the United States. Martin succeeded beyond his wildest expectations, creating C. F. Martin and Company, which evolved into one of America's leading guitar manufacturers. During his short but storied career Jimmie Rodgers was known to favor Martin guitars. After the Civil War, Martin had competitors as guitar production in the United States soared. Founded in 1871 in Jersey City, New Jersey, by Oscar and Otto Schmidt, the

Oscar Schmidt Company produced guitars and a host of other string instruments which sold very well, as did the Harmony Company, founded in 1892 in Chicago by William Schultz. Like many other blues performers of his era, Charley Patton usually played an inexpensive but durable Stella Brand guitar, which was manufactured by the Schmidts in New Jersey. Orville Gibson of Kalamazoo, Michigan, was also an influential guitar designer who contributed to the rise of the modern guitar. In the 1880s he began tinkering with new designs for mandolins and guitars that would become standard issue for both instruments. He sold the rights to his designs to several investors who in 1902 formed what would become the Gibson Guitar Corporation. By the turn of the twentieth century American manufacturers were producing more guitars than ever before and the price of individual guitars fell accordingly, allowing almost anyone access to the instrument.[51]

The banjo, fiddle, and guitar came into widespread use in the nineteenth century in part as a result of minstrel shows that emerged during the 1830s as a popular form of entertainment in both the North and the South. A manifestation of acute racism, a minstrel show was usually some form of variety show that included comedy and a great deal of singing and dancing. The shows were initially performed by white men who used burned cork or some other substance to blacken their faces, and who imitated and parodied black forms of music and dance. While the musical performances could be genuine, the shows promoted every negative stereotype that many whites held toward African Americans, lampooning blacks as loud, simple-minded, and lazy. In many cases they also presented a fictional and extremely romanticized version of plantation life in the Old South, steeped in paternalism and complete with characters including the kind master and the ignorant, ever-loyal "darkie." The typical minstrel show consisted of several white men in blackface "armed with an array of instruments, usually banjo, fiddle, bone castanets, and tambourine." The shows varied in length but usually included raucous singing, satirical monologues, and slapstick comedy in addition to narrative skits. Ironically, as time wore on many minstrel shows became an outlet for African American performers who, despite the racial overtones, found performing in such a manner preferable to making a living as an agricultural laborer. Because these shows were almost always performed by a traveling troupe, minstrel shows affected both blues and country-music culture in the South by exposing blacks and whites to many songs that they had never heard before. Songs written by professional songwriters poured into the South's musical melting pot via what would later be considered one of the most racist forms of entertainment that ever existed in the United States.

Many traditional tunes associated with the South first became popular as minstrel songs, including "Oh Susannah," "Old Dan Tucker," "Blue Tailed Fly," the Stephen Foster standard "Old Folks at Home (Suwannee River)" and, of course, "Dixie." According to historian Edward Ayers, "The minstrel shows, always on the lookout for new material, brought a steady infusion of the latest songs from vaudeville, Tin Pan Alley, and ragtime to the South." Researcher Eric Lott has pointed out that these shows had a huge impact not only on American music but on white American culture in general. "From *Oh! Susanna* to Elvis Presley, from circus clowns to Saturday morning cartoons," Lott wrote in his study of minstrelsy in the United States, "blackface words have figured significantly in the white [imagination]. Without the mistral show there would have been no *Uncle Tom's Cabin* (1852), *Adventures of Huckleberry Finn* (1884), and John Howard Grifin's *Black Like Me* [1961]." One of the most famous minstrel songs of the pre–Civil War era, "Jump Jim Crow," lent part of its name to the so-called "Jim Crow" laws of the twentieth century that codified segregation in the southern United States.

Despite the harsh racial imagery, many African Americans attended minstrel shows and, at least to an extent, appropriated this form of entertainment for their own purposes, laughing at private jokes among themselves and, in the case of black musicians, seizing the opportunity to make a good living at anything other than field labor. For African American minstrels, any type of performing was preferable to picking cotton all day, and they relished the opportunity to both perform and travel. It offered them, in a backhanded way, more freedom in a world where freedom was a commodity. They were forced to "play along" and conform to racial stereotypes, lest they agitate white audiences, but in so doing they benefited by acquiring mobility. By taking on the guise of a non-threatening, buffoonish character, the black minstrel gained freedom of movement in a way that average African Americans in the South could not. Renowned Delta blues musician Joseph Lee "Big Joe" Williams was among the early blues musicians who took advantage of any opportunities that the minstrel show provided. "Everywhere, we went everywhere," he later remembered. "They had dancing, cracking jokes, blackfaced comedians—we all used to do that. Take flour and soot to make you dark; we had wigs we wore sometimes; we had them old high hats and them long slop [frock] coats and a walking cane and them button-type spats." For anyone whose people were oppressed, mobility of any type signified independence and freedom, irresistible luxuries in the nineteenth-century black world. In addition, the minstrel show allowed black musicians on the road the opportunity to associate with one another and collectively hone their talents. It was also a training ground for many blues musicians, serving as a unique vehicle through which black performers could safely tour the South and gain experience entertaining large crowds.[52]

While it seemed to some a rather primitive form of entertainment, the minstrel show was of great importance in the South because it represented a vehicle for the blending of white and black culture and musical styles. According to W. T. Lhamon Jr., in most minstrel performances "race relations were their constant topic, in all modes." Minstrel skits and music highlighted interaction between whites and blacks in both exaggerated and subtle contexts. White pretension was a common theme in concert with black clowning. While minstrel performances never challenged white authority, those portraying the African American subordinate in skits were sometimes able to win the day, outsmarting their white antagonists by using nonthreatening foolishness and an ability to "make an art of talking back under cover of playing stupid." The music that was always part of these spectacles had a distinct racial mix. In his book on blackface minstrelsy, Eric Lott stated that the minstrel show's humor, songs, and dances were culturally mixed to the extent that their racial origins were difficult to distinguish. This included African American folklore interspersed with southwestern humor; black banjo techniques and rhythms mixed with folk music from of the British Isles; and the relentless "earth-slapping footwork" of the black dances alongside jigs and reels of Irish origin. According to blues historian Francis Davis, "as a defining episode in American race relations, the minstrel show is a rich and ambiguous topic. . . . Minstrel shows provided scores of white Americans with their first taste of black music, no matter that it was secondhand." Among those white performers who "blackened up" for minstrel-style performances was a young Jimmie Rodgers in the days before he became famous. In fact, yodeling, which was a Rodgers trademark on record and a trademark device of early country music, was a musical device used in minstrel shows dating back as far as the 1840s.[53]

The old-style "medicine show" was also an entertainment staple for blacks and whites in the rural South during the nineteenth and early twentieth century. Predating minstrel shows, the medicine show was usually a traveling wagon affair that hawked various "miracle cures" and other types of alleged medications from settlement to settlement, town to town, and city to city. Usually the miracle drug was a pill of some sort or some type of bottled, colored liquid that included a generous dose of alcohol. Blues performer and Patton contemporary Furry Lewis, who started off in medicine shows, once told an interviewer, "We sold Jack Rabbit syrup, we sold corn salve. And we sold, like they got now aspirins, but they was the best aspirins in the world, you know. That's what they say on the doctor's show." Likewise, as a young man country-music legend Roy Acuff worked in a medicine show for an alleged healer named "Doc" Hauer who sold a product called Mocoton Tonic that (according to the label) cured "dyspepsia, sick headaches, constipation, indigestion, pain in the side, back and limbs, torpid fever, etc." "That's the best experience a boy can get," Acuff recalled many years later. "I didn't make much money at it, but I got a pretty good background in show business. . . . I found out that I could fiddle and I found out that I could sing a song, or sell a song, and I found out that the people appreciated me." To draw a crowd, medicine shows used various forms of entertainment that could include singers, musicians, dancers, jugglers, and magicians. Some medicine show performers also performed in blackface and, as with the minstrel show, African American musicians sometimes toured with the groups.

Early in his career, bluesman Aaron Thibeaux "T-Bone" Walker toured with a medicine show and later recalled, "Dr. Breeding hired me and another boy, Josephus Cook, to ballyhoo for him. . . . I'd play and feed jokes to Seph, and he'd start in to dance. Then we'd stack up the bottles and Doc would come on." Not long after the end of the Second World War, B.B. King, fresh from the Mississippi Delta and a Walker devotee, began his storied performing career in Memphis singing a simple radio jingle that promoted a health tonic called Pepticon. The medicine show was another vehicle for exposing rural audiences to songs that they would probably never have heard in the era before recorded music. Many songs from Tin Pan Alley—a prolific group of musicians and music publishers centered in New York City around the turn of the twentieth century—made their way South via the medicine and minstrel shows, where they became very popular. Among the Tin Pan Alley tunes that became American classics were "In the Good Old Summertime," "Shine On Harvest Moon," "Down by the Old Mill Stream," "They'll Be a Hot Time in the Old

Town Tonight," and "Hello! Ma Baby (Hello Ma Ragtime Gal)." In many cases
the traveling medicine show was the only form of entertainment that many
rural people saw in the course of a year, so naturally the shows drew very big
crowds that included whites and blacks. According to Francis Davis, the medicine shows, like the minstrel shows, created a musical backdrop for racial interaction that was otherwise restricted. "Though prevented from meaningful
contact by custom and law," Davis has argued, "whites and blacks increasingly
shared a taste in music—another way of saying that what was eventually called
'country' and what was eventually called 'the blues' shared a similar genesis in
these medicine shows."[54]

By the turn of the twentieth century, legal separation of the races was the
norm in Mississippi and the rest of the South, but in reality cultural separation
could never be completely accomplished. While whites and blacks might not
be allowed to eat together in the same restaurants or stay in the same hotels,
they still walked the same country roads and city streets, saw the same scenery and breathed in the same air. They lived side by side, within literal earshot
of one another, and they had been listening to each other's music for generations. In many ways the music of white southerners and black southerners was
the same at its core, with layers of environmental factors creating the social
and cultural distinctiveness. It was no coincidence that the themes and tensions that propelled country music—loneliness, vice, struggle, escape, God,
the devil, and love—also dominated the blues. It is a testament to the fact that
they were universal folk themes held not by blacks and whites in a segregated
South, but by southern human beings, all of whom were forever culturally
linked. In the early twentieth-century South, music was a great manifestation
of emotions that were universal and not restricted by race. Both blacks and
whites experienced happiness and sadness, joy, regret, and heartache. Individuals of both races had the ability to reflect on their past and contemplate
their future. They could view and comment on the things going on around
them with either laughter or disgust, and they reacted to life's ups and downs
in a similar fashion. And they were all moved by music, which is as universal
as the emotions it conveys. Rather than serve as a divisive force, music tends
to promote interaction through cultural ebbs and flows that are both constant
and unpredictable. It can be a means of communication between two races
that have trouble communicating on other levels because of their social environment. "As a tool for arousing feelings and emotions, music is better than

language." neuroscientist Daniel J. Levitin wrote in his study of the effects of music on the human brain. "The multiple reinforcing cues of a good song—rhythm, melody, contour—cause music to stick in our heads."[55]

In 1900, Charley Patton and Jimmie Rodgers were children. Patton was nine years old and about to begin his musical education. Rodgers was still a toddler at age three, destined for a job as a railroad man, and later a musical career unmatched by any country artist of his time. In the parlance of notoriety, neither man "came out of nowhere." They were both a product of their times and the environment in which they grew up. They were a product of their race and of the racial divide that existed in the United States during their lifetimes. They were also the product a unique society that could be officially fractured by law and custom, but not always culturally segregated in practice. Long before blacks and whites in the South mingled legally in public places, music was already helping in its own way to subtly integrate the region. The ironies are many and varied. The tension and turmoil of a segregated South in the early twentieth century created a sense of place and culture that fostered great artistic focus. This sense created fertile soil where blues and country music could both put down roots, and it fostered creative exchange between white and black artists that was all the more intense because it went against rigid social norms. The music itself drew people together in a world where man's law tried to force them apart, and it began breaching the walls of segregation in an era when those walls were high, strong, and sometimes dangerous. As blues researcher Tony Russell wrote: "Consider the landscape. A musician would be open to sounds from every direction: from family and friends, from field and railroad yard, lumber camp and mine; from street singers and traveling show musicians; from phonograph records and radio; from dances and suppers and camp meetings and carnivals; from fellow prisoners in jail, from fellow workers everywhere. . . . In all but the most tightly enclosed communities, there was some degree of interaction, and, as the twentieth century grew older, and group isolation rarer, the threads of the two traditions were more and more often entangled."[56]

★★★★ 2 ★★★★

COMING OF AGE

I will sing with the spirit, and I will sing with the understanding also.
—1 CORINTHIANS 14:15

While they were born a generation after the Civil War's end, Charley Patton and Jimmie Rodgers both came into a world completely immersed in the fallout from the conflict. The environment in which both grew up was little different from the antebellum era when many whites were poor and African Americans were denied their full civil and political rights. Though they lived in a legally segregated world, most whites and blacks in turn-of-the century Mississippi had settled into a pattern of life that revolved around the simple concept of survival. Sharecropping was a common occupation, and little hard money circulated through the state. A rigid social system separated the races, and African Americans were denied influence in the political process. Public schools, white and black, were consistently underfunded, and illiteracy rates among both groups were high.

While Charley Patton lived most of his adult life in the Mississippi Delta, he was born in Hinds County, Mississippi, in the central part of the state near the small town of Edwards, about halfway between the state capital at Jackson and the port city of Vicksburg on the Mississippi River. Edwards and the surrounding vicinity had been hit particularly hard by the Civil War. Situated near the Pearl and Big Black rivers, the land around Edwards produced a great deal of cotton before the conflict, and the Edwards railroad depot, situated as it was on the Vicksburg and Montgomery railroad line, was a major focal point for local cotton shipping. The war came to the area in force on May 16, 1863, when 32,000 Union troops under the command of Ulysses S. Grant clashed with 22,000 Confederates under General John C. Pemberton at the Battle of Champion Hill near Edwards in the pivotal battle of Grant's campaign to take Vicksburg. Thousands of men fell during the Union victory, and before they left the

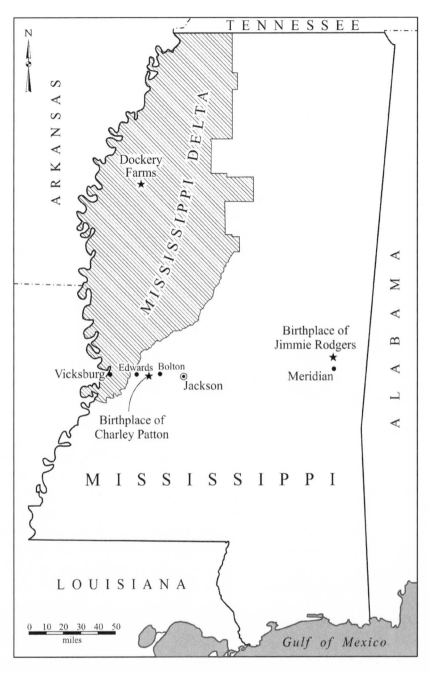

Mississippi: The Home of Charley Patton and Jimmie Rodgers.

area Federal troops burned the Edwards railroad depot. After the war, Mississippi's economy was still based in agriculture and Hinds County continued to produce a great deal of cotton and other crops with African American share-croppers rather than slaves serving as the area's primary labor force. By the turn of the twentieth century, two-thirds of the county's population was black.[1]

Tracing Charley Patton's heritage can be a fairly convoluted process due to a combination of sketchy records and decades of rumors and gossip about the man. Even Patton's birthdate is in dispute. According to federal census records, Charley Patton was born in April of 1891, and his headstone, which was placed on his grave many years after his death, gives the same date. The years 1881, 1885, and 1887 have also been given by various sources as his year of birth. I have given the greatest weight to the federal census records stating that Patton was born in April 1891 in Hinds County, Mississippi. Questions also revolve around the actual spelling of Patton's first name. While his record label and many who later wrote about him spelled the name "Charley," which I also use, others suggest that he may have preferred "Charlie." Even on his death certificate the spelling of his first name is difficult to discern, although on his tombstone the name is spelled with the "ey."[2]

Many of Patton's distant ancestors originally came from Africa, brought to America as slaves, but like so many individuals labeled "black" in the bifur-cated Jim Crow South, the bluesman was actually of mixed heritage. His father's lineage included some white and perhaps Native American ancestry, but no one, including Patton himself, could identify precisely all of the blood that flowed through the bluesman's veins. Patton's contemporaries frequently com-mented on the singer's light complexion and speculated as to its origins. David "Honeyboy" Edwards, a fellow musician who saw Patton perform many times, later recalled that "he was a yellow mulatto, with curly hair," while Chester "Howlin' Wolf" Burnett, who became a blues icon in his own right after work-ing with Patton, once told an interviewer that in appearance "Charley Patton was more Indian than Negro. He was a half-breed, you know." Patton's mixed race heritage was significant in the African American community where social strata could be determined by the lightness or darkness of the skin. Accord-ing to researcher Paul Oliver, African Americans were influenced by skin hue, "about which they were almost pathologically self-conscious by the very fact that they were perpetually reminded of its existence as a social barrier. . . . 'white' attributes were often much admired." If black and white were legal distinctions in the South as a whole, various shades of "yellow," brown and black, many times defined status in the African American community. While the notion that "lighter" was somehow a better station, or more attractive, or more sophisticated, was not universal per se, in the primitive world of many of the South's black communities at the turn of the twentieth century it was a solid societal component. Charley Patton himself bore this out when, commenting on the type of women that he preferred, he sang in "Pony Blues," "brownskin woman like something fit to eat, but a jet black woman don't put your hands on me."[3]

Quiet controversy in the form of whispers and raised eyebrows also surrounded Patton's more immediate heritage. According to one version of the Patton story, the first Patton in the South to know freedom was Charley's grandfather John, who was born around 1841 in Tennessee, most likely as a slave. Following the Civil War, John Patton made a rough living as a sharecropper in the Mississippi Delta, first in Desoto County and then Coahoma County. John had a number of children, one of whom was Charley Patton's father, who was born in March of 1864 and named Bill.[4] According to another account, Bill Patton was actually the product of a sexual liaison between a white slave owner also named Bill Patton and one of his slaves who was of African and Native American ancestry. If a white slaveholder was indeed Charley Patton's biological grandfather, as formidable blues researcher David Evans suggests, it could have been a white man named William E. Patton, who was forty-six years old and living with his family in the Mississippi Delta at the time of Bill Patton's birth. According to federal census records, William E. Patton was a South Carolinian who had lived in Tennessee and moved to Mississippi around 1847.[5]

Bill Patton, Charley's father, grew up in the Mississippi Delta, in the northwest part of the state, but in his teens he moved south to the vicinity of Bolton and Edwards, Mississippi, in Hinds County, where he married Annie Martin and began a large family that eventually included at least seven children. Bill Patton was a large man, probably weighing in the neighborhood of 350 pounds, and he had a relatively light complexion that some of his grandchildren later described as "bright" and "red." Devoutly religious, he preached from time to time and had a reputation as a dependable fieldworker. Charley's mother Annie Martin was born in 1861, and according to most accounts was "a short, brown-skinned woman with strait hair, of partial Indian ancestry."

The couple lived and worked on a local plantation known as "Heron's Place," named for its owner, Sam Heron. There, in 1891, their eldest son, Charley Patton, was born.[6]

As was the case with his father, questions also arose as to the biological origins of Charley Patton. While most people who knew the family always regarded Bill Patton as Charley's father (as did Charley himself), an alternate version of the bluesman's origins also made the rounds in Delta. According to some sources, Charley bore Bill Patton's surname, but not his blood. When he was younger Bill Patton was far from the quintessential family man, and tended to spend long stretches away from home, leaving his wife Annie to care for their children and earn a meager living on the Heron place. During one of these separations, Annie allegedly began spending time with Henderson Chatmon, a former slave who sharecropped on a neighboring plantation and was the patriarch of a large family there. The Chatmon clan later claimed that Charley Patton was actually one of their own, fathered during one of Bill Patton's lengthy sojourns away from home. Sam Chatmon, one of Henderson's musician sons sometimes referred to Patton as his "brother," and bluesman Houston Stackhouse, who knew the Chatmon clan, once told an interviewer that Henderson's sons "were Charley Patton's half-brothers" and that Patton was one of Henderson's "outside boys." The story was plausible to many, particularly after Patton made a name for himself as a musician. In addition to being a noted womanizer, Henderson Chatmon was an expert fiddler, and several of his sons became prominent blues performers in their own right. To those who chose to believe the story, the source of Charley Patton's musical prowess was obviously genetic.[7]

Regardless of whether Henderson Chatmon was Charley Patton's biological father, the Chatmon family had a significant musical influence on Patton during his formative years. They were a musical family who made the most of their considerable talents. Henderson Chatmon was born a slave around 1850 and learned to play the fiddle as a young man, taught by a white plantation owner named Robert Lacy. He became such a proficient fiddler that after the Civil War he was in demand to play rural square dances and other events for both white and black audiences in and around Hinds County. "My daddy, he was a slavery-time man," one of Chatmon's sons once told an interviewer. "He went by Chatmon 'cause his master was Old Man Chatmon. . . . He worked in the field awhile, but he played music in slavery times."[8] Like many blues artists who were already familiar with the music of the cotton fields, Chatmon also learned "white" music to play for his white audiences. Many of these songs were barn dance standards such as "Can't Get the Saddle on the Old Grey Mule," "Little Liza Jane," and "Granny Will Your Dog Bite?" Chatmon had a large family that included a number of gifted musicians who later became part of a prominent touring band called the Mississippi Sheiks. Formed in the 1920s and taking their name from the famous Rudolph Valentino movie of the period, the Sheiks were, for the most part, a string-and-fiddle outfit. They were very popular in and outside of Mississippi and in the years leading up to the Second World War were one of the most successful African American acts to come out of the region. They toured the southeastern United States but also roamed as far north as Chicago and as far west as San Antonio, playing blues and country music along with popular Tin Pan Alley standards of the day. "We played parties everywhere," Sam Chatmon later recalled, "for colored and white, too. All we wanted was the money. If we could play two and a half hours we would get five dollars a man. When we'd get through with crops, late · on 'bout June or July, we'd all get together and take a tour all up through Memphis and Chicago and different places like that." The Sheiks were pioneers in the blues genre who had great influence on American popular music in their own right. For instance, they wrote "Sittin' on Top of the World," a well-known blues standard later recorded by Bill Broonzy and Howlin' Wolf as well as the "King of Texas Swing" Bob Wills and his Texas Playboys. Whether he was actually part of the family or not, Charley Patton grew up around the Chatmons and was exposed to their musicianship early on. He also kept up with several members of the family later in life and reportedly played with them occasionally.[9]

Not only were the Chatmons likely a great musical influence on Charley Patton, they also may have shown him the more practical powers of music in the segregated South. Anyone who could generate income from performing music could conceivably avoid a typical sharecropper's life of mundane agricultural labor. A good musician was not completely tied to the monotony of the plantation. He could travel from place to place performing, which was an enticing prospect and a unique opportunity for a young African American male in the South during the first decade of the twentieth century. An African American musician who sometimes performed for whites might also be able to "get along" a little better than his contemporaries in a world that was dominated by whites. With regard to the Chatmons, "the scope of Henderson's repertoire appears to have been shaped by his long-standing interaction with whites in Central Mississippi," Christopher A. Waterman explained. This allowed Chatmon and his family "to weave a set of socio-economic relationships that crossed the color line." Patton could not help but notice that the Chatmons were somehow different from other agricultural laborers that he came in contact with. They moved a little more freely and with a little more confidence through the world of the white man than did the typical sharecropper who silently navigated row after row of cotton each day. They enjoyed a less tense relationship with many whites and were admired by many blacks as well. According to musician and author Ben Sidran, with the end of the Civil War, African Americans began to equate freedom with mobility, and as time wore on the traveling musician in many ways "became the ultimate symbol of freedom. Escape from the static monotony of black employment, combined with the ability to make a living without having to rely on the white man— beating the white man at his own game, in other words—kept the musician's status high."[10]

At some point shortly after the turn of the twentieth century Bill Patton chose to move his family from Hinds County to the Mississippi Delta, in the northwestern part of the state. As with other details surrounding Charley Patton's early life, the date of this move is in dispute. Some sources say the Pattons moved to the Delta in 1897 although according to United States census records the Patton family was still living in Hinds County as of June 16, 1900.[11] The reasons for the move have also been debated through the years. There is little doubt that Bill Patton chose to move his family to the Mississippi Delta because he thought he could make a better living there. However, some said the move was the result of his being jealous of some of his wife's local suitors, particularly Henderson Chatmon. Others have maintained that the family moved in part to get young Charley away from members of the Chatmon clan who the religious Bill Patton considered bad influences. For whatever reason, the Pattons packed their belongings and moved to a unique region that ultimately produced some of America's most legendary musicians, Charley Patton among them.

What is traditionally referred to as the Mississippi Delta by those interested in blues music is technically misnamed. A delta is defined as an area composed primarily of silt deposits that have built up over an extended period of time at the mouth of a river. These deposits usually form a geographic pattern resembling the shape of a triangle, the same shape as the fourth letter of the Greek alphabet, delta. The actual delta region of the Mississippi River is located around New Orleans at the river's mouth, some three hundred miles south of the area where Charley Patton made music. The region that was Patton's home and the cradle for generations of blues musicians is more properly called the Yazoo-Mississippi Delta, or simply the Yazoo Delta. Shaped more like a diamond than a triangle, it is actually an alluvial floodplain between the Mississippi River and one of its important tributaries, the Yazoo River in northwestern Mississippi. The soil there has always been exceedingly fertile, the result of thousands of years of silt deposits from Mississippi and Yazoo river floods. In his definitive study of the region, titled *The Most Southern Place on Earth,* historian James C. Cobb described the land's physical boundaries: "The Mississippi River, which runs southward from Memphis to Greenville, where it then bends slightly eastward toward Vicksburg, forms the western boundary of the area. On the east, the Yazoo Delta is defined by a line of bluffs, some reaching two hundred feet in height. These bluffs run from slightly below Memphis south to Greenwood and then southwesterly along the Yazoo River, which meets the Mississippi at Vicksburg. The Yazoo-Mississippi Delta is approximately two hundred miles long and seventy miles across at its widest point. The area within its boundaries is approximately 7,110 square miles."[12]

Regardless of the semantics involved in defining the geological and geographic ebbs and flows of two rivers and their alluvial flood plains, the area became popularly known as the Mississippi Delta, with Mississippi natives and many blues enthusiasts usually referring to it simply as "The Delta." The land within its borders would come to define not just a geographic region, but a way of life as well. For most of its history the Mississippi Delta was a swampy, impenetrable wilderness of various types of trees, tall grasses, and tangled vines. William Faulkner once described it as a "vast flat alluvial swamp of cypress and gum and brake and thicket lurked with bear and deer and panthers and snakes."[13] The first whites who settled the Delta in the 1820s were confined primarily to the areas adjacent to the rivers, particularly the Mississippi, because there were no passable roads in the region. Despite the inclination of some writers to romanticize the area's first European settlers as hearty pioneers looking for an opportunity to pull themselves up by their own bootstraps, many of the first settlers were actually men with means. Many people knew that the Delta was extremely fertile, but the swamps were so dense and the forests so thick that the chore of clearing the land for cultivation was labor intensive and, for most whites, cost prohibitive. As a result, while many of the first Deltans were white, many more were black. As noted Mississippi writer and Delta native David L. Cohn stated in his memoirs, "The men who came to the Delta were the embodiment of a seeming contradiction—pioneers with means. They were the sons of wealthy and moderately wealthy planters. . . . Traveling like princely patriarchs of the Orient, they brought with them their slaves and their household goods." Planters with resources brought in slaves to clear land and cultivate cotton, rice, and other staple crops. Suddenly the land began to produce, and over time some began to perceive the Delta as a potential planter's paradise. More planters entered the region, as did many more slaves. By 1840 the population of Washington County, in the heart of the Delta district along the Mississippi River, included only 654 free whites among 6,637 slaves. Delta slaves usually toiled dawn until dusk, performing difficult manual labor on endless acres of bottom land and swamps that needed clearing, draining, and cultivating to produce profits for their masters. The difficult nature of the work lowered life expectancies among the slave population, as did the insect-borne diseases that sprang from the Delta swamps.[14]

The Civil War temporarily interrupted the development of the Delta, but afterwards cotton planters made a concerted effort to continue transforming the area into a vast cotton kingdom. In so doing they also sought to turn back the clock and reinstitute an economic and social system that was more antebellum than modern. It was a simple equation. In the Delta a relatively small number of whites controlled most of what remained very fertile land, but they could not profit from their holdings without a large number of agricultural workers to pick and process cotton. Their ideal was a large labor force permanently tied to the land that was paid as little as possible for their work. Under this system all the profits would flow to the landowner while the workers would live a hand-to-mouth existence. Obviously, the problem with creating such a system was that the Civil War and the Thirteenth Amendment to the United States Constitution had ended slavery. Workers had to be paid, and they could not be held against their will.

For the major landowners there was also a problem linked to simple supply and demand. As long as there was a high demand for laborers, African American workers would have to be given some kind of consideration. Because demand was such that many plantations needed labor, a landlord who abused his workers might not have workers for very long. As early as 1868 the Freedman's Bureau was reporting that in the Mississippi Delta "the demand for labor is greater than the supply, there being applications in this office for several thousand more laborers than can be processed." While planters certainly hoped to keep their workers' pay at a minimum, and in so doing keep their profits higher, some felt that they must exercise a certain degree of "kindness and forbearance" toward those who worked their fields "in order to retain them as laborers." While planters clearly held the upper hand in the region, there was room for negotiation and, depending on the circumstance, some African American farmers did have a degree of leverage in dealing with landlords. This leverage had to be exercised judiciously, of course, as there was always a line that African Americans were not allowed to cross, no matter what the circumstance. As time wore on, however, and the Jim Crow system became more firmly entrenched, the door to land ownership and limited prosperity began to close. By 1920 only a crack in the door remained as many moderately successful African American farmers "fell back among fellow blacks who had long ago relinquished their hopes for a brighter future in the Delta." Similar to the docile slave of the antebellum period, the docile agricultural worker of the early twentieth century had little chance of economic advancement in the Delta, but he could survive without significant trouble and maybe even make a little money as long as he "knew his place" and remained there. Deference and anonymity were important survival tools, as was a general rootlessness that allowed workers to pick up stakes and move from one place to another. Movement signified independence as well as escape. Even if the move was not far, it was a victory of sorts.[15]

Immediately following the Civil War there was a brief period during Reconstruction when it seemed that, rather than a vast cotton kingdom controlled by a few major landowners, the Delta might be a place where yeoman farmers, white and black, could put down roots and make a good living. The war disrupted the plantation economy of the South, and there was talk of major land redistribution as a result of the end of slavery. Some white and black farmers moved into the area once the war ended, but the small farmer's paradise never developed. Instead, as Reconstruction ended, ultraconservative politicians and their friends regained control of Mississippi. They held most of the state's resources and used their political connections at the state and national levels to benefit themselves financially. While some yeomen whites and blacks remained in the Delta after Reconstruction, many were financially insecure and did not have the resources to clear and cultivate large holdings. In the meantime, wealthier Delta planters began building levees, clearing land, and draining swamps to increase their acreage and influence. They successfully appealed to the state and federal governments for resources, and for funding for subsidies to railroads who built lines through the region to haul cotton to lucrative markets in New Orleans, Memphis, and beyond. In a relatively short time the region began to expand economically. Land values increased and the rich got richer. Massive cotton plantations developed, and a relatively small group of planters came to dominate this new plantation kingdom. "The Delta that emerged from this process was not the open, competitive agricultural society that had been the promise of the early 1870s," Cobb has observed, "but the undisputed domain of an ambitious and grasping planter-business-professional elite." These men dominated politics in the region and controlled most of the Delta's financial resources. They ruled the poorer whites and the massive number of African American who eventually came into the region to work the cotton fields.[16]

In addition to controlling the area's economy and the black workers who toiled on their land, the Delta planter class was also very image-conscious. They crafted for themselves in the New South a world that, in their minds, mirrored the idealized version of Old South plantation life that would later be depicted in films such as *Gone With the Wind*. They saw themselves as benevolent patriarchs whose fair but firm hand had created a thriving industry. As for how they viewed their African American labor force, the planters echoed the self-serving notions and illusions of antebellum slave owners. White supremacy was the foundation of the society that the planters controlled, and as far as they were concerned their workers were engaged in the only type of labor that suited them. They maintained that the African Americans who worked on Delta plantations were not capable of functioning in society without rigid supervision. By the turn of the twentieth century, in the seventeen counties that lay completely or in part in the Delta, African Americans were approximately 80 percent of the total population.[17] In some counties whites represented 10 percent of the population or less. When Charley Patton's family moved to Sunflower County in the Delta around the turn of the century, blacks outnumbered whites there three to one. Regardless of what they thought about their workers, white planters lived among thousands of them in an atmosphere that generated anxiety among whites who wanted to remain in control, and violence against any African American who challenged the Delta's social system.

African American migration to the Mississippi Delta began after the Civil War as word circulated about the area's rich soil and overall potential. Some former slaves were able to acquire small plots of land to call their own, but many would end up working as sharecroppers on land owned by wealthy whites. Encouraged by the planter elite who needed workers to make their land profitable, impoverished African Americans from other parts of the state came into the region looking for work. The sharecropping system that developed in the rest of Mississippi and the Deep South was particularly severe in many parts of the Delta. Most black workers who envisioned working for the white landowner until accumulating enough money to purchase their own farm saw that dream evaporate as the sharecropping system took root and flourished. African Americans who borrowed money from a landowner or purchased goods on credit from local merchants at the beginning of the growing season found it more and more difficult to pay off their obligations once they sold their crop. Most of the ready cash they accumulated went to the landowner or merchants to pay off debts, leaving the workers with little or nothing at the end of the cycle. Fluctuating crop prices and the ability of some unscrupulous landowners and merchants to manipulate credit terms added to the misery. The "evils of the plantation system have kept the 'emancipated' sharecropper in debt, poverty, and peonage since the Civil War and are continuing to do so," the National Association for the Advancement of Colored People reported in 1935. "Settlements at the end of the year are often figured with a 'crooked pencil' to keep the sharecropper in debt." Some African American farmers were able to make a fair living under the system, but most could not. The 1910 U.S. Census of Agriculture did not explore in detail the economic and social plight of black sharecroppers in the region, but it did report that "the plantation system is probably more firmly affixed in the Yazoo-Mississippi Delta than in any other area of the South. The fertile soil and climatic conditions favorable for cotton raising, together with the large negro population, make the plantation the dominant form of agricultural organization in the Delta."[18]

Although some sharecroppers lived better than others, many were barely able to sustain themselves and their families. Typically, sharecroppers lived in unpainted wooden shacks scattered around the landowner's holdings. These dwellings usually had no more than three rooms and served as the home to a family of between five and fifteen individuals. There was usually no glass in the windows or screens on the doors, with insects coming and going as they pleased during the hot summer months. In the winter, sharecroppers usually heated their homes with a single wood or coal stove. Their crude and often inadequate diet revolved around rice, peas, cornbread, coffee, and occasionally small game such as squirrels or rabbits. Males in the family wore simple denim overalls and the females cheap cotton dresses. Because flour and feed sacks were frequently used to make clothing, including diapers, for the sharecropping family, many mills put their products in colorful sacks in an effort to increase sales.[19]

While planters usually did not fear individual African America workers per se, they certainly felt uneasy about blacks significantly outnumbering whites in the Delta. As a result, they created and maintained a strict social system in which the white minority subordinated the black population through economic and sometimes physical intimidation. White supremacy and violence were the twin foundational pillars that supported the Delta social system. African Americans in the Delta depended on white landowners for their livelihood, and blacks were not allowed to vote in large numbers. They were expected to work dawn until dusk on land that was not their own, generating profits that flowed primarily into the white community. Any worker who complained about the system did so at his own peril, risking significant injury and even death. "You couldn't argue with them," one thirty-year veteran of the sharecropping system in Mississippi told an interviewer about the white landlords, "I have been living in the Delta thirty years and I know that I have been robbed every year; but there is no use jumping out of the frying pan into the fire. If we ask any questions we are cussed, and if we raise up we are shot, and that ends it." The instances of lynching in the Delta increased after the turn of the century, with the region averaging about one extralegal killing every six month from 1900 to 1930. Many times these executions were public, held in front of cheering crowds, with the victim or victims being tortured before they were killed. Such events were part mayhem, part murder, and part ceremony designed to serve as a reminder of how the system worked and who was in charge. The message for the black community was simple. Quiet workers who did not complain and who recognized the supremacy of the white man had less to fear. Submissive workers might even make a little money for themselves during a good crop year if they worked hard. On the other hand, regardless of how hard he worked, any African American sharecropper who challenged the social system could potentially suffer dire consequences.[20]

Despite the harsh social system that was developing in the region, Bill Patton decided to move his family to the Mississippi Delta around the turn of the twentieth century. The Delta system, as restrictive as it was, was in principle the same system that existed in Hinds County, in the rest of Mississippi, and in the rest or the states of the former Confederacy wherever cotton was grown. It seemed more pronounced in the Delta in part because of the extraordinarily large percentage of African Americans who lived there. Patton had the reputation of being a hard worker who did not complain. He was exactly the kind of worker that Delta planters liked and exactly the kind of worker who might be able to curry favor with local landowners. Because the demand for labor in the Delta was high, a smart, industrious black farmer who knew how to work within the system might be able to improve his station in life somewhat if he moved there and played his cards right. During good years, when cotton prices were stable, some tenants and sharecroppers who worked on plantations with reputable owners were able to negotiate reasonable terms for their employment, and a few were even able to break the cycle of debt that kept them from owning their own farms. This small glimpse of hope was enough of an incentive for Bill Patton and many others to move into the region. Delta plantation owners also sent labor agents around the state to recruit farmers to come to the big plantations. One of these agents might have encouraged the Pattons to move north, or they might have heard tales of the Delta's rich soil by word of mouth. Regardless, Charley Patton left Hinds County, Mississippi, soon after the turn of the twentieth century and moved with his family to the Mississippi Delta, where he began a journey that would make him a musical legend. The family moved on to the Dockery plantation, which would later become famous worldwide as monument to blues music.[21]

A North Carolina native from a prosperous family, Thomas Covington Dockery moved to DeSoto County in the Mississippi Delta shortly before the Civil War. He established himself as a successful farmer, and when the war came he helped raise an infantry company, the "DeSoto Rebels," that served as part of the Twenty-second Mississippi Infantry. He entered Confederate service as a captain and later received a promotion to major. Wounded at the Battle of Corinth in 1862, Dockery survived the war and later served as DeSoto

County sheriff and as a member of the Mississippi legislature. As was the case with most successful north Mississippians, he sent his son William Alfred Dockery to the University of Mississippi, where he rubbed elbows with the sons of the state's elite. Will Dockery left the university after his sophomore year and eventually received a degree from Leddin Business College in Memphis. He returned to the Mississippi Delta, where he worked for a while as a bookkeeper. Taking advantage of his family connections and family resources, Will established himself in the little Delta town of Cleveland. He made considerable money in the timber business and by 1895 had acquired thousands of undeveloped acres in Sunflower County. There Will Dockery established Dockery Farms, the famous plantation that many blues enthusiasts would later consider a shrine to the music they enjoy.[22]

Improving the area was no easy task. Sunflower County at the time was one of the least developed counties of the Delta, and wilderness conditions still prevailed. According to Dockery himself, what he found in the Sunflower County swamps was a far cry from the flat cotton farmland that it would become:

> There was a small amount of cleared land then and it was on bayous, lakes and rivers. The country was covered with blue cane fifteen to twenty feet high and the land was rich as cream. Woodland was being sold by the Y&MV railroad at $5.00 per acre on long time terms, but it was expensive to clear and lots of people, both white and black would quit after a year or so and sell out for small equity. I remember seeing one forty-acres of land being traded for a cow and another forty acres for a Winchester rifle. . . . Rosedale, Mississippi was the county seat and hard to get to as there were no roads worth considering. . . . I remember going to Rosedale in a two-wheeled cart with a single horse. My wheels got stuck and I had to pull the cart out in the cane, and hang the harness on a tree and lead the horse several miles.[23]

Through perseverance and years of hard work by Dockery and the wage laborers he employed to do the heaviest lifting, the end result was a ten-thousand-acre cotton empire, one of the most formidable in the Delta. Dockery Farms became a self-sufficient community with its own cotton gins, multiple stores, an infirmary, a post office, and a train depot that Charley Patton would later make famous in the song "Pea Vine Blues." The Kimball Lake Branch of the Yazoo and Mississippi Valley Railroad began at the Dockery depot, and the line was known locally as the "Peavine Branch" because of the twists and turns along its route. Like other large spreads, the Dockery plantation printed its own scrip that the paymaster used to pay the renters and sharecroppers who worked the place. The scrip was good only at the Dockery stores, which made it difficult for a worker, even if he was able to accumulate a small amount of cash, to leave the plantation for greener pastures. Once he left Dockery's, the worker's scrip was worthless. Still, the Dockery plantation attracted many laborers, with as many as four hundred families living on the place at any given time. Many preferred Dockery's to other Delta plantations, and Will Dockery had a reputation for treating his workers more fairly when compared to some of the other landowners.[24]

Bill Patton moved his wife and children to the Dockery plantation soon after the turn of the twentieth century and established himself as not just an industrious laborer, but as an entrepreneur as well. Unlike many others tenants and sharecroppers, Patton came to the Delta from Hinds County with at least a few resources, and he never got mired in the unending cycle of debt that kept so many African American workers tied to the land with little return. He made a tidy living in the Delta and, later, was actually able to find several tenants to whom he sublet his Dockery acres. He eventually opened his own lumber-hauling business, a small store, and also became more domestic in the way that he conducted his life. Where he had come and gone as he pleased on the farm in Hinds County, he tended to stay put in the Delta, and he remained associated with the Dockery plantation for the rest of his life. He continued to preach from time to time and had the reputation of being a strict disciplinarian when it came to his children. His daughters seemed to flourish under their father's strong hand. One eventually married a stable African American farmer who had miraculously been able to accumulate seven hundred Delta acres of his own, while another married a man that ran the grocery store at Dockery Farms. However, it seemed that Bill Patton's religious leanings had little effect on his son Charley. In fact, the frequent whippings that the boy endured for "low behavior" in the eyes of his father apparently had the exact opposite effect that the lay preacher intended. From the start, Charley Patton was determined to avoid agricultural labor if at all possible, but his options were limited.[25]

The racial tension in Sunflower County, where the Pattons lived, and the surrounding area was acute because African Americans outnumbered whites there to such a great degree. At the turn of the twentieth century 4,007 whites lived in the county alongside 12,078 blacks. Many whites felt constantly threatened just by the sheer number of African Americans who lived in their midst. Any incident, large or small, had the potential for boiling over into the most hideous sort of violence. While Delta lynchings were not common occurrences, they were not rare, either. In 1904 one of the worst lynchings in Mississippi history took place in Sunflower County when a black man was accused of killing the son of a local white planter. After being hunted down by a mob of around 200 whites, the suspect and his wife were tied to a tree and tortured. While the couple was still living and conscious, their fingers and ears were cut off and distributed as souvenirs to local whites who had gathered to watch the execution. Dismissing hanging as too quick an end, those involved in the lynching finally dowsed the couple with gasoline and burned them alive. No one was ever convicted of the crime, and the message was clear. Any African American accused of challenging the existing social system might face the death penalty without benefit of trial, and no one would do anything about it.[26]

Charley Patton did not want to become a farmer in a dangerous world where even the most successful black person was a second-class citizen. He did not want to do agricultural work, but he also did not want to draw the ire of local white authorities who were always suspicious of any African American who was not going to, coming back from, or working in a cotton field. This left him with few alternatives other than trying to make a living as a musician. Like no other member of the African American community, black musicians were able to establish some sort of rapport with local whites. It was a testimony to the power of music in general that the ability of black musicians to entertain disarmed local whites to a great extent, even in the Delta. Some black musicians played for white social functions and, while they were not treated as equals, the periodic contact with whites tended to smooth over some of the rougher edges of racism so prevalent in their society. When whites listened to the music of black musicians they felt good, not threatened. Indeed, one of the most famous tales in the history of American blues involved legendary musician Huddie William Ledbetter, better known as "Lead Belly," and Pat M. Neff, the white governor of Texas during the early 1920s. In 1924, Lead Belly was far from the well-known blues icon that he would later become. Instead, he was a convicted murderer serving a seven-to-thirty-year sentence in a Texas prison. That same year Neff, who was elected governor on a progressive platform, toured the state prison system and by chance heard Lead Belly sing and play his guitar. The governor enjoyed the performance to such an extent that he made several more visits to the prison to hear Lead Belly play, and eventually issued the prisoner an official pardon. Most good African America performers of the period realized that their music generated good will, and a smart, talented musician like Charley Patton could use that good will to his advantage. While most guests at white parties preferred that Patton and his friends play popular standards of the day such as "Let Me Call You Sweetheart," they were not averse to faster-paced blues numbers. Eddie James "Son" House, a significant blues performer himself who collaborated on stage with Patton, later remembered, "White people liked our music just fine. Anything fast and jumpy went over. "[27]

There were other less complicated reasons that the life of a musician appealed to Charley Patton. Good musicians usually did well with women, and they could travel from place to place doing well with women. The Delta plantations provided built-in, captive audiences for their music and, while the work during the planting and harvesting cycle was difficult for plantation labor, there was also an extended off season during the fall and winter months during which workers could enjoy some leisure time. And, there were always Saturday nights throughout the year. On most Delta plantations the landowners took little notice of what their workers did during their off hours, particularly on weekends, as long as their daily work schedules were not disrupted. Many plantations had their own "juke joint," typically a decent-sized, weatherworn building used as a bar, a venue for live music, and a general gathering place for black workers on the weekend. Mississippi planters tolerated the juke joints because they provided workers with a self-contained outlet for entertainment in an era when the state of Mississippi practiced prohibition. On Saturday nights workers could procure illegal liquor, get drunk, dance, mingle with the opposite sex, and generally raise hell without attracting local law-enforcement officers who usually did not challenge planter authority on the plantation. Rather than having to spend time and effort on Sunday mornings bailing workers out of the local jail, most landowners preferred that those workers who liked to drink and carouse do so on property. As Joe Rice Dockery, Will Dockery's son, once told an interviewer, "It was just kind of understood that Saturday nights belonged to them."[28]

Charley Patton's early musical influences are up for conjecture. He was certainly exposed to the Chatmon family in Hinds County as a child, and the Chatmon's musical repertoire was wide and varied, everything from blues to popular standards of the day to dance music aimed at white audiences. He heard hymns as a child while attending worship services with his family. By living among agricultural workers during his formative years, he was certainly familiar with the music of the fields, the "call and response" hollers and song fragments that had helped time pass for decades in the land of cotton. Patton came of age musically at Dockery's, and his artistic education began in earnest once he arrived there. "We moved from Edwards to Dockery's when Charley was still a young boy," Viola Cannon, Patton's sister, once told an interviewer. "He didn't start to play the guitar until we were on Dockery's." On the plantation Patton eventually came under the tutelage of an older musician named Henry Sloan. Born in 1870, Sloan was a shadowy figure in blues history. Some researchers believe that he was a major influence on Patton, that he was a mentor of sorts who took the younger man under his wing and taught him the basics of blues music and composition. Some of Patton's contemporaries later claimed that Patton was constantly at the older man's side and that it was from Sloan that Patton learned the foundations of the music that would make him famous. Others dispute Sloan's influence on Patton or as a blues player in general. According to Gayle Dean Wardlow, a noted authority on Patton's life and music, Sloan "was just a chorder. He played what you would call pre-blues, just chords for dance music." Sloan apparently left the Dockery plantation for good around 1918 and settled in Chicago. Researchers have also identified another blues player, Earl Harris, who lived near Cleveland, Mississippi, as a possible early influence on Patton. Harris apparently worked and played music at Dockery Farms during the first decade of the twentieth century but, like Henry Sloan, little is known about him.[29]

Charley Patton did not invent the blues, although some credit him with doing so. What Patton did was take a type of music that was already popular in the Mississippi Delta's black community and make it his own. His individuality created a model for others to follow, and he seemed to personify the essence of rural blues music and the entire wicked environment from which the music rose. The famous African American musician and band leader W. C. Handy, who was credited in the early twentieth century with giving raw blues some commercial polish that made it more palatable for the masses, once told the story of his travels through the Mississippi Delta in the early twentieth century, and his first experiences with Delta blues at its source. According to Handy, who led a large string-and-brass band that played at social events in the region, he had a revelation one night in 1906 when he and his outfit played a Delta dance. After entertaining the audience with a mix of standards and what he called "old time southern medleys," he received a note from one of the patrons that he at first thought was a song request. Instead, the patron asked Handy if some local blues musicians might be allowed to play some music "native to the area" during his band's next break. Somewhat curious, the classically trained Handy obliged and was astonished at what transpired. At the next break, three men in tattered clothes and worn-out shoes took the stage with an old guitar, a mandolin, and a stand-up bass. According to Handy, their music was as rough around the edges as their style of dress. "They struck up one of those over and over strains that seem to have no beginning and certainly no ending at all," he later remembered. "The strumming attained a disturbing monotony, but on and on it went, the kind of stuff that has long been associated with cane rows and levee camps." As the men played, the dancers at the party became more animated, stomping their feet to the rhythm and voicing their approval in loud, boisterous tones. The raucous crowd further amazed Handy by literally showering the musicians with tip money. It was then that Handy realized the raw force of what he was witnessing: "A rain of silver dollars began to fall around the outlandish, stomping feet. The dancers went wild. Dollars, quarters, halves—the shower grew heavier and continued so long that I strained my neck to get a better look. There before the boys lay more money than my nine musicians were being paid for the entire engagement. Then I saw the beauty of the primitive music. They had the stuff people wanted. They touched a spot. . . . My idea of what constitutes music was changed by the sight of that silver money cascading."[30]

By the time W. C. Handy first experienced the full power of Delta blues music, Charley Patton already knew a good bit about it. In 1906, the year Handy witnessed the shower of coins, Charley Patton was fifteen years old. He was already playing music and already familiar with what went on in the Delta after sundown on Saturday nights. Over the next decade he would write some of his most famous songs, many of which were based on his personal experiences. Like good musicians of any era, Patton had a gift that allowed him to view the world through a special lens. He could experience life and then take those experiences and write a song about them that stirred the emotions of others. As Samuel Charter wrote in *The Poetry of the Blues*, "The blues, as a poetic language, has still the direct, immediate relationship to experience that is at the heart of all art. It is here that poetry begins, in the response of the artist to life." In many ways the whole Mississippi Delta was Charley Patton's muse. He wrote about the lifestyle there, the people and places that were part of the scenery. In 1930 in Clarksdale, Mississippi, a Delta town where Patton frequently played, the building that housed Borman Lumber Mill, a major local employer, burned to the ground, and not long afterwards, the bluesman recorded the song "Moon Going Down," which included the lyrics:

> Oh well, where were you now, baby,
> Clarksdale mill burned down.
> Oh well, where were you now, baby,
> Clarksdale mill burned down.
> I were way down Sunflower,
> With my face all full of frowns.[31]

Patton could make a complicated song about something obvious or a simple song about something monumental, and everything was fair game. As Handy put it, "Southern Negroes sing about everything. Trains, steamboats, steam whistles, sledge hammers, fast women, mean bosses, stubborn mules— all become subjects for their songs. They accompany themselves on anything from which they can extract a musical sound or rhythmical effect." Patton did just that, but he also chronicled in his songs actual events that took place in the region where he lived and performed. His music sometimes included the real names of local characters and places. One example was "Dry Well Blues," about a severe drought that devastated the country around tiny Lula, Mississippi, one of the Delta communities that Patton repeatedly rambled through:

> Way down in Lula, hard livin' has done hit
> Way down in Lula, hard livin' has done hit
> Lord, your drought come an' caught us,
> an' parched up all the trees. . . .
> Lord, the citizens around Lula,

aw, was doin' very well
Citizens around Lula, aw, was doin' very well
Now they're in hard luck together,
'cause rain don't pour nowhere.

In addition to writing and performing music that appealed to others, Patton was also adept at playing to crowds with on-stage antics including a host of dance steps and body gyrations. In short, he was musically talented, but he could also put on a show.[32] Patton started out playing street corners in the tiny Delta communities surrounding the Dockery property. Although his father had him out in the fields picking cotton at an early age, the fledgling bluesman avoided manual labor whenever he could. Bill Patton reportedly beat his son on a regular basis in hopes of instilling in him a more conventional work ethic, but to no avail. The younger Patton was quick to realize that one of the draws of being a musician was that a good musician was able to make money without resorting to strenuous physical labor. According to Son House, a Patton contemporary, "Charley hated work like God hates sin. He just natural-born hated it. Charley called himself 'smart' 'cause he didn't like to work." For Patton, playing for nickels and dimes on the street corner was preferable to facing row after row of cotton each day. Plus, it was more fun.[33]

As he became a more experienced performer, Patton took to traveling from community to community playing in local barrelhouses or juke joints, or at house parties in black neighborhoods. Generally speaking, a barrelhouse was a type of nightclub filled every Friday and Saturday night with African American patrons in search of a good time. They were typically located near one of the major Delta plantations and relatively close to a railroad depot. The barrelhouses of the Mississippi Delta were often owned by whites but run on a daily basis by blacks, and local law enforcement allowed them to operate because the police were usually paid to look the other way. Barrelhouses usually stood within walking distance of the town's railroad depot so that patrons from many miles distant could come and go as they pleased. Like the juke joints, barrelhouses were lively centers for gambling, drinking, dancing, and prostitution, and musical acts were hired to play these establishments based on their ability to draw a crowd.[34] The barrelhouse was also loud, and any musician who hoped to appeal to the crowd had to play and sing music that carried. There was no electric amplification of the entertainer's voice, so he had to rely solely on his vocal chords and the sound of his instrument to penetrate the club's severe ambient noise. The atmosphere seemed tailor-made for Charley Patton, who became a popular barrelhouse performer despite being a small man, about five and a half feet tall and probably weighing not much more than a hundred pounds. "He had a big voice," bluesman David "Honeyboy" Edwards, who saw Patton perform many times, later remembered. "He didn't need no mike. To hear him singing you'd think he weighed two hundred pounds. He broke them country houses down!" Apparently Patton's personality also fit the barrelhouse perfectly. According to Edwards, Patton "liked to fight and get drunk. He was a hell raiser, always drinking a lot of whiskey and fighting, every Saturday night. He'd fight at his own dances, when he was playing."[35]

Patton's predilection for rowdy behavior was also part of his overall persona as a blues performer. His illicit comings and goings, his drinking, and his tumultuous relationships with women collectively represented a pattern of questionable but colorful behavior that made some wandering blues players, and decades later major rock stars, larger-than-life characters. Of course the type of behavior exhibited by Patton was also self-destructive and contributed to the health problems that would ultimately kill him. From all accounts, Patton was a heavy drinker and smoker who held little sway over his own vices. "I never knowed him to do nothing but pick that guitar and crack jokes," Reverend Frank Howard, a Delta minister who knew the bluesman, remembered, "He just believed in playing his guitar, having a big time with his women, and drinking his whiskey." Like the establishments where he played, he could be belligerently loud, cursing, bragging, and holding one-sided conversations, especially when he drank. According to Son House, "He'd drink anything if it wasn't poison. All he wanted to know, was [if] people supposed to drink it. . . . Charley was 'whiskey-headed,' and of course when he got to drinking whiskey you couldn't tell him too much." Whether Patton's drinking affected his performing was always up for debate. Some later claimed that they saw him pass out from drinking during performances, while others claimed that, the more Patton drank, the better he played and sang. Some said he could not hold his liquor while others thought he had a hearty constitution when it came to drinking. "I like to fuss and fight, I like to fuss and fight," he wrote in "Elder Greene Blues," "Lord and get sloppy drunk off a bottle and walk the streets at night."[36]

There is little doubt that Patton's drinking had a great effect on his relationships with women. Patton was a volatile romantic partner to say the least, usually never staying with one woman for a significant period of time. "Something to tell you when I get a chance," Patton sang in "Stone Pony Blues," "I don't wanna marry, just wanna be your man." In the barrelhouses and even on the street he considered any black woman, married or single, a potential bedmate. Drunk or sober, he was consistently bold in his advances. "He'd call anybody's wife 'honey' or 'sugar,'" guitarist Willie Young later reported. "A jealous man didn't have no business around Charley Patton." Indeed, Patton's "meddling" with the wives or girlfriends of others reportedly caused him to sustain at least two serious wounds during his lifetime, one from a knife and another from a gun. Patton went from woman to woman in much the same manner that he went from whiskey bottle to whiskey bottle, picking one up, indulging himself, and then discarding it when he was finished. In what could be considered a foundational example of what decades later would be referred to as "rock star decadence," he apparently had more than a dozen women during his lifetime who some people called his "wives," and innumerable one-night conquests during his travels as a performer. Blues scholar David Evans uncovered at least six marriage certificates in the Mississippi Delta with Patton's name on them, with the bluesman being married to some or perhaps eventually all of the women at the same time. He reportedly fathered at least seven children, both in and out of wedlock.[37] "Heap of time you'd mostly meet him he'd have a different wife," Patton's nephew Tom Cannon said. "He'd just put one down, and pick another one out. . . . He could play good music and everything, and they'd fall for him." According to some, Charley Patton in his younger years was also physically abusive to the women who were attracted to him, almost as if he lost all respect for them once they showed their interest. Stories circulated through the Delta that he could be horribly violent, routinely beating women, either with his fists or with a stick or a whip. "They said he was awful cruel," Sara Garrett, one of the cooks from the Dockery plantation, later told an interviewer in reference to Patton and his relationship with women.[38]

Patton, like Jimmie Rodgers, reserved a special place in many of his songs for women, and the universality of the romantic relationship tied many of Patton's blues and Rodgers's country tunes together thematically. In their lyrics, both men dealt with various types of women, some of whom they obviously revered, and others that they did not care for, or at least did not respect. Some of the songs dealt with the hunt for a relationship, others with the throes of a relationship, and still others with the breakup of a relationship punctuated by a spectrum of emotions—love, hate, lust, fidelity, infidelity, sadness, and remorse. Both Patton and Rodgers sang about wild women. For instance, in Patton's song "Going To Move To Alabama," he boasts:

> Aah, I got a woman, she's long and tall
> The way she do the boogie, makes a panther squall. . . .
> Well I got a woman , she's long and tall
> But when she wiggles, she makes a panther squall. . . .

while in "Blue Yodel No. 3 (Evening Sun Yodel)" Rodgers sings:

> She's long she's tall she's six feet from the ground
> She's long she's tall she's six feet from the ground
> She's tailor made, Lord she ain't no hand me down.[39]

These stanzas sung by two different artists, one "blues" and one "hillbilly," also highlighted the murky origins of both genres and the relationship between the two. A "long tall woman" or a "long tall gal" appeared in various incarnations of early folk, jazz, blues, and country music predating the recordings of Patton and Rodgers. Newman Ivy White, in his collection of early twenty-century African American folk songs, cited a number of lyrics collected from around the South in 1915–16 that referenced a "long and tall woman," and folklorist John Lomax traced a version of the lyric back as far as 1909 as part of a tune called "Dink's Song," although "Dink" was actually a woman singing about a "long tall man." The phrase appeared in various versions of "I'm Alabama Bound," an old ragtime number written in 1909 by Robert Hoffman that had many other similarities to Patton's "I'm Going to Move to Alabama." Regardless of its origins, the phrase seemed to flourish in the twentieth century, crossing and recrossing the color line. Robert Johnson mentions a long tall girl in his 1937 recording "They're Red Hot," and the same year blues singer Kokomo Arnold recorded "Long and Tall," about a woman who was long and tall but "shaped like a cannonball." A little later, in the 1940s, the famous western swing musician and songwriter Bob Wills wrote a song titled "Nancy Jane," about a woman who was "long and tall and sweet as she can be," and during the same period Woody Guthrie and Lead Belly both recorded versions of "Yellow Gal," about a woman who was equally statuesque. Not to be outdone, the flamboyant rock-and-roll icon "Little Richard" Penniman used the phrase in the title and lyrics of one of his most famous numbers, "Long Tall Sally," in 1956.

While Patton and Rodgers sang about wild or loose women who might of-fer temporary companionship, they also sang about women that they sincerely cared for, as in the Patton song "Screamin' and Hollerin' the Blues," recorded in 1929:

> No use a-hollerin', no use a-screamin' and cryin'
> No use a-hollerin', no use a-screamin' and cryin'
> For you know you got a home, mama, long as I got mine
> Hey, Lord have mercy on my wicked soul
> Oh, Lord have mercy on my wicked soul
> I wouldn't mistreat you, baby, for my weight in gold

The previous year Rodgers recorded the song "My Little Lady," which mirrored the sentiments of the Patton tune. The similar language in the songs indicated that they had, at least in part, similar lyrical origins:

> You know I love you, you know it's true
> Give you all my love , babe, tell me what more can I do
> I'm walkin' by myself, I hope you'll understand
> I just walk to be your lovin' man
> I love you, yes, I love you with my heart and soul
> I wouldn't mistreat you for my weight in gold

The universal themes of love and sex were pervasive throughout the re-cordings of Patton and Rodgers, and both men handled these themes with similar flair. Recording in the early twentieth century, when the explicit men-tion of sexual intercourse was taboo in polite society, and certainly something that record companies would censor, both Patton and Rodgers used innuendo, metaphor, and other creative phrasings to get their point across. The ability to veil, however thinly, sexually explicit material on record for Patton and Rod-gers was both an art form and a commercial tool. Record companies of the period viewed "race" and "hillbilly" tunes as music marketed to an unsophisti-cated but nonetheless large audience whose heads could be turned quickly by the mention of sex in one form or another. As would be the case in all forms of media and advertising throughout the twentieth century and beyond, sex or sexual imagery could move product. "In order to meet the demand of the market," Paul Oliver wrote, "record companies appear to have evolved a double standard in which they accepted, and may have invited, sexually suggestive material but suppressed direct speech which might be interpreted as obscene." Hence, in the cases of Patton and Rodgers, the experiences they gleaned from their nomadic, philandering lifestyles as musician intersected neatly with the marketing needs of record companies and gave way to a number of songs.[40] While there were no explicit obscenities in the lyrics, there was really no mistaking what Patton was referring to in the provocatively titled "Love My Stuff" when he sang:

> I love my stuff babe, I want to give it a hop
> And my rider[41] got the shivers, swear it just won't stop
> Oh I know she want it hard babe, sure don't want it chawed
> It would break my heart, if [she don't] need no more
> And I keeps on telling my rider, well she was shivering down
> Lord that jelly-baking strut, will make a monkey-man leave his town

or in "Jersey Bull Blues," when he sings:

> And my bull got a horn, baby, long as my arm
> And my bull got a horn, long as my arm
> I've an old five pound ax and I'll cut two different ways
> I've an old five pound ax and I'll cut two different ways
> And I cut my little women both night and day.

By comparison, as with Patton's recordings, some of Rodgers's songs did not require a great deal of imagination to get the point across, "Pistol Packin' Papa" being a prime example:

> I'm a pistol packing papa, and when I walk down the street
> You can hear those mamas shoutin' 'Don't turn your gun on me!'
> Now girls, I'm just a good guy, and I'm goin' to have my fun
> And if you don't wanna smell my smoke, don't monkey with my gun!

Like a hobo when he's hungry; like a drunk man when he's full
I'm a pistol packing papa, I know how to shoot the bull.[42]

When not plying his trade in the barrelhouses, Patton frequently entertained at "house parties," which were common weekend occurrences in Delta
neighborhoods that could be as wild as anything in a beer joint. As the name
implies, these were simply social gatherings of varying sizes held at someone's
private home, where the owner—or renter, as was many times the case—
might attempt to make a few dollars by selling food or moonshine liquor.
"They would have the parties just where they lived at," Muddy Waters later recalled. "They would put the beds outside and have the whole little room to do
their dancing in. They'd pull up a cotton house [a covered trailer used during
harvest] and that's their little gambling shed. And they made lamps with coal
oil." Similarly, blues performer James "Son" Thomas once told an interviewer,
"Those are them old raggedy houses way back out in the country. We didn't
have but one night to have a good time. We'd stay up all Saturday night and try
to get some rest on Sunday."[43] Roebuck "Pops" Staples, who lived at Dockery
Farms when Patton did and went on to fame as the patriarch of the legendary
Staples Singers, described a typical weekend routine for Delta blues performers of the period:

> On Saturday afternoons everybody would go into town and those fellows
> like Charley Patton . . . would be playin' on the streets, standin' by the rail-
> road tracks, people pitchin' em nickels and dimes, white and black people
> both. The train come through the town maybe once that afternoon, and
> when it was time, everybody would gather around just to see the train pull
> up. They'd play around there, before and after the train came in, and an-
> nounce where they'd be that night. And that's where the crowd would go.
> [At the house] they'd have a plank nailed across the door to the kitchen
> and be sellin' fish and chitlins, with dancin' in the front room, gamblin'
> in the side room, and maybe two or three gas or coal-oil lamps on the
> mantelpiece in front of the mirror—powerful light. It was different peo-
> ple's houses, no clubs or nothin'.[44]

Patton's early performing style was as wild as the crowds he entertained.
Twenty years before the birth of rhythm and blues icon James Brown, Patton

was considered "the hardest working man in show business," at least in the Mississippi Delta. The songs he chose to sing at bars and parties, both those he wrote himself and those he covered, were not overly introspective, nor were they sad. Most of the tunes, such as "Going to Move to Alabama," "A Spoonful Blues," or "Love My Stuff," were designed to get people moving, either toward the bar or the dance floor, and to make people scream and shout. Many, if not most, including the Patton classic "Shake It And Break It (But Don't Let It Fall Mama)," had sexually suggestive lyrics:

> You can shake it, you can break it
> you can hang it on the wall
> Throw it out the window, catch it 'fore it falls
> You can shake it, you can break it
> you can hang it on the wall
> Throw it out the window, catch it 'fore it falls
> My jelly, my roll, sweet mama, don't let it fall. . . .

Patton used his guitar and his voice as rhythm instruments that could cut through and accelerate the lively dance-floor rancor all at the same time. Patton was also a very animated performer with a natural presence who drew attention to himself through his movements onstage. He stomped his feet and sometimes jumped in the air as he performed, playing the guitar behind his head or between his legs. Howlin' Wolf, who saw Patton perform many times, later recalled, "He was a real showman. When he played his guitar, he would turn it over backwards and forwards, and throw it around over his shoulders and between his legs, throw it up in the sky." Authors Harry Shapiro and Caesar Glebbeek have drawn comparisons between Patton's performing style and rock legend Jimi Hendrix's seminal 1967 performance at the Monterey Pop Festival, where Hendrix treated an awestruck audience to a variety of "guitar gymnastics" that left a lasting imprint on rock music. Shapiro and Glebbeek emphasize the "tradition of showmanship in the blues . . . done for effect, to grab attention. . . . An element of showmanship was expected by all black audiences." From all accounts, if early twentieth-century audiences in the Delta expected showmanship, then they got their money's worth from Charley Patton. He seemed to feed off his audiences, and the wilder they got, the wilder he became. As Elijah Wald has pointed out, blues performers of the period like Patton were also masters of improvisation who "would simply play and sing, often for twenty minutes or more without a break," routinely falling into a lively mix "of 'floating verses'—couplets heard from other singers, many of which were popular throughout the South—with an admixture of original lines, sometimes improvised on the spot." Later examples of this type of more free form blues were Bill Broonzy's "When Will I Be Called a Man" and "Mannish Boy" by Muddy Waters, both of which abandon the traditional AAB configuration common to traditional blues songs.

While the blues of Charley Patton was pulsating through the Mississippi Delta, an equally formidable musical force was emerging in another part of the state. Jimmie Rodgers was born near the city of Meridian, in the east-central part of Mississippi, about ninety miles east of Jackson. Located in Lauderdale County, Meridian owed its existence more to industry—specifically the railroad industry —than agriculture. Although there were several significant plantations in Lauderdale County before the Civil War, it was the coming of the railroad that literally put Meridian on the map. The soil in Lauderdale County was not conducive to large-scale cotton production, so local farmers grew a great many food crops, and the slave population in the area was relatively low. Settlers began trickling into the Meridian area in the 1830s, and twenty years later the settlement found itself at the crossroads of two major rail lines. The Mobile and Ohio Railroad ran north and south through the town, and the Vicksburg and Montgomery line, which also passed through Edwards, near where Charley Patton grew up, ran east and west. Meridian was incorporated in 1860, and it became a bustling center of activity during the early years of the Civil War. A constant stream of men and supplies flowed through Meridian along the rail lines as Mississippi and the rest of the Confederacy prepared for war in 1861. Warehouses, public buildings, saloons, and hotels sprung up overnight, but Meridian's notoriety as a strategic railroad center would have terrible consequences as the war wore on.

In 1864, Union General William Tecumseh Sherman captured the town and destroyed much of it over the course of five days. "Meridian," the general eventually reported, "with its depots, warehouses, arsenals, hospitals, offices, hotels, and cantonments no longer exists."[45] Despite the disaster, Meridian rebuilt rapidly after the war and with the help of the railroads evolved into one of Mississippi's major cities. By 1900 the city had more than fourteen thousand residents, which qualified it by Mississippi standards as an urban center, complete with a recently constructed library and an opera house. During the first decade of the twentieth century, an observer reflected on the city's progress: "One of the first advances of Meridian into city life was the introduction of mule street cars, and then gas lights. In due time these were merged into electric lines and electric lights and power. . . . Meridian now has ten miles of electric street railway, and many miles of gas pipes, water pipes, sewerage, paved streets and paved sidewalks. It is the metropolis, and the most important railroad center in eastern Mississippi. Its rapid growth having taken place since the war, and chiefly during the last two decades."[46]

Jimmie Rodgers's heritage was little different from that of any other white Mississippian who was born toward the end of the nineteenth century. Most of his early ancestors had immigrated to the British colonies before the American Revolution, and with successive generations had jumped the Appalachians and moved steadily south and west. Rodgers's forebears, along with hundreds of thousands of others, were constantly on the move in search of opportunity, either to better themselves and their station in life or simply to survive. Year after year, decade after decade, they pushed the frontier steadily westward toward the Mississippi River and beyond.

Both of Rodgers's grandfathers served the Confederacy, but in very different ways. Samuel Bozeman, who was the singer's maternal grandfather, was twenty-three years old when he volunteered during the war's opening months as a private in Company B of the Fourteenth Alabama Infantry. As time wore on, his regiment took one beating after another during major engagements in Virginia, as well as during the Battle of Gettysburg in Pennsylvania. Bozeman was captured at Gettysburg in 1863 and spent almost two years as a prisoner of war before receiving a parole after the conflict ended. Following the war, he came back to his home in Lowndes County, Alabama, and then moved a few miles west over the state line into Lauderdale County, Mississippi. Bozeman settled just north of Meridian, where he made a living as a farmer and carpenter, and married a young widow named Virginia Robinson. Sam and Virginia had several children, among them a daughter, Eliza, who was born in 1868.[47]

Zachary Rogers (who spelled his name without the "d"), Jimmie Rodgers's father's father, was born in 1841, and his service to the Confederacy during the war was brief, and far less heroic. After somehow managing to avoid service for more than three years, in late 1864 he became part of what amounted to a home-guard unit in Alabama that operated as a local police force in a region where the rule of law was tenuous. The group was charged with rounding up deserters and keeping the local peace in general. Rogers was either a conscript or one of many adult male southerners who late in the war formed or joined existing home-guard units to avoid regular service in the Confederate Army. Regardless of his reason for joining the unit, he quickly decided that the work did not suit him. Zack Rogers deserted after less than a month, not long before the Confederacy itself disappeared. After the war he settled in Choctaw County, Alabama, where he took up farming and married Martha Woodberry, a Georgia native. The union produced more than a half-dozen children, including a son, Aaron, who was born in 1870.[48]

When he was a teenager, Aaron Rodgers signed on as a section hand for the Mobile and Ohio Railroad that ran through Meridian. At the time the Mobile and Ohio (M&O) was an established company with a history that spanned several decades. Chartered in 1848, the line was originally designed to connect Mobile, Alabama, with the Ohio River near Cairo, Illinois. Construction began quickly at Mobile with the first section of track opening for business between Mobile and Citronelle, Alabama, in 1852. Within a few years the line reached Meridian, where it crossed the Vicksburg and Montgomery line to create a significant railroad junction. In 1861 workers completed the northern terminus of the line at Columbus, Kentucky, on the Mississippi River, rather than at Cairo as originally planned. During the Civil War federal troops virtually destroyed the sections of the line running through Mississippi, but the railroad company rebuilt and flourished in the decades after the conflict. New investors eventually completed the connection with Cairo, and from there the M&O met another line that went into St. Louis. The end result was a major commercial artery that connected the South with the Midwest, moving thousands of people and millions of dollars in freight over its rails.[49]

The heavy traffic on the southern end of the line, along with structural pressures brought on by the weather, soil erosion, and the general contours of the southern landscape, meant that the M&O tracks were in frequent need of repairs. Like many of young men of the period who hoped to escape farm work, Aaron Rodgers signed on to be part of a section crew that monitored and repaired the M&O rail lines in the region. A section crew usually consisted of about a dozen men who were responsible for the maintenance of a particular section of track. They frequently moved up and down the lines at a moment's notice, helping other crews at various locations as needed. The men usually resided in dismal camps, sleeping in boxcars, hastily constructed shacks or heavy tents provided by the railroad company. Even though the paycheck was steady, it was hard work and a hard way to live. Still, Aaron Rodgers stuck with it and developed a reputation as a dependable employee. He moved to Meridian, and within a few years he was promoted to section foreman responsible for organizing and leading his own crew of men.

Aaron Rodgers took on a different set of responsibilities in 1884 when he married Eliza Bozeman and began a family. The newlyweds lived a transient life at first, with Aaron traveling up and down the railroad lines and Eliza joining him as often as she could. As they began having children, the couple established a more permanent home in the Pine Springs community, just north of Meridian, on land given to them by Sam Bozeman. Their first son, Walter, was born in 1886 and was joined in 1890 by another son, Talmadge, who the family called "Tal." On September 8, 1897, they welcomed their third child into the world, a son named James Charles "Jimmie" Rodgers, who would grow up to become "The Father of Country Music." Later, after he became famous, Mississippi and Alabama would both claim to be Jimmie Rodgers's birthplace. The latter's claim was based on the fact that some of his mother's relatives lived in Geiger, Alabama, in the extreme western part of the state, where Eliza spent some time during her pregnancy. The more credible, or at least the more accepted version of Rodgers's beginnings, states that he was born about forty miles southwest of Geiger, across the state line in Pine Springs. Nolan Porterfield, who penned the singer's definitive biography, stated that Rodgers was born in Pine Springs, and Rodgers himself always claimed Meridian as his hometown.[50]

The nomadic life of a railroad man was not conducive to the quiet domesticity that Eliza Bozeman longed for, but she attempted to maintain some type of "normal" life despite her family's circumstances. At first she accompanied her husband on his sojourns up and down the rail lines, setting up housekeeping in one of the line shacks or occasionally in an abandoned boxcar. If life for Aaron was difficult on the road, for Eliza it was almost unbearable. The product of a comfortable upbringing, she had never been exposed to the harsh life of a railroad worker and was not accustomed to living among the great unwashed in the railroad camps. Once the children began arriving, she was quick

to realize that she had to move to a more stable environment. She returned to
Pine Springs and lived among family in a house provided for her by her father.
Aaron continued to work on the railroad, visiting his family in Pine Springs
whenever he could, but his frequent and sometimes extended stays away from
home put a strain on the household. Things changed during the 1890s when
Eliza's health began to deteriorate and she found it more and more difficult to
look after the Rodgers clan on her own. She needed her husband at home on
a regular basis, so Aaron quit his job with the M&O and moved back to Lauderdale County to try his hand at farming, a profession he had been trying to
avoid all of his life.[51]

In 1903, when Jimmie Rodgers was six years old, tragedy turned his life
upside down. His mother passed away at Pine Springs at the age of thirty-five.
There has been some speculation about the cause of Eliza Rodgers's death, but
many researchers believe that she died from complications brought on by tuberculosis, a disease that was not uncommon among the poverty-stricken in
the turn-of-the-century South. Always frail, she likely contracted the disease
during her stays in the damp, dingy railroad camps that were a natural breeding ground for all types of human maladies. At the time, a person diagnosed
with tuberculosis, or what many referred to simply as "T.B.," knew that he
or she was living under a death sentence. The disease killed slowly, sometimes over a period of years. Early symptoms included a persistent cough,
night sweats, and weight loss followed by progressive shortness of breath and
finally, in the disease's latter stages, heavy fever and hemorrhaging. It was not
a pleasant way to die, as one researcher described: "The disease continues to
invade the lung tissues about it. This slow spread throughout the lungs, scar-
ring and ruining them by infiltration, is the common pattern for tuberculosis,
taking years to kill its victim. This was how it acquired its ancient name, *consumption*, which aptly describes the wasting of the body and the final consum-
ing high fever. . . . When this happens the bleeding may be so torrential that
the victim dies of exsanguinations or from drowning in his own blood."[52]

The death of Eliza Rodgers had a tremendous effect of her youngest son.
Of course Jimmie Rodgers grieved over his mother's death and, as with any
other terrible family event, a great natural sadness enveloped him for some
time. "My mother she's in heaven, where God and the angels smile," he later
sang, "and now I know she's watching, her little orphan child." Like any child,
he missed his mother, and her loss would weigh heavy on him for the rest of

his life. His earliest memories would always involve a great, tragic loss and a sudden, permanent sense of insecurity that would color his view of the world. Contemporary scholarship on the effects of the death of a parent on children seems to bear this out. Researchers Nancy R. Hooyman and Betty J. Kramer maintain that from a psychological perspective children are particularly vulnerable after the death of a parent. They are "forced to deal with a feeling of complete discontinuity with what previously existed," and a "terrifying insecurity since if a loved parent can die, then nothing is safe, predictable or secure. . . . A parent's death separates the world into 'before and after.' In fact, even thirty, forty or fifty years after the early death of a parent, adults still refer to this as the central event of their lives." Eliza Rodgers's death also left her youngest son without the stable maternal influence that could have led him over time into a more settled life than that of a railroad man or traveling musician. As an older child and teenager Jimmie Rodgers would be free to walk the streets of Meridian without much adult supervision, peeking into tavern doorways and down darkened alleys. Temptations such as drinking, smoking, gambling, and loose women were part of Rodgers's universe from an early age, and he later made reference to this rowdier side of life in some of his songs. "For years and years I've rambled," he sang, "drank my wine and gambled."[53] As the central, tragic event of his youth, the death of his mother fostered in Rodgers a sense of independence and an acute sense that life was indeed short and that nothing was permanent. People or things that you love might be taken away at any moment, so living for the moment might be the best, and least painful, alternative to a life tempered by constraining responsibilities. This made it easier for him as an adult to take on the transient life of a railroad worker and subsequently the life of a traveling musician.[54]

While the psychological effects of losing a parent at the age of six would certainly color the perceptions of any child through his or her adulthood, the effects were particularly acute in the case of Jimmie Rodgers. Not only had Rodgers watched helplessly as his mother died from a dreadful disease, but he was destined to suffer with the same disease himself. Rodgers learned from doctors in 1924 that he had contracted tuberculosis. He was only twenty-seven years old at the time and was yet to make a single record. The disease forced him to give up railroading and concentrate full-time on a musical career. The situation also created one of the great, tragic ironies in the history of popular music and of American culture in general. By the time he began his legendary recording career in 1927, Jimmie Rodgers had known for some time that he was a dead man. He played every chord on his guitar and sang every verse of every song with the knowledge that a slow, grinding death was on the horizon. "I've got that old T.B., I can't eat a bite," he wrote in 1931, "got me a worried soul, I can't even sleep at night."[55] Rodgers lived for nine years after the original diagnosis and for the last few years of his life was in the throes of stardom and a slow death all at the same time. He had watched tuberculosis ravage his mother, and he knew that one day the disease would claim him. Those who saw Jimmie Rodgers perform after he became famous routinely commented that he seemed so genuine, and that his voice always seemed packed with emotion. Little did they know that he was singing every song, literally, as if it might be the last song he ever performed. "Don't let that old T.B. ever get you down," Rodgers sang a year before his death in his composition "Whippin' That Old T.B.," "first they want you insurance, then they plant you in the ground."[56]

Eliza Rodgers's death broke up the Rodgers family. Afterwards, Aaron Rodgers went back to riding the rails and his oldest son, Walter, at the time a teenage, also took up railroad work. Younger sons Tal and Jimmie were shuttled around from relative to relative in their father's absence and for a year or so lived with family in Geiger, Alabama, and Scooba, Mississippi. In 1904 Aaron took a second wife, a widow from Pine Springs named Ida Smith, and eventually tried another short, unsuccessful stint as a farmer. In 1906 he found a new job with the New Orleans and Northeastern Railroad, a line spanning almost two hundred miles between New Orleans and Meridian, and his long trips away from home again grew more frequent. With their father away, sixteen-year-old Tal and nine-year-old Jimmie came under the thumb of their stepmother, with whom they did not always get along. Already tough, independent children, they did not listen when she spoke to them and resented any efforts Ida made to bring discipline into their lives. The situation grew untenable, and the family decided that Ida would go with Aaron as he moved up and down the rail lines while Tal and Jimmie would move in with their mother's sister, a maiden aunt named Dora Bozeman. Tal only lived with his aunt for a year or so before he married and started a life of his own, but Jimmie lived with his aunt for some time during what would prove to be one of the most stable periods of his young life. Bozeman became Rodgers's surrogate mother, providing him with love and discipline at a critical time in his life.[57]

While on the surface Dora Bozeman seemed like a typical old maid, she was actually educated and cultured. She had attended a local school for girls near Meridian where she earned diplomas that allowed her to teach English and music. She enrolled her nephew in school, cleaned him up for church on Sundays, and gave his life the structure it had lacked up to that time. An accomplished pianist herself, she may have contributed to her nephew's early musical development. According to Nolan Porterfield, "Her musical training was not the sort of thing that would have appealed to or much affected a rapscallion like Jimmie Rodgers. On the other hand . . . Dora's background in language, literature, and melody, her training in rhyme and rhythm, may well have been factors, however subliminal, in his development."[58]

In 1910, when Jimmie Rodgers was thirteen, his father made another attempt to establish a permanent home, this time in Meridian, where he rented a small house near the railroad yards. Jimmie moved back in with his father and away from the discipline and structure of his Aunt Dora's home. At the time Meridian was still experiencing considerable growth. It was Mississippi's largest city and the closest thing the state had to a major economic center. While Jackson, ninety miles to the west, was the state capital, it played second fiddle to Meridian as a vibrant city of the New South. According to one observer, Meridian in 1910 was "a bustling town that boasted lumber mills, cotton gins, factories, and seven railroad lines with attendant warehouses, shipping facilities and repair shops." Multi-storied buildings framed the city's downtown area, electric streetcars carried passengers from place to place, and telephones in the central business district were becoming commonplace. At night the city glowed from gas and electric lighting. For an unsupervised thirteen-year-old like Jimmie Rodgers, Meridian was a wonderland of adventure and discovery. He had never taken direction or discipline from his stepmother, and his father continued to spend a great deal of time away from home, which allowed the boy to come and go as he pleased. He frequently played hooky during the school year, and during the summer he spent much of his time with a sympathetic bachelor uncle, Tom Bozeman, his mother's younger brother. Bozeman owned a barbershop in Meridian that became his nephew's home away from home. Rodgers spent hours in the shop listening to and trading stories with the older men who came in. It was all a part of his broader education.[59]

In addition to general vices of the street, Rodgers was also exposed at a young age to a good deal of music. As a major railroad center with, for the region, a significant population, the city was considered a Deep South cultural center. By the 1890s Meridian had a large opera house and other theaters downtown that hosted a variety of traveling entertainment ranging from actual opera performances to national and local vaudeville productions. All types of acts came and went through Meridian. The city was a significant stop on the touring circuit for medicine shows, minstrel shows, and for all types of traveling bands that performed in venues large and small, indoor and outdoor. Their repertoires included old, familiar songs along with new tunes almost literally picked out of the air as they traveled around America. Black music, white music, fiddles, banjos, and guitars were all part of a musical environment that Jimmie Rodgers was intrigued with from an early age. According to Nolan Porterfield, "Young Jimmie, apparently star struck from birth, was fascinated by any type of show; he was particularly excited when the Gem and Elite theaters [in Meridian], both nominally vaudeville houses, began to show the newfangled moving pictures between acts." Of course Meridian also offered other types of musical entertainment that were equally enticing though not quite as sophisticated. Local street-corner, beer-joint, and pool-hall performers were also part of the mix, and as a roaming teenager Jimmie took great pleasure in familiarizing himself with the entertainment options in some of the town's seedier saloons.[60]

As with Charley Patton, it is difficult to pin down the precise early influences that led Jimmie Rodgers to pursue music. His course was likely the product of a combination of circumstance, environment, and perhaps even heredity. Rodgers's grandfather Zach played the fiddle, as did members of his mother's family. His Aunt Dora was a properly trained pianist, and her musical influence may have had an effect. Brother Tal learned to play the banjo at an early age, which would seem to indicate that the playing of a musical instrument was encouraged, or at least tolerated, in the Rodgers family. According to his wife, Jimmie Rodgers had some of his first significant musical experiences in the railroad yard, where as a boy he was occasionally employed to carry water to the workers, many of whom were black. In a highly romanticized biography published after Rodgers's death, she wrote that, "during the noon dinner rests, they taught him to plunk melody from banjo and guitar. They taught him darkey songs: moaning chants and crooning lullabies."[61] Regardless, when he was old enough to wander the streets of Meridian making many of his own decisions he gravitated to music and musicians. Performing appealed to Rodgers for the same simple reasons that it appealed to Patton or any other like-minded young artist. He had a talent for music, playing and singing was fun, and his musical abilities set him apart from the crowd. His music caused people in general and women in particular to take notice of him. It made him popular. How could a young man not be attracted to that?

By 1911 Rodgers gave what many believe was his first "official" public performance, entering an amateur talent contest sponsored by the Elite Theater in Meridian. Even at a young age he was apparently able to impress a crowd as well as the contest judges. He won first prize for renditions of two Tin Pan Alley hits of the day, "Steamboat Bill" and "I Wonder Why Bill Bailey Don't Come Home." Both songs were frequently sung by performers in traveling medicine shows and minstrel shows that passed through Meridian, which may have been where Rodgers first heard them. His choice of those particular songs as a public showcase for his talents also spoke volumes with regard to Rodgers's personality and his general lifestyle to date. Rather than choosing to perform a sentimental ballad or a novelty song of some sort, the still thirteen-year-old Rodgers chose two songs that featured dynamic characters who led what he considered to be exciting lives. "Steamboat Bill" was a brave and daring steamboat captain who died an untimely death in a spectacular boiler explosion while racing his boat up and down the Mississippi River, while "Bill Bailey" was always on the move, either leaving home or coming home as the result of a tumultuous relationship with a woman. Brimming with confidence after his victory at the Elite Theater, Rodgers was somehow able to latch onto a traveling medicine show that passed through at about that same time. A little later he wrote to his uncle Tom Bozeman that he was "making a little money and having a good time too," but his first foray into life as a traveling singer did not last long. He quit the show after a falling out with the owner, and soon he was back in Meridian with his father. [62]

Alone after the recent death of his second wife and wanting to keep an eye on his youngest son, Aaron Rodgers took Jimmie on the road with him and began teaching him railroad work. From that point on, the future Father of Country Music was a railroad man. Many years later after he became famous many myths related to the railroad became part of the Jimmie Rodgers persona, one of the most prominent being that he had been first and foremost a railroad man who had lived an exciting life of travel and begun a musical career only after health issues had forced him to retire. As the story went, he then took the experiences that a lifetime of travel had given him and poured them into his music. The contrast between the rugged railroad man and the sensitive artist made for a good story and, even decades after his death, many would continue to refer to Rodgers with admiration as "the Singing Brakeman," a name that he never really cared for. In reality, the opposite was true with regard to Rodgers's career paths. While from his earliest memories he was exposed to the railroad life through his father, his first love was performing, and his initial dreams and aspirations involved riding the rails only to the extent that those rails carried him to his next show. At the first opportunity he had run away from home with a traveling medicine show, not a railroad section crew. Only after his first adolescent attempt at a show business career failed did he come back to Meridian to pursue life as a railroad employee. At the time he was under pressure from his father and other family members to "grow up," accept the responsibilities of adulthood, and pursue some type of legitimate work. Although crowds certainly attended and enjoyed musical performances in Meridian during the early twentieth century, a career in show business for a young man was viewed by many as unseemly and perhaps not completely masculine.

Still, had he not lived much of his life as a railroad worker, Jimmie Rodgers might never have been a successful singer. Working on the railroads allowed him to travel, meet new people, and experience new things, which no doubt provided him with subject matter and inspiration later on as he wrote songs. Some of his most popular recordings had travel and trains as their themes. On the road and in the railroad yards he gravitated to music and musicians, trading licks and lyrics with other performers whenever and wherever he could. For Rodgers, sunset in the railroad yards was not a signal to eat supper and go to bed. Instead, sunset signaled that it was time to start living, time to strap on a guitar for informal musical interplay with other railroaders, black or white, who liked to play and sing. Ironically, this type of musical and social interaction between black and white maintenance workers in the railroad yards was in direct contrast to Jim Crow laws that by day rigidly segregated southern railroad passengers by race. At other times, nightfall meant that it was time to find a local saloon where an enterprising performer might play alone or with other musicians for tips. In the process of carrying out these types of evening activities Rodgers apparently mastered the guitar, banjo, and mandolin. "He rode the railroads and lived in towns all over the South with his father, coming into contact with the free life and the sordid life and the lonely life," country-music scholar Paul Hemphill wrote. "He learned a lot about music from the work-gang Negroes along the way. He saw honky-tonks and hobo camps and train wrecks." Moving constantly with the railroad allowed Rodgers to live in a much larger universe than most of his contemporaries in Pine Springs or Meridian, which likely broadened within him the creative impulses that made him a star.[63]

From the outset the railroad was an important part of Rodgers's life. In fact, in many ways it defined his life and his musical career. As the son of a railroad man, and later as a railroad man himself, he would rarely spend very much time in one place. For long stretches he traveled the rail lines with no fixed address, and he never knew where the railroad might take him from week to week or month to month. Up and down the lines, north, south, east, and west. That was Jimmie Rodgers's life for many years. In a way he was better off than most of the farmers who eked out a living around Lauderdale County in that he had regular wages and got to see places that most of the people where he was from could only dream about. In an era when many Mississippians rarely left the state, Rodgers might see four or five states in a single month. He got to see new people, experience new things, and live his life in a way that some people back home considered exciting, and maybe even sinful. Stops in new towns meant visiting new street corners, saloons, and beer joints where musi-cians plied their trade and honed their skills. Life on the road exposed Rodgers to different types of music that later had a great impact on his own writing and performing style. He heard black blues from African American workers in the rail yards, guitar and fiddle music in local beer parlors, popular stan-dards from string bands entertaining at barn dances or outdoor events. Add these to the hymns that he heard as a child in church and Rodgers's musical education was extensive. Traveling from town to town was also an attractive prospect because it offered him a sense of freedom that the typical Meridian farmer or shopkeeper could never experience. He could pick up and go when-ever he liked, and if he did not care for the town that he was in, it never really mattered. There was always another town just over the horizon. In his record-ing "The Brakeman's Blues," he sang that "Portland, Maine is just the same as sunny Tennessee, any old place I hang my hat is home sweet home to me," and in 1929 he recorded a song with a title, "I've Ranged, I've Roamed and I've Travelled," that seemed to sum up his entire existence.[64]

Rodgers's life of "rambling, railroading and drifting" both affected his music and lent itself to comparisons with Charley Patton and other African American bluesmen who likewise could never seem to stay in one place for very long. Just as mobility defined a lifestyle for Rodgers and Patton, it also served in a broader sense as a common thematic resource for both country and blues music. Though discussing African Americans in general, Mark Twain could have easily been describing the Delta's black musicians when he wrote in 1883, "These poor people could never travel when they were slaves; so they make up for the privation now. They stay on the plantation until the desire to travel seizes them, then they pack up. . . . Not for any particular place; no nearly any place will answer; they only want to be moving." Johnny Shines, who traveled many performing circuits around the Delta with the legendary Robert Johnson during the 1920s and 1930s seemed to confirm Twain's assessment, at least as far as musicians were concerned, when he told an interviewer, "We would walk through the country with our guitars on our shoulders, stop at people's houses, play a little music. Walk on. . . . We might hear about where a job was paying off—a highway crew, a railroad job, a levee camp along the river. . . . I didn't have a special place then. Anywhere was home." He was speaking of his travels with Johnson, but the descriptions of wandering aimlessly fit the Rodgers mold as well. It also fit the mold of Patton, who many described during and after his lifetime as "always on the move," or as a "rambling bluesman."[65]

The idea of mobility looming large in the life and work of both the white country singer and the black bluesman was no coincidence. A certain restlessness and an urge to pick up stakes and relocate gave black and white southerners in the poorer classes something in common during the latter part of the nineteenth and early twentieth centuries. Because a lack of resources and no clear path to prosperity held them all back, poor blacks and whites had many shared daily experiences that sprang from common forms of economic distress. As the United States advanced rapidly during the age of industrialization, it became apparent that the wonders of modernization were not affecting everyone in a positive way, and that large groups of individuals, including minorities and poor whites, were being left out. In rural areas many whites and blacks in the poorer classes were trapped on land that barely supported them, while in the cities menial laborers were also trapped in monotonous jobs. One of the great themes of country and blues music is movement, the ability to pick up stakes and leave at a moment's notice—leave a job, leave a town, or leave a romantic relationship that has soured. The ability to break away and be independent has traditionally been a cherished freedom, particularly for the oppressed. Any group that is held back or held down, black or white, suffers a form of societal humiliation that only the ability to control one's own destiny can cure. This is a concept that knew no color line. Just as an African American farm laborer in the Mississippi Delta of the early twentieth century might want to exercise his independence and display his manhood by leaving the employ of an unscrupulous landlord, a working-class white might want to accomplish the same thing by quitting his job and telling his difficult foreman to go to hell. As Lawrence Levine wrote, "the rootlessness and alienation which were so well conveyed in the blues and the work songs were not solely the reflection of Afro-American culture, but of the larger society as well, which was at its heart rootless and deeply afraid of the rapid changes that were transforming it."[66]

In such an environment a primary dream of the oppressed, regardless of color, was to one day escape, move away to a new location where there were fewer problems, and where a better living could be made. The ability to move, to not feel trapped, was the ultimate status symbol for whites and blacks in the poorer classes, which is one of the reasons that mobility is such a foundational theme of early country and blues music. As Cobb maintained in his treatment of southern culture, "Surely no point of comparison between blues and country music is so striking as the common emphasis on mobility, whether in the form of travel or aimless 'ramblin.' Not surprisingly, country singers were as fascinated by trains as were bluesmen, and, more often than not, they were ambivalent, longing for escape on one hand, searching for a place to call home on the other." Class trumped race in themes related to travel and general mobility. It was usually only the poor or those who perceived themselves as being oppressed who sought relief through movement, while the financially secure had no reason to flee their circumstance. The train was the central image for those longing to move because it unlocked the imagination of small-town or rural Americans with regard to the wide world that existed outside the borders of their county. For people black and white whose lives were localized, train travel was not just a potential means of getting from one place to another. It could open up a whole new world that was literally as boundless as the horizon. In short, the train represented freedom. For African Americans the railroad would help move along the Great Migration to the North that began around the time of the First World War and would continue for decades. Early blues researcher Howard W. Odum observed that not only were trains mentioned frequently in blues lyrics, but the musicians would also evoke the "musical image of a running train" through their guitar playing. "The train is made to whistle," Odum recalled. "By a prolonged and consecutive striking of several strings, while the bell is rung by the striking of a single string. As the listeners imagine themselves observing the train, or riding on it, the fervor of the occasion is increased. . . . The Negroes thus create their train. They hear it and see it as if it were reality." The same can be said for country music, where many train songs have traditionally been enhanced using techniques on the guitar and fiddle to imitate the sounds of train wheels and whistles. Probably the most famous use of this technique in the realm of country music is "Orange Blossom Special," a fiddle tune crafted by Ervin T. Rouse during the 1930s, which became one of the most famous country train songs of all time.[67]

Thematic imagery in the songs of Rodgers and Patton bore out the notion that mobility as a class-based concept could trump race in southern culture. Patton sang about "travelin' down the dirt road" and evoked the image of the railroad in some of his most prominent recordings, such as "Green River Blues," "Hammer Blues," "Pea Vine Blues," and "Pony Blues." Other blues singers and players carried on the tradition, such as "Tampa Red" Whittaker, who sang "Nobody knows that I.C. [Illinois Central Railroad] like I do. Now the reason I know it, I ride it through and through," in the song "I.C. Blues," or Lead Belly, who took the traditional train songs "Midnight Special" and "Rock Island Line" and made them his own during the 1930s. As for Jimmie Rodgers, he eventually crafted an entire public image for himself based on the character of the "singing brakeman," and many of his songs used the freight yard, the freight train, or the railroad depot as a starting point of an autobiographical adventure set to music. One of his most famous publicity photos, reprinted through the years to the point that it has become iconic in the history of country music, featured a smiling Rodgers in a railroad costume, holding his guitar and giving the double "thumbs-up" sign. "When a woman gets the blues, she hangs her head and cries," Rodgers wrote in "Train Whistle Blues," "but when a man gets the blues he grabs a train and rides."[68] Later, Rodgers fan Johnny

Cash penned "Folsom Prison Blues," one of the most famous songs ever to use the train a symbol of freedom and escape.[69]

Of course while life riding the rails could be exciting for a young man, there was also a downside—a sad side—to Rodgers's career as a railroad worker. Life on the road could be very lonely. Without a fixed home to cling to, Rodgers developed a sense of rootlessness that never quite went away even after he became famous and had a big house and a family to call his own. Some of these feelings were summed up in a song he recorded in 1932, after fame had struck, called "Miss the Mississippi and You":

> I'm growing tired of the big city lights
> Tired of the glamour and tired of the sights
> In all my dreams I am roaming once more
> Back to my home on the old river shore
>
> I am sad and weary far away from home
> Miss the Mississippi and you dear
> Days are dark and dreary everywhere I roam
> Miss the Mississippi and you.[70]

The happy and sad duality of the road created a great deal of friction in Rodgers's life that he later turned into music which could be lively and celebratory, or melancholy and distant. As his biographer Nolan Porterfield later put it, "Whether a song was humorous or bluesy, sentimental or bawdy, Rodgers sang it like a testament, as if he'd lived every line and suffered every change." A wide range of emotions was always reflected in Rodgers's repertoire, which was part of the magic that made him so popular. For instance, in "My Rough and Rowdy Ways," an upbeat number heavy on bravado, he told listeners, "I may be rough, I may be wild, I may be tough, but that's my style," while in the touching country lullaby "Sleep Baby Sleep" he may have been thinking of his own daughter when he sang, "Sleep baby sleep, while angels watch over you, listen to your mother, while she sings to you."[71]

From 1911 Rodgers worked for several years on the Mobile and Ohio Railroad line with his father as well as the New Orleans and Northeastern and other lines. Starting as a member of a section crew that repaired track, he also worked as a flagman, baggage handler, and brakeman as needed. The road was his life, and he had few responsibilities until 1917 when a friend introduced him to Stella Kelly, an eighteen-year-old whose parents owned a small farm in Noxapater, Mississippi, a Winston County hamlet about fifty miles north of Meridian. After a quick courtship, Rodgers and Kelly married and the railroad man pledged to settle down. The couple moved to Durant, another railroad town located about ninety miles northwest of Meridian, where Rodgers hoped to find permanent employment as a mechanic in one of the local shops. The job never materialized, and after supporting himself and Stella for a time doing odd jobs, he went back to working on the rail lines, taking temporary employment doing any job necessary. Once again he was away from home for long stretches and because of their precarious financial situation Stella was forced to move into a boarding house near her family.[72]

From the start the marriage was doomed. While Rodgers was charming, charismatic, and fairly proficient at the art of courtship, his ability to commit to anything long-term was suspect to say the least. Extended stays away from home took a serious toll on the marriage, and rumor had it that, much like the sailor with a woman in every port, Rodgers collected girlfriends up and down the rail lines. "I'll eat my breakfast here, and my dinner in New Orleans," he later sang on one of his most prominent recordings, "I'm gonna get me a mama that I ain't never seen."[73] Rodgers also was a seasoned drinker by the time he married Stella, and while he may not have been a hopeless drunk, his frequent tippling probably did not help his domestic situation. According to an acquaintance, Rodgers and his friends like to "drink, they'd shoot dice—little bit of everything, I guess."[74] Stella was also light years ahead of her husband in her ambitions. Where Rodgers had only gone to school off and on growing up, Stella had graduated high school by the age of sixteen and attended college at Mississippi A&M (now Mississippi State University), an unusual feat at the time for a young girl in Mississippi. It was obvious that she expected big things, and it was just as obvious that her husband was easily content. The friendly, informal qualities that made Rodgers a great drinking companion did little to help his marriage and quickly wore down his wife's patience. The couple rarely had any money and depended on relatives to pay many of their bills. To make matters worse, Stella did not like Rodgers's music. "I didn't think it would ever amount to anything," she said many years later. "I didn't think he was very good." It did not take long for her to realize that she and her husband were mismatched, and that by marrying Jimmie Rodgers she had made a serious mistake. The union did produce one child, a daughter, Kathryn, who was born in 1918, but by the time of her birth the marriage was already all but over. Rodgers and his wife had separated some time before, and Stella supposedly never told her husband that she was pregnant or notified him when she had the child. Her parents moved to Oklahoma, and she followed them to start a new life. The divorce was finalized, and apparently Rodgers did not know of his daughter's existence until a contentious 1932 lawsuit filed by Stella after he became famous.[75]

After his first marriage dissolved, Rodgers continued to work with the railroad. For a couple of years he shared with his cousin a small apartment near the Meridian rail yards and stayed either there or with his aunt Dora Bozeman during layovers in the city. When he was home he routinely made the rounds in Meridian and the surrounding area, visiting with old friends and drinking and playing music in old haunts. During one of his stays in Meridian a friend took him to an unlikely gathering place for someone like Jimmie Rodgers, a Methodist preacher's home. Reverend Jesse T. Williamson and his wife, Kizzie, were flexible in their social habits compared to many other ministers and ministers' wives in the area. They liked to entertain and have fun, and they loved music of all kinds. Their house was a neighborhood social center, a community gathering place where people congregated to enjoy each other's company. "Ours was a religious family," one of the Williamson children later wrote, "but none of your stern, sour fanatics. Ours was a happy home with good clean fun with good music, the classic and popular music, as well as church songs."[76] The music drew Rodgers and his friend to the Williamson household in the summer of 1919, and it was there that Rodgers met the sixteen-year-old girl who would become his second wife.

Carrie Cecil Williamson was the seventh of nine children in the Reverend's household, and she was immediately caught off guard by Rodgers's charm. She later described herself at the time she met her future husband as a "school girl, a minister's daughter, I was not thinking of young men, nor of marriage. My lessons and my church and Sunday school work were to me not dull, but happy, enjoyable duties." From all accounts Carrie Williamson, like Stella Kelly before her, was dissimilar from Rodgers in attitude and work ethic. Shy but strong willed, she was a hard worker with a full-time job at a department store in downtown Meridian. Once Rodgers met Carrie he began stopping by the

Williamsons' home on a regular basis, sometimes with his guitar or banjo. Welcomed with open arms at first, the Williamsons grew suspicious of Rodgers as his romance with Carrie began to blossom. They knew his reputation and were uncomfortable with the notion that he could potentially become a member of their family. Their fears were realized on April 7, 1920, when Jimmie Rodgers and Carrie Williamson married at the home of one of Rodgers's friends in a hastily arranged ceremony that her family did not find out about until several days later. Once confronted with the harsh reality that Rodgers, a vagabond railroad man with a reputation as a fun-loving drinker and womanizer, had joined their clan, they tried to make the best of the situation. As was the case with Rodgers's first wife, Carrie Williamson subordinated any personal aspirations that she may have had to life with her husband. Unlike Stella Kelly, however, she accepted her situation and quickly gave up on trying to change or reign in Jimmie Rodgers.[77]

For much of the next few years after their marriage the couple lived a hand-to-mouth existence. While Rodgers found a good bit of part-time work with the railroad, fulltime jobs were rare, and even when he did have money he tended to spend it frivolously. When Carrie was not on the road with her husband she usually stayed in Meridian with her parents or other family members who also helped the couple with their bills. Even the birth of his first child, Carrie Anita Rodgers, on January 30, 1921, failed to curb Rodgers's penchant for road life. Though he had a wife and child, he rarely acted like a man with familial responsibilities. Rather than dreading the prospect of being away from his new baby for an extended period, Rodgers welcomed any railroad job that gave him the opportunity to travel, no matter how meager the wages or how long the job would keep him away. When he was home he spent some time with his family, but he also made the rounds, visiting local bar rooms and pool halls, just like always and more in the manner of a single man than the head of a household. Through it all one thing remained constant: Jimmie Rodgers almost always carried a guitar or banjo with him everywhere he went, on the road or in town, and he rarely passed up an opportunity to play with other musicians. "He learned to play the banjo and guitar at a very early age and often entertained his fellow workers during lunch and rest breaks," country-music authority Bill C. Malone later commented. "In his off hours he often played with black musicians down around Tenth Street in Meridian."[78]

In 1923, when he was between railroad jobs, Rodgers made an attempt to break into what he considered big-time show business. That year a traveling tent show passed through Meridian, and the aspiring singer latched onto it for about a month. Tent shows, more formally called tent-repertoire or "tent-rep" performances, were common during the early twentieth century in rural areas that had access to the railroad. While the show could feature many types of entertainment, the basic formula involved visiting a community for about a week and performing a different play—dramas, comedies, and everything in between—each night under a large tent. Between acts of the plays, many shows employed vaudeville performers or musicians to keep the patrons entertained and give them the feeling that they were getting their money's worth. According to Mary C. Henderson, "hundreds of companies took to the road every summer, each carving a slice of vast territory, cultivating audiences with a ten cent admission fee, offering a different program in one-week stands." The shows that toured the countryside typically employed around thirty actors and other performers, and some outfits enlisted local talent from time to time in an effort to draw crowds. At the end of the week, the show would literally fold up the tent and move to another location. The tent-rep show grew out of the earlier tradition of the traveling theater troupe that moved up and down the rail lines performing plays, usually in some type of indoor facility. Some promoters, especially those involved with troupes that moved through the South, later chose the tent-rep format because an outdoor tent provided better summertime ventilation than an enclosed, indoor facility in the era before air conditioning. In addition, those who ran the shows did not have to pay a large fee, usually in advance, for renting a hall. Tent shows were generally looked down upon by the "legitimate" theater community, but they were very popular and thousands flocked to see them every year.[79]

The tent show that caught Rodgers's attention in Meridian in 1923 was owned and operated by a seasoned tent-rep performer named Billy Terrell. Terrell was a show-business veteran who appeared for years with a number of companies before organizing his own troupe in 1921 called "Billy Terrell's Comedians." Known for producing comedy pieces, Terrell and his group were successful at a time when many such troupes quickly came and went. In his travels throughout the country Terrell frequently encountered local musicians or other performers who wanted to join his show and escape boring lives in the tiny, sleepy towns they called home. Usually these young performers were woefully underpolished, even for the tent-show circuit, and were sent back to the farm. When Rodgers approached Terrell during his troupe's 1923 stop in Meridian, the showman saw him as just another thin, dusty country boy with more aspirations than talent. Still, he gave Rodgers a tryout and was impressed enough to give him a small spot on the program. According to an interview with Terrell that took place many years later, Rodgers told the showman that he could "[p]lay the banjo, guitar some. Do blues on the guitar, and 'blue yo-deling.'"[80] Later on Rodgers would become famous as "America's Blue Yodeler," but at the time Terrell was not certain what the term meant.

After Jimmie Rodgers became famous, many tried to describe the type of trademark yodel that Rodgers put on record. He eventually recorded thirteen so-called "blue yodel songs" during his career in which the yodel punctuated stanzas and played an important part in the general tenor of the song. Rodgers himself described his yodels simply as "curlicues I can make with my throat," but they had a great impact on the early history of recorded music in the United States. Once Rodgers's records began to sell, yodeling became virtually synonymous with country music and scores of country entertainers mimicked his delivery. Rodgers did not create the yodel, but he certainly popularized it once he began making records, and his yodeling abilities eventually became part of his legend, copied by white and black performers alike. Music scholar and author Jocelyn R. Neal analyzed the famous Rodgers "falsetto warble":

> The single biggest factor in Rodgers' stardom was his yodel. . . . All the dis-cussion in the world cannot possibly do it justice; there is simply no substi-tute for hearing Rodgers yodel, and for a country fan, that sound is a means of venturing back into the 1920s and 1930s. . . . There are two fundamen-tally different types of yodeling in country music: one occurs when a singer jumps into a falsetto register in the middle of a word or inserts a warble in an otherwise normal line of lyrics. Rodgers used this occasionally, and it is this type of yodeling that resurfaces most famously in Hank Williams' mu-sic two decades later. This type of yodel is neither the most prominent in Rodgers' music nor the most discussed. The second kind of yodel is a stand alone musical phrase that occurs after the regular lyrics. . . . This yodel is sung on its own nonsense syllables (such as 'yo-del-lay-ee-o'). Over the

span of his career, Rodgers yodeled on many different melodic patterns, which grew more elaborate as he gained confidence and experience.[81]

While it is difficult to discern exactly where the Rodgers yodel came from, the African American influence among the European is unmistakable. "Swiss yodels were cheery," country-music writer Colin Escott maintained, "but the blue yodel owed more to black field hollers and the lonesome tones of railroad whistles." The origins were ancient, certainly predating the Civil War. Ethiopian scholar Ashenafi Kebede wrote that the calls, cries, and hollers of slaves in the field were "performed in a free and spontaneous style; they are often ornamented and employ many African vocal devices, such as yodels [and] echo-like falsetto." In the 1853 book on his travels through the South, Frederick Law Olmsted mentioned what he called "Negro Jodeling" and the "Carolina yell" that he heard as he passed through slave communities. In the context of a Rodgers live performance or recordings, the yodel was part improvisational expression, part theatrical device, and part musical punctuation. Ultimately, it also served as another evidentiary link between black (blues) and white (country) musical culture in the South. "Yodeling is known to be common in many areas of Africa in addition to being similar to the 'field hollers' of African American folk tradition," Joseph E. Holloway stated. "Thus we can postulate a partial African origin for Jimmie Rodgers' distinctive 'blue yodel' style of singing, so important in the development of Country Music." While ethnomusicologists have attempted at length to distinguish between the European yodeling tradition and the "falsetto leaps" of the African tradition, the early adoption of this form of expression by both country and blues musician tended to quash any elements of racial distinction that applied. According to early Mississippi blues performer Herb Quinn, during the 1930s "anybody who could pick a guitar," black or white, wanted to imitate the Rodgers's "blue yodel" in some form or fashion.[82]

Whether it was his ability to "blue yodel," or the self-assurance that he outwardly displayed as he asked for the job, Rodgers won Terrell over during his audition with a series of standards, including "Hot Time in the Old Town" and "The Daring Young Man on the Flying Trapeze." Rodgers left town with Terrell's troupe in November of 1923, leaving his wife behind to care for their two children, two-year-old Carrie Anita and five-month-old June Rebecca who was born the previous June. Leaving his family was not an unusual occurrence for Rodgers, who had done so many times during his years with the railroad. He routinely counted on the charity of relatives to help his family survive in his absence. Rodgers gave his first performance with Terrell's group during a stop in Hattiesburg, Mississippi. He played a railroad song that included his trademark blue yodel, along with the upbeat standard "Frankie and Johnny." From all accounts the appearance—basically a brief musical interlude performed between acts of a play—was well received. [83]

On the surface it seemed that Rodgers might have his dream of becoming a traveling performer in sight, but ultimately his short time with Billy Terrell's Comedians ushered in a horrible period in the aspiring singer-songwriter's life. Rodgers lasted only about a month with Terrell. Life on the road was not as glamorous as it seemed. Getting from place to place with all the performers and equipment was sometimes difficult, and while shows were usually welcomed in a community, show people were many times looked down upon, especially by local hoteliers and other merchants who worried that a traveling troupe might leave town without settling their bills. Rodgers also made very little money with the troupe. Even with a successful company like Terrell's, the bulk of the pay went to the actors who performed in featured skits and plays. For someone like Rodgers, a novice performer who was allowed to play only two or three songs between acts, there was little left over at the end of the night. By comparison, it made his sporadic railroad work seem almost lucrative.

While the low pay contributed to Rodgers leaving Billy Terrell's Comedians after just a few weeks, he was also summoned home by his wife, who was dealing with a devastating family tragedy. On December 22, 1923, the couple's youngest daughter, June Rebecca, died in Meridian. When Rodgers got the news he was in New Orleans, and he immediately hopped a freight train back to Mississippi, where he borrowed money from his wife's family to pay for the funeral. Grieving and broke, he fell back on the only life he knew, eventually finding part-time work on the railroad in early 1924. He spent much of the rest of the winter away from home, making his way as far west as Colorado and Utah. During the course of his travels he fell ill with what he believed at first was a serious cold. As time wore on, however, he developed a cough that he was never quite able to shake. [84]

By the summer of 1924 Rodgers was back in Mississippi with his family, where it was becoming obvious that he had a health problem. His cough turned more ominous, rattling his chest and occasionally causing him to spit up blood. He tried to ignore the symptoms, but on a visit with Alabama relatives the following autumn he suffered a severe hemorrhage that almost killed him. He was hospitalized, and the doctor's diagnosis was swift, severe, and terrifying. Rodgers had contracted tuberculosis, a horrific lung disease that killed slowly, and a disease for which there was no cure. In the early twentieth century a diagnosis of tuberculosis was a death sentence. In an instant Rodgers knew that he was doomed, and that for the rest of his life he would have to find a way of making a living other than with the railroad. "For three months my boy lay there, in a charity hospital, fighting for his life," his wife later remembered. "When he was released after those three agonizing months—we knew. Knew that never again would he be a ladder climber, never again ride the decks and test his lungs against the roaring winds and clattering empties; never again collect a railroader's stake." For the rest of his life Rodgers outwardly tried to ignore his illness even at times when he was very sick, keeping up a happy-go-lucky facade and pretending that he was not bothered. Inwardly, however, he could not ignore his condition. Not only did he wake up every morning with the knowledge that his days were numbered, but he also knew that when he was a child his mother suffered a painfully slow death from the same disease. As was the case with anyone who was terminally ill, trying his best to ignore the malady and pretending that everything was fine served as an emotional defense mechanism that Rodgers used to keep himself going.[85]

Despite the diagnosis, Rodgers in 1925 made one last attempt at railroad work, trying to land a permanent job in the yards, but nothing came of it and he turned his full-time attention to music. He made an initial foray into featured entertainment by forming a trio with himself on banjo and guitar, his sister-in-law Elsie McWilliams on piano, and his friend Slim Rozell on violin. For several months the group served as the house band for a resort at Lauderdale Springs, just north of Meridian. The resort was well known regionally and attracted many well-heeled patrons to its mineral baths. According to one publication of the period, "The Lauderdale Springs are situated on the Mobile and Ohio Railway, about eighteen miles north of Meridian. There are a number of springs and a good hotel with ample facilities." The trio played slow to medium- tempo dance music, mostly old standards and popular waltzes, at an outdoor pavilion. The job ended once winter set in and fewer patrons were willing to brave the elements at an outdoor performance. While the engagement did not last long, it was significant in that it sparked a professional relationship between Rodgers and his sister-in-law Elsie McWilliams that eventually bore musical fruit.[86]

Elsie McWilliams was destined to become an important figure in the Jimmie Rodgers saga as his songwriting partner, and together they penned a number of his most popular tunes. Born in 1896, Elsie grew up in the same music-filled household as her sister, Rodgers's wife Carrie. In 1917 she married a Meridian policeman named Edwin Richard McWilliams, who most people in town referred to with affection as "Uncle Dick," and took a job as a schoolteacher. She collected sheet music and wrote songs for her own enjoyment. Before her appearances with him at Lauderdale Springs, Elsie had performed informally with Rodgers many times at the home of her parents. Later, after Rodgers began recording, he called on her to help furnish him with material. While she received a writing credit on only nineteen of her collaborations with Rodgers, McWilliams helped him with many other compositions. She outlived Rodgers by more than half a century and in 1979 was inducted into the Country Music Songwriters Hall of Fame in Nashville.[87]

Rodgers was disappointed when his trio's run at Lauderdale Springs ended, but he did his best not to show it. He simply moved on to try something else. Still desperate to forge an entertainment career, he played at local functions in Meridian or for tips in the city's bars or pool halls. To pay the rent he looked for legitimate employment but ended up working a succession of odd jobs, none of which lasted very long. Had it not been for his wife, who sometimes worked as a clerk in a department store, and the kindness of her family, the Rodgers clan might have starved to death. Occasionally, Rodgers was able to find temporary work with small-time traveling medicine shows that frequented the area, sometimes performing in blackface. These engagements were short-lived, but they did give Rodgers an opportunity to practice his craft and develop his skills as an entertainer.

By the mid-1920s Charley Patton and Jimmie Rodgers were both trying to sustain themselves as musicians. At the time, Patton was the older and more popular performer, or at least he had more dedicated followers. He had caught on with black audiences in the Mississippi Delta and seemed to be able to draw a good weekend crowd regardless of where he played. For an African American country-blues performer of the period, Patton was close to the pinnacle of success. But regardless of how popular he was in the nightclubs, there was always a glass ceiling for black artists, especially someone as unrestrained as Patton. Limited regional notoriety in the black community was about as high as a Delta blues player could expect to climb on the ladder of success in the Jim Crow South. Already in his thirties, Patton seemed destined for a life of routine touring in the Delta as a live performer who, for all practical purposes, was always on the road, growing older and older with each passing day. Many people at the time believed that Charley Patton would not live much longer anyway, with either his general lifestyle or a jealous husband eventually doing him in. As for Rodgers, he had yet to establish himself as a solo artist, performing primarily for nickels and dimes at local events, or as a temporary member of one traveling show or another. He was quick to display his talents to anyone who would listen in hopes that somehow he might catch a break, but for Rodgers any form of luck seemed elusive. He suffered from an incurable disease, he had never been able to adequately support his family, and he had been a part-time husband and father at best during his travels with the railroad. Singing and playing the guitar, along with a few drinks, were among the few activities that seemed to move him, and his happy-go-lucky persona was beginning to wear thin with his family and his creditors. The irresponsibility of youth did not translate well into a man approaching his thirties. Instead, it branded him a failure. Most people who knew Rodgers liked him, but few believed that he would ever amount to anything. By the mid-1920s Patton and Rodgers looked as if they had both gone as far as they could with their music, and both men seemed trapped, Patton in a Jim Crow society that would always hold him back, and Rodgers in a physical body that was slowly betraying him. Regardless of any talents they had, it looked as if both men would eventually die in obscurity. No one, including Patton and Rodgers themselves, could have guessed that each man was already on a path to musical immortality.

Members of a traveling minstrel show, some in blackface. While minstrel shows were racist in their content, they disseminated song lyrics and tunes throughout the South and elsewhere in the era before recorded music. Author's collection.

Crowd assembled to watch a medicine show. Musicians and other entertainers both black and white performed in traveling shows like this one. These shows were another vehicle that spread song lyrics and tunes throughout the South and elsewhere. Author's collection.

An early advertisement for the Edison phonograph. The advent of recorded sound made exceptional performers like Charley Patton and Jimmie Rodgers immortal. Courtesy of Neil Lerner.

Workers picking cotton in the Mississippi Delta in an era before mechanization, the type of difficult farm labor that Charley Patton spent a lifetime trying to avoid. Library of Congress.

Modern photograph of the entrance to Dockery Farms, called by some the "cradle of the blues," in Sunflower County, Mississippi, where Charley Patton and other blues greats lived and worked. Blues fans from all over the world regularly travel to Dockery Farms to have their photograph taken in front of this iconic sign. Author's collection.

The only full-length portrait of Charley Patton known to exist. From the collection of John Tefteller / Blues Images. Copyright 2004. Used with permission.

The face of Charley Patton. Cropped from the larger photo, this image was used by Paramount Records in their publicity material. Courtesy of John Tefteller / Blues Images.

A typical southern juke joint where musicians like Charley Patton drew large crowds on Saturday nights. Library of Congress.

Depression-era advertisement for Patton's "Pony Blues" that appeared in the *Chicago Defender*.

This ad for the Patton Song "Screamin' and Hollerin' the Blues" appeared in the September 14, 1929, edition of the *Chicago Defender*. It billed the singer as "The Masked Marvel" as part of a promotional contest to guess his true identity.

Downtown Meridian, Mississippi, the hometown of Jimmie Rodgers, during the 1930s. Author's collection.

Publicity photo of Jimmie Rodgers. Courtesy of the Jimmie Rodgers Family, Meridian, Mississippi.

Jimmie Rodgers, "the Father of Country Music," with one of his prized, custom-made guitars. Courtesy of the Jimmie Rodgers Family, Meridian, Mississippi.

This ad for the Jimmie Rodgers's song "Blue Yodel No. 9 (Standin' on the Corner)" appeared in the September 11, 1931, edition of the *Memphis Commercial Appeal*.

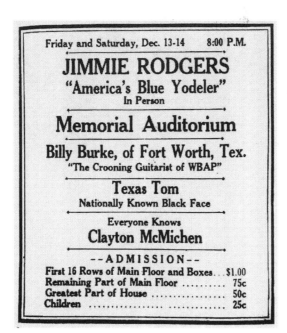

This ad for a Jimmie Rodgers personal appearance appeared in the December 13, 1929, edition of the *Chattanooga Times*.

Still image from Jimmie Rodgers's 1929 film short titled *The Singing Brakeman*. Courtesy of the Jimmie Rodgers Family, Meridian, Mississippi.

Postcard depicting the Taft Hotel in New York City, where Jimmie Rodgers passed away on May 26, 1933. Author's collection.

★★★★ 3 ★★★★

FOR THE RECORD

That Mississippi sound, that Delta sound is in them old records.
You can hear it all the way through.
—MUDDY WATERS

Jimmie Rodgers had to be a strong personality. . . . People connected
with him. They could identify themselves with him.
—JERRY LEE LEWIS

T he success and influence of Charley Patton and Jimmie Rodgers did not rest on sheer chance or luck, but both men happened to be in the right place at the right time. Had they been born a generation earlier, when recording technology was yet to be refined and the commercial music industry yet to be created, they would probably be long forgotten, regardless of their talents. Had they been born later, they would not have been among the first generation of recording artists in the history of American popular music. Patton and Rodgers both came of age at a time when the recording industry was finding its legs, desperate to find new artists in a variety of genres and looking everywhere for new sounds. While personal success was one thing, Patton and Rodgers also had lasting influence because they came of age at a time when the concept of recorded music was fresh and exciting. A recording allowed a person to listen not just to their favorite music, but to their favorite individual musical performance as well, over and over again. It also allowed individual performances to survive outside the memory of those who were listening. For the first time in human history a musical performer was able to make music for his or her contemporaries, and literally for generations unborn. "The novelty of the phonograph," Andre Millard explained, "was that it could preserve a part of life that had previously been a fleeting experience. Live music lasts only as long as the performance. . . . With proper care a recording can last a lifetime or longer, preserving the music many years after the musician is dead." Very quickly recorded music became more than just a new method of preserving an art form. It was also a saleable commodity, one that could be packaged and marketed for profits that would flow to individuals other than the artist. To record companies, an audience was not just a group of individuals who enjoyed a particular artist or a particular type of music. An audience constituted a market to be exploited, and although artists like Patton and Rodgers created the music, it was the record companies that disseminated the music on a grander scale. Of course this all meant that, in addition to being heard by generations of the music-buying public, a good performer could influence generations of musicians as well, allowing the phonograph to both preserve musical traditions and shape the future of music all at the same time.[1]

Like most great inventions, the phonograph was not the product of a single person's efforts. On December 6, 1877, prolific inventor Thomas Alva Edison first recorded the human voice using a machine that he had created in his laboratory in Menlo Park, New Jersey. He captured the simple phrase "Mary had a little lamb" on a cylinder wrapped in tinfoil, and the event represented the birth of recorded sound in America. While Edison would forever after be credited with producing the first phonograph, his machine actually was a synthesis of different technologies that already existed. Improving on Edison's design, inventors Chichester Bell (Alexander Graham Bell's cousin) and Charles Sumner Tainter produced their own version of a recording machine in 1885 that recorded onto wax cylinders. Two years later still another inventor, Emile Berliner, produced a machine that recorded sound onto flat disks. This represented an important innovation as the disks were easier to mass produce and distribute. It was an assistant working for Berliner, Eldridge Johnson, who during the 1890s significantly refined the process of recording sound and duplicating records. Johnson formed his own company, which he dubbed "Victor," supposedly in celebration of a legal victory over Berliner, who had filed a lawsuit claiming patent infringement. Soon the Edison Phonograph Company, Bell and Tainter's organization, and Victor were major competitors in the phonograph industry.[2]

The phonograph industry in the United States grew quickly as the result of major marketing efforts by manufacturers and a general upturn in the economy that took place in the waning years of the nineteenth century. In the decades following the Civil War, America industrialized, building great factories that by the turn of the twentieth century employed large numbers of workers to mass produce goods for the public. At the same time, as Court Carney

pointed out, "increased urbanization, regional mobility, technological innovation, and a rapidly expanding economy eroded the Victorian moorings that
underpinned American culture." It was an era when Americans opened up to
new forms of entertainment in an environment where new forms of entertainment could be disseminated more widely than ever before. With the rise of the
phonograph, as well as dependable player pianos, piano rolls, sheet music, and
eventually radio, the music of the emerging modern era could be recorded,
preserved, packaged and sold on a grand scale. Once the applicable technology was invented, the production and distribution of phonographs was little
different from the production and distribution of any other consumer good.
Mass production made items more affordable, and therefore more Americans
were able to purchase phonographs for their homes. Originally sold by traveling salesmen off the back of a cart or wagon, phonographs soon made their
way onto the floors of department stores, hardware stores, and furniture stores
where they sat next to another "miracle" invention of the period, the Singer
Sewing Machine. Merchants marketed phonographs as a multipurpose machine that no home in America could do without. According to sales pitches
of the era, the phonograph could turn any living room into an opera house
or music hall, generating entertainment for adults and children alike as it
brought families closer together in the warm embrace of popular song.[3]

By the first decade of the twentieth century, discs were replacing cylinders
as the industry's primary recording medium and phonographs were being used
more often for widespread distribution of musical performances. Because of
the technological restraints of the era, early musical recordings were usually
limited to dance bands, opera, marching bands, and other performances that
produced sound at high volume, as opposed to balladeers or more delicate
performances with light string arrangements. Early recording studios were
crude, to say the least, and the recording process was tedious. Even under the
best of circumstances and with the best equipment of the day it was difficult
to produce a high-quality recording. Most of the time the "studio" was little
more than a large room with most of the furniture removed. The acoustics
were usually poor, and because there initially was no electronic amplification
or audio mixing, performances were recorded live, over and over again, until
an acceptable version of a song was produced. A finished recording was almost
always the culmination of a painstaking process of trial and error, take after
take, during which performers and instruments were arranged and rearranged

at various points around the room in hopes of producing the proper blend of sounds. If an instrument was too loud, it was simply moved further away from the microphone, sometimes across the room or outside into a hallway, and a complicated system of large horns was used to funnel sound in one direction or another. Under the circumstances, the process of making a record was rarely a pleasant experience for those involved.[4]

By the end of the First World War, advances in technology had significantly improved and streamlined the recording process, virtually creating the modern music industry. According to author Nelson George, "From World War I through the mid-1920s, advances in technology permitted an explosion in record sales, causing music historians to dub this period the 'golden age.'" Performers sang and played into more sophisticated microphones, and their performances could be manipulated electronically. More sensitive equipment recorded sound with greater clarity and captured the subtleties that distinguished an outstanding artist from those who were simply adequate. The sheer number of records being produced increased as small, independent recording companies sprang up and attempted to compete with existing industry leaders. At the same time markets for recorded music were evolving, and fledgling radio stations began featuring recorded music in addition to live musical broadcasts. In the never-ending quest for profits, recording companies sought to create new market niches based on performers' regional appeal, ethnicity, or race. Irish ballads became popular, as did the songs of Jewish performers. Records by black entertainers were marketed directly to African American audiences in northern cities and the southern countryside, and primitive country music was targeted toward whites in rural areas.[5]

Developing slowly at first, recorded music by black artists later took off once it became apparent that there was money to be made by marketing African American artists to the African American buying public. The first African Americans to record did so for white audiences and came out of the vaudeville or medicine-show traditions that often lampooned black culture. George W. Johnson, called by some the "first black recording star" had a hit in 1890 with a song title "The Whistling Coon," which he followed up with a record called "The Laughing Song." A Virginian by birth, Johnson recorded for local companies in New Jersey and New York and for several years was very popular, though also very non-threatening to whites. The period also saw a number of whites record novelty songs using exaggerated African American dialects in much the same manner that whites sometimes performed in blackface in traveling medicine shows.[6]

Some very dramatic developments in the history of southern music began unfolding around the turn of the twentieth century as ragtime and jazz came of age. Music labeled "ragtime" originated with house bands and pianists in the red light districts of New Orleans. It was then transported by traveling musicians up the Mississippi River to Memphis, St. Louis, and eventually New York. Its nickname came from what many viewed as the "ragged" nature of the music's beat, and it was this "raggedness" that drove people to either love or hate the genre with equal ferocity. Ragtime was very popular during the early twentieth century, and music publishers did their best to take advantage of what some have described as one of the earliest waves of "pop music." By far the most famous name associated with ragtime was the African American composer Scott Joplin, who in 1899 wrote "Maple Leaf Rag," a national bestseller that helped broaden ragtime's appeal. As ragtime emerged as a popular musical genre, jazz music was also coming of age in the Storyville District of New Orleans. Located two blocks off the French Quarter, the Storyville District was created by the city in the late 1890s in an attempt to regulate prostitution by limiting the practice to one specific location. The district quickly grew to include a wide variety of brothels, dance halls, and saloons that used musical entertainment as a marketing device. Musicians who played all different mixes of music with African and European origins flocked to the area, among them early jazz pioneers like Charles "Buddy" Bolden and Ferdinand "Jelly Roll" Morton. The musical exchange that took place in the district was rapid and electric. While scholars have struggled to identify and define the musical nuances of ragtime and jazz, one general distinction between the two was that ragtime performances were more often than not limited to the piano, banjo bands, and some brass bands while jazz players used a wide range of instruments from pianos and guitars to woodwind instruments, saxophones, and trumpets. As with ragtime, jazz musicians exported their music up the Mississippi and beyond, making it one of the most popular forms of music that America ever produced.[7]

Music labeled as blues began circulating widely through sheet music beginning around 1912, which marked the beginning of a "blues craze" during which sheet music labeled as blues became very popular. Though called blues, the music was more jazz-based than the raw blues being played by Charley Pat-

ton and others in the Mississippi Delta. Some recognize "Memphis Blues" by
W. C. Handy as the first significant blues record although it seemed to come
from a more ragtime or jazz tradition. The tune started out as a campaign song
for Edward Hull Crump, the powerful mayor of Memphis, Tennessee, who
ran the city like a dictator during the early twentieth century. Later, Handy
discounted the song's political importance but reflected that "its musical setting, which I later published under the new title 'Memphis Blues,' was the first
of all the many 'blues,' and it set a new fashion in American popular music
and contributed to the rise of jazz or, if you prefer, swing, and even boogie-
woogie." Handy himself was dubbed "the Father of the Blues" although he
consistently maintained that he did not invent the genre. Some of the more
polished music that he called blues was based to a great degree on the earthy,
primitive music of the Mississippi Delta that he had heard as a touring musician in the South.

Part of what Handy—and other innovators like Charley Patton—did was
take a variegated body of work and create with it a more standardized form
with musical parameters that could be labeled and sold commercially in various permutations. From there, the heterogeneous processes—artistic creativity, social change, modernization—resulted in new developments and
branches made by future generations of musicians. In the end, Handy personified a strong link between primitive folk culture and modern commercialization that in the twentieth century created more opportunities for musicians in the South's poorer classes. Handy followed up "Memphis Blues"
with "St. Louis Blues" (which became his most famous composition), "Yellow
Dog Blues," and "Beale Street Blues." Publishers producing sheet music soon
noticed that music with the name "blues" in the title usually sold well, so it
was added to as many titles as possible by other artists, including many white
songwriters. While African Americans bought these records, they were still
distributed mainly to white consumers with most of the major record companies holding fast to the belief that most whites but few blacks had enough
disposable income to buy phonographs or records.[8]

Another significant development in the spread of African American music and culture was the rise of the "chitlin' circuit," a network of exclusively
African American performance venues that sprang up in the South and elsewhere around the turn of the twentieth century. For decades performers on
this circuit plied their trade in large tents, churches, nightclubs, or, especially

in some larger cities, major black-owned theater buildings. Sometimes referred to as "Negro vaudeville," the chitlin' circuit included various types of entertainment but always featured music. While the circuit nurtured young entertainers and gave experienced performers a place to showcase their talents, it also provided black audiences with an opportunity to share their collective culture away from the prying eyes of whites and among other individuals with whom they shared common societal experiences. The all-black entertainment venues promoted African American unity and allowed members of the audience to relax and, in essence, let down their cultural guard. As Christine Acham explained, the white-dominated society in which African Americans lived "led to the creation of black communal spaces. These sites often nurtured African American culture and resistant politics. The example of the chitlin' circuit . . . demonstrates the importance of these spaces within African American society, culture and politics." Many early African American musicians, including jazz and blues performers, cut their teeth on the chitlin' circuit beginning just a few years before commercial recording took off. "As soon as there was a visible network of black vaudeville theaters in the South," Lynn Abbot and Doug Seroff pointed out, "the first identifiable blues pioneers appeared in the footlights. . . . These self-determined vaudevillians gave specific direction to a new vernacular form, including the so-called classic blues heard on the first crashing wave of race recordings"[9]

The "first crashing wave of race recordings" began its initial swell in 1920 when Mamie Smith, a veteran vaudeville performer, recorded "Crazy Blues," which some call the first true blues record although, like Handy's music, it had more of a jazz feel. While scholars argue over whether recorded blues began with Smith, she was an important character in the history of recorded music in that her version of "Crazy Blues" was the first big hit by a black artist that sold primarily in the African American community. Born Mamie Robinson in Ohio in 1883, Smith began touring as a vaudeville performer at the age of ten. By the time she entered her twenties she was a seasoned musical performer who could sing, dance, and play the piano as the need arose. On August 10, 1920, she recorded with a jazz band several songs written by African American songwriter Perry Bradford for Okeh Records, a small, independent label in New York that later became part of the Columbia recording empire. Among the songs that Smith recorded was "Crazy Blues," which helped transform the music industry. The song sold around seventy-five thousand copies in its first month of release, catching the attention of major American record-company executives who quickly began making plans to market black artists to black audiences. While "Crazy Blues" was more jazz than blues to those interested in making the distinction, the historical importance of the song as a catalyst for record companies recognizing the African American market is beyond dispute. The song was enshrined at the Grammy Hall of Fame in 1994 and in 2005 was selected for permanent preservation by the National Recording Registry at the Library of Congress. In another example of how "black" blues and "white" country music perpetually cross-pollinate, Smith's recording was supervised by a man named Ralph Peer, who had recently been hired as Okeh's director of recording after spending several years with Columbia. Peer, who was white, also made a number of early country-music recordings and later, in 1927, supervised the first recordings made by Jimmie Rodgers.[10]

With the success of "Crazy Blues," companies throughout the fledgling record industry took notice of what they considered a raw, untapped market for their products. Soon recordings by African American artists, called "race records" in the industry, were being produced and distributed throughout the South and elsewhere. Many of the first commercially viable performers of music labeled in this manner were women. Smith's success led other companies to rush to find female artists to make records. Cabaret singer Mary Stafford, backed by a jazz band, recorded "Royal Garden Blues" in 1921 for Columbia Records, and the label also recorded jazz singer Edith Wilson's "Nervous Blues" that same year. Ethel Waters recorded "Down Home Blues" during the same period, which was a significant record in that it was produced by Black Swan Records, the first widely distributed black-owned label marketing specifically to African Americans. Harry H. Pace, a singer, lyricist, and entrepreneur who had been in the music publishing business with W. C. Handy, ran the label. In 1923, two women who would become famous in the annals of American music made their first recordings. Gertrude "Ma" Rainey was marketed by Paramount Records as "the Mother of the Blues," and the incomparable Bessie Smith, called by many the best female blues singer of them all, recorded for Columbia Records. Originally headquartered in Washington, DC, Columbia began as a regional company that distributed phonographs for Thomas Edison. As early as 1891 the company had a section in their catalog called "Negro Music," which at the time was viewed primarily as novelty music. After Mamie Smith's success the label actively pursued black artists including Stafford, Wilson, and Bessie Smith along with a number of males who would make their mark on the blues world. In 1929 Columbia merged with another major player in the race-records market, Okeh Records.[11]

German Otto Heinemann founded Okeh in New York City in 1918 and began recording popular songs, dance tunes, and vaudeville-styled musical performances. Always in search of new markets, Heinemann made records that appealed to the large immigrant communities that had recently come into the major cities on the East Coast. These included existing recordings leased from European distributors and original recordings in German, Polish, Swedish, and Yiddish. Like Columbia, Okeh actively pursued black artists, male and female, after "Crazy Blues" proved that a significant African American market existed. The company created a separate division for race recordings and hired noted jazz pianist and composer Clarence Williams to oversee the venture. Credited by many as having coined the term "race records," Okeh advertised in African American newspapers that it produced "The World's Greatest Race Artists on the World's Greatest Race Records." Other companies that specialized in recording music for African Americans included Bluebird, a subsidiary of the Victor Recording Company, Gennett, which also recorded early country artists, Ajax, an offshoot of the recording empire founded by Emile Berliner, and the legendary Paramount Records.[12]

Paramount was the most prominent race-records producer of the early twentieth century. The company was founded in 1916 by the New York Recording Laboratory of Port Washington, Wisconsin, a subsidiary of the Wisconsin Chair Company, a successful furniture-manufacturing enterprise that produced, among many other things, wooden phonograph cabinets and their own line of phonographs. Paramount initially recorded simple compositions as a marketing tool, giving away copies of their records to anyone who purchased a phonograph. In 1924 the company purchased financially troubled Black Swan Records and began making records targeted to black audiences. To oversee the release of their race records, Paramount hired Jay Mayo Williams, the most successful black talent scout and producer of the period. During the early 1920s the label boasted, "Whether your musical tastes crave beautiful spiritual melodies, stirring band marches, or up-to-date jazz, Paramount gives you the best there is. The greatest stars of the Race—singers and players— artists everyone, record only with Paramount."[13]

Once multiple labels committed to producing black artists, a massive race to recruit talent took place between the competing companies. All the labels sent men into the field, and particularly into the South, in search of commercially viable African American musicians. New, portable equipment allowed talent scouts to record artists in their own environment, or in hastily prepared audition rooms in southern cities and towns. Advertisements in local newspapers or simple word of mouth attracted musicians to the sessions. Most had no concept of the recording process, or how records were distributed, but they had heard that by recording their songs they might be able to make a few dollars. Other southern artists were brought north to record in better equipped studios in places like New York or Chicago. The successful labels developed national networks that passed on information about artists whose work might sell. According to Giles Oakley, "All the recording companies had their talent scouts in the field—musicians, record store proprietors, whites and blacks in all parts of the country would be constantly recommending some new singer or group. Some were brought up North to record, but increasingly it was a matter of going down to the location with portable equipment."[14]

The race to find solo "country blues" or "rural blues" performers took off about midway through the 1920s. Country blues as a genre was difficult to define because so many different influences helped create it, but in general it was a highly personalized form of blues from which much of modern music labeled as blues evolved. Traditionally, it was personified by the lone, usually male, artist who performed with little accompaniment other than a guitar played finger style and occasionally with some type of glass or metal slide. Some argue that original blues was a type of African American folk music, while others believe that the personal nature of the music distinguished it from other forms of African American song. Still others claim that the word "blues" has always been little more than a marketing vehicle designed to sell music, be it the word printed on the front of sheet music in the early the twentieth century or the "blues" festivals routinely held decades later at various locations throughout the South and elsewhere. Thematically, rural blues drew from many sources, although the ancient relationship between men and women provided many bluesmen with material. According to Giles Oakley: "The principal theme of the country blues, and probably all of blues, is the sexual relationship. Almost all other themes, leaving town, train rides, work trouble, general dissatisfaction, sooner or later reverts to the central concern. Most often the core of the relationship is seen as inherently unstable, transient, but with infinite scope for pleasure and exultation in success, or pain and torment in failure. This gives the blues its tension and ambiguity, dealing simultaneously with togetherness and loneliness, communion and isolation, physical joy and emotional anguish."[15]

Regardless of the countless nuances involved in this style of music, the Mississippi Delta early on was credited as the cradle of country blues, although some early performers hailed from elsewhere. A sightless blues player named "Blind" Lemon Jefferson was a primary catalyst in the development of country blues as a commercial entity. Born blind in Freestone County, Texas, around 1894, Jefferson learned to play the guitar as a child and began playing for local social events as a teenager. After his family moved to Dallas, he played on street corners and later in bars and pool halls, where he reportedly made a significant amount of money in tips. A record store owner recommended him to Paramount and, beginning in 1925, he made several records that sold very well to African Americans in both the South and some of the North's large cities. Jefferson's style came to be labeled "Texas Blues," which differed generally from the "Delta Blues" of Charley Patton in that it had a somewhat faster tempo and was influenced to an extent by early Texas "swing" music. Jefferson recorded dozens of tunes, mostly with Paramount, between 1925 and his death in 1929, of which forty-three were issued. While his style was not necessarily imitated to the same extent as Delta players like Patton, Jefferson was undoubtedly an influence on everyone who heard his records, including many of the early Delta players. Once Jefferson's records hit, Paramount and other labels doubled and tripled their efforts to find talented blues singers, and the search led them to the Mississippi Delta, and to Charley Patton.[16]

As the recording industry began to evolve, Patton continued performing to enthusiastic crowds in the Delta, developing a reputation as the region's greatest showman. He never settled in one place for very long, playing occasional dances at Dockery's and in juke joints and house parties on a circuit that included many Mississippi Delta communities. "He'd go out into the country and play at some juke," Honeyboy Edwards later remembered. "He didn't play at Dockery's all the time. He'd go to Scott, Lula, Rosedale, Merigold. . . . Go out in the country and play for them people giving the country dances for three dollars a night and all the whiskey he could drink. He'd put on a big show, take that guitar and play it behind his back clowning around." Patton knew his audience and knew what pleased them. He played some Delta standards and many original compositions that reflected Delta life and his own personal experiences. Patton sang, shouted, laughed, and moaned onstage, sometimes beating on his guitar without plucking a string. According to Delta blues singer J. D. "Jelly Jaw" Short, a Patton contemporary, the bluesman "used to play the guitar and he'd make the guitar say 'Lord have mercy, lord have mercy, pray brother pray, save poor me.' Now that's what Charley Patton'd make the guitar say." Patton was a true showman, but as he gained popularity among the juke-joint patrons of northwest Mississippi, he also gained a reputation among some as a troubled, even sinister figure. He lived much of his life in a sundown-to-sunup world fueled by cheap whiskey and filled with loose women and volatile men, many of whom were jealous of the way their wives or girlfriends were attracted to the bluesman. In 1921, Will Dockery threw Patton off of his plantation for being a bad influence on the fieldworkers and because of rumors concerning the way that the bluesman mistreated some of the women on the Dockery place. Naturally, Patton wrote a song, "34 Blues," about the situation in which he sings and sighs that "they run me from Will Dockery's."[17]

Exiled from Dockery's, Patton simply moved on to another plantation and kept up the lifestyle to which he had become accustomed. Two years later a jealous husband shot him after Patton had made a play for the man's wife in a barrelhouse, leaving the bluesman with a permanent limp. It was not the last serious wound that the bluesman sustained during his life. Despite a tainted reputation, there were others who saw Patton in a different light. To many he personified nothing more than a good time, his music representing not mayhem but a vehicle that allowed an oppressed people to have a little fun at the end of a work week. A number of Patton's acquaintances later referred to him consistently as a "nice fella" who never meant any harm. As for the bluesman's periodic and sometimes violent indiscretions, his defenders blamed alcohol, claiming that Patton was only incorrigible after drinking. "He wasn't on the mean side none," Booker Miller, a younger musician who admired Patton later claimed, "but if you didn't understand him, you'd think he was."[18]

Patton's unpredictable personal demeanor was in large part the product of the way he grew up and the environment he chose to live in as a traveling musician. At times he was not able to control his drinking in an era when alcohol abuse was not identified as a disease but rather as an acute moral failing. However, Patton's proclivities to live life on the edge, more or less as if it were a perpetual party, and his sometimes erratic behavior, may have been the result of a deeply ingrained streak of fatalism. Some of the lyrics in his songs bore this out, including "Prayer of Death (Part 1)" in which he sang:

> I want to be prepared to die
> In any kind of weather
> I want for you to be ready too
> We'll fly away together
> If you think your life will have no end
> Your foolish days are numbered
> Go and waste your time trying to pretend
> Still you're bound for eternal slumber.

According to one source, Patton once told an acquaintance that he was examined by a doctor at Dockery's plantation around 1917 and was disqualified from military service in World War I because "he had a bad heart. That's what the doctor told him." From that point on Patton knew, or at least suspected, that he was living on borrowed time because of his health. Coupled with the general sense of hopelessness that many African Americans felt at the time in the poverty-stricken Mississippi Delta, this created in the singer a pattern of behavior that revolved around living every day as if it were his last, unburdened by major responsibilities. This certainly gave him something in common with Jimmie Rodgers, who was diagnosed with tuberculosis in his twenties, in that before either man had recorded a single song, both suspected that they would not live long lives.[19]

Through all the tumult of Patton's life, one thing remained constant. He was always able to compose and perform music that appealed to people. He never lost the ability to communicate with an audience, or later on records, through song. He was known primarily for writing and playing blues, but he also played standards and even penned a few religious songs. His themes were typical of the blues—love, loss, escape, trouble, salvation—but he wove them into songs in a highly personalized way that made his music unique and set a musical template for blues performers that followed. According to blues researcher and author Francis Davis, "To a greater extent than any of his contemporaries, Patton drew on personal experience, reshaping verses in common usage to his own ends. But his lyrics were observational rather than autobiographical." His earliest compositions were some of his most animated, written for a noisy dance-floor audience, and he used his voice, his guitar strings, and his guitar's body as rhythm instruments.[20] They included songs such as "Running Wild Blues," "Shake It Don't Break It (But Don't Let It Fall Mama)," and "Banty Rooster Blues," which drew howls from the crowded dance floor when he delivered the lines:

> Gonna buy me a hammock, carry it underneath through the tree
> Gonna buy myself a hammock, carry it underneath through the tree
> So when the wind blow, the leaves may fall on me
> Go on, baby, you can have your way
> Ball on, baby, you can have your way
> Sister, every dog sure must have his day.

After being thrown off Dockery Farms, Patton landed on the nearby Cottondale Plantation, a twenty-five-hundred-acre spread about a dozen miles southeast of Dockery's that was owned by George Kirkland. Kirkland liked the idea of having a musician on his place and was impressed enough by Patton's talents to let him move into an abandoned sharecropper's shack on the property. Initially, Kirkland seemed amused by Patton, treating him as somewhat of a curiosity. The landowner even made it a point to come to Patton's first official performance in his new surroundings, a Saturday-night Christmas party with several dozen local tenants in attendance. According to a witness, "First Saturday night they had a big time. Mister George himself come down; they had a great time. That was a little bit before Christmas. . . . The Christmas affair took place on the lawn in front of Kirkland's house and lasted an entire day and night." Sensing that he might have a good thing going at Cottondale, Patton cut back on his alcohol consumption for several months, but then backslid. He began drinking as heavily as ever, which led to fights with both men and women. He participated in a legally binding marriage ceremony in 1922 to a woman named Mandy France, whom he then reportedly began beating on a regular basis. Not long afterward, the bluesman got into a dispute with George Kirkland, who was probably unhappy with the singer's increasingly hostile behavior. In the process Patton ridiculed Kirkland after the landowner threatened to put him to work in the fields. The two exchanged harsh words, and Kirkland threw Patton off the plantation, a relatively light punishment considering that in the Mississippi Delta of the 1920s insubordinate African American who talked back to members of the white power structure often found themselves in jail or, on occasion, dangling dead from the end of a rope.

After leaving Cottondale, Patton moved around for several years, even returning to Dockery's for a short time, living with this woman or that woman and then moving on. According to one acquaintance, the musician sometimes chose his bed partners on the basis of how well they could keep him fed. He was particularly enamored with any woman who worked as a cook for local whites, because he knew that she would have regular access to food. "He'd try to be slick. He'd take up with the white folks' cook," one man who knew Patton later recalled. "He'd fool them up and play to them like he was so much in love with them, and she was toting them pans [of food] from the white folks' kitchen. He was a slicker, you know." Patton stayed in the Mississippi Delta most of the time, although he occasionally ventured into Memphis or across the Mississippi River into Arkansas or Louisiana to perform. Wherever the bluesman went, barrelhouse audiences welcomed his music with enthusiasm. [21]

Many of Patton's early songs were heavy on sexual innuendo—perfect material for the barrelhouse crowd—but some were filled with social comment on Delta life. Among his most popular tunes was "Pony Blues," which was later heavily covered by other blues artists, and "Down the Dirt Road Blues," a song of sex and transience that included the classic Patton line "every day seems like murder here," a general assessment of the oppressive conditions under which many African Americans in the Delta lived, as well as a specific comment on the violent nature of some of his Saturday-night audiences. Adam Gussow wrote that, when Patton sang that line, "he was speaking not just about his chances of being lynched by a white Mississippi mob, but about the dangers he faced from his black blues audience at plantation frolics or jukes." In another one of his more popular compositions, "A Spoonful Blues," Patton used a slide to replace words, making his guitar "talk" in a technique later used by a host of other blues performers. The song, which was reputably about cocaine consumption, became the foundation for a later version by Chester "Howlin' Wolf" Burnett, which in turn was covered by the noted rock band Cream, featuring Eric Clapton, in 1966. [22]

Another popular Patton tune was "High Water Everywhere, Part 1," a song about the great Mississippi River flood of 1927 that wreaked havoc up and down the Mississippi River Valley as the most destructive flood in the history of the United States. During the disaster, flood waters breeched the river's levee system in almost 150 places, flooding more than twenty-five thousand square miles, displacing more than 600,000 individuals, and killing several hundred. The flood devastated the Mississippi Delta, where it quickly became apparent that local authorities were unprepared for the breadth of the disaster. Racial tension ran high in the region as relief organizations eventually evacuated many whites but rounded up African American farm laborers and forced them into refugee camps similar to prisons without adequate food, water, or sewage facilities. Patton chronicled the flood's progression and his own movements from community to community in a quest to find high ground, first to the Delta town of Sumner, then Leland, Greenville, Rosedale, and beyond. In a second incarnation of the song titled simply "High Water Everywhere, Part 2," Patton went to great lengths to chronicle the pain and anguish of those individuals suffering through the flood and those who did not survive it:

> Man, the water was risin' at places all around,
> boy, they's all around
> It was fifty men and children come to sink and drown
> Oh, Lordy, women and grown men drown
> Oh, women and children sinkin' down Lord, have mercy
> I couldn't see nobody's home and wasn't no one to be found.

The Patton song that perhaps more than any other showcased both the bluesman's wit and his ability to weave local experiences and personalities into an appealing whole was "Tom Rushen Blues." An embellished account of one of Patton's periodic arrests for drunkenness, the song was set in Merigold in Bolivar County, Mississippi, where the bluesman spent a good deal of time. It was part documentary and part satire that included a cast of real characters including Bolivar County Sheriff Tom Day, who was up for reelection at the time Patton composed the tune, and an African American bootlegger named Holloway. The star of the song was Deputy Ottis Washington "Tom" Rushen Sr., whose last name was actually spelled "Rushing" and who had picked up the nickname "Tom" as a child. It was standard practice in the Delta shortly before elections for the sheriff and his men to lock up local black bootleggers and their patrons in an effort to create the impression that they were being tough on crime, and then release the prisoners once all the ballots had been cast and counted.[23] At the beginning of "Tom Rushen Blues" it was Tom Rushen himself who wakes Patton up from a drunken stupor:

> I laid down last night, hopin' I would have my peace,
> I laid down last night, hopin' I would have my peace,
> But when I woke up, Tom Rushen was shakin' me
> When you get in trouble, it's no use to screamin' and cryin',
> When you get in trouble, it's no use to screamin' and cryin',
> Tom Rushen will take you, back to the prison house flyin'.

Many years later the real Tom Rushing told his grandson that he had known Charley Patton fairly well and had liked him although he had to lock him up several times for "getting drunk in town." Rushing confirmed what others said about the musician with regard to his drinking, mainly that "Charley was like two people, his sober self and his drunk persona. He could be a 'mean drunk' as they say and that was the primary reason for his recurring arrests."[24] Patton later reworked "Tom Rushen Blues" to describe a similar incident in Belzoni, Mississippi, another Delta town. In the song, titled "High Sheriff Blues," Patton admitted, "It takes booze and blues, Lord, to carry me through." A penchant for strong drink and a habit of writing about it were also thematic threads that ran through the work of Jimmie Rodgers. Both Patton and Rodgers were comfortable in the barroom, be it a juke joint or a beer joint, and the music that both men performed was comfortable there as well. For instance, in "Elder Greene Blues," Patton sang, "I like to fuss and fight, I like to fuss and fight, and Lord get sloppy drunk on bond and walk the streets at night," while Rodgers, in "Gambling Bar Room Blues," offered a similar sentiment, singing about not only vice, but the self-destructive nature of turning on one's friend while under the influence of liquor:

> I strolled back to the barroom for another drink of gin,
> but the first thing I knew I was reeling, rocking drunk again
> I kept drinkin' gin and liquor, 'till way up in the night,
> When my pal walked into the barroom, we had an awful fight.[25]

While Patton was known as a solo performer, he did play with other musicians from time to time. One of his most significant performing partners was Willie Brown, who would also become a legendary character in the eyes of many blues enthusiasts. A little younger than Patton, Brown was born around 1900 near Robinsonville in the Mississippi Delta and began hanging around with Patton as the older man was gaining popularity on the Delta circuit. Patton reportedly taught Brown to play the guitar, with Brown being a quick study. While he could not match Patton's sheer force as a performer, it did not take Brown long to become a technically better guitar player than the man he idolized. Patton appreciated Brown's talents, and the two began to perform regularly together. According to Robert Palmer, Brown's forte was "fast, clean, aggressive picking" that eventually made him one of the most sought-after sidemen in the Delta. Brown consistently stayed out of the limelight, content in the shadows, but he eventually performed with many of the Delta's early blues masters, including Robert Johnson, who mentioned Brown by name in his seminal masterpiece "Cross Road Blues." Patton also performed occasionally with a Sunflower County trio of string musicians, a fiddler named John Nance, a mandolin player named James Hardy, and a mysterious musician known as "Kid" Bailey or sometimes "Killer" Bailey, who some researchers believe was actually Willie Brown using an alias. Not much is known about these men, but according to some they teamed with Patton for a few remarkable appearances.[26]

Charley Patton was a confident performer who believed in his own musical abilities, but by 1929 he was also aging rapidly. He had been touring for years and had already influenced a host of up-and-coming Delta bluesmen, some of whom had actually had their work recorded. Toward the end of the 1920s word circulated through the Delta that there was a white man in Jackson, Mississippi, who was willing to pay black artists for their music and put that music on records. This caught Patton's attention for a combination of reasons. He was generally drawn to any situation where he might be paid for playing and singing, and his ego probably led him to pursue recording because younger Delta players who had learned from him had already done so. Whether he saw recording as a way to preserve his work after he was dead is up for conjecture, but Patton certainly never would have envisioned a situation where more than a half-century later blues enthusiasts and collectors would covet his original records as if they were gold or precious jewels. Motivated by money, ego, a continued desire to express himself artistically, or by a combination of all three, Patton at some point in late 1928 or early 1929 wrote a letter to the white man in Jackson requesting an audition. The letter was addressed to Henry C. Speir.

Speir was an entrepreneur. Born in Prospect, Mississippi, in 1895, Speir was thirty years old when he opened his furniture store on Farish Street in downtown Jackson. In addition to standard furniture, Speir sold phonographs and records in his store and soon became a successful freelance "talent broker" for a number of record labels. At the time, the competition was fierce among labels that produced "race" records, with everyone desperate to sign new talent that offered something different and innovative. "They didn't want you bringin' no sheet music up there," Louisiana-born musician Eurreal "Little Brother" Montgomery later remembered. "They wanted original things from you." Although Speir was white, his store was located in the first block of Jackson's downtown black business district, so he had many African American customers and he came to know their tastes in music. Rather than a royalty, Speir received a set fee from the record labels for each artist and record that he produced, along with money to cover expenses.[27]

In 1926, Speir installed a recording machine in his store where he made personal recordings for the general public and demo recordings of the musicians that he recruited for record labels. He specialized in finding blues artists who could write and perform their own material, and his association with the genre eventually made history. "No other legend stands out as indelibly across the grooves of recorded music and in the memoirs of blues and sanctified music as does Henry C. Speir," Gayle Dean Wardlow wrote. "This man was a giant among talent scouts. He not only knew the artists, he knew what record companies wanted and he gave it to them." Speir had a simple but effective way of doing business. He would hear about a performer, many times through word of mouth, and he would then go and listen to that performer. If he liked what he heard and thought the artist's music would sell, Speir would make a demo record for one of the labels, or send the performer north to record in one of the studios maintained by the record companies. In hindsight, the process was filled with irony as Speir, a white businessman, for the most part chose the black blues artists he wanted to promote and record based on his own personal tastes and his vision of what would sell to black audiences. Some artists would recommend other players, but Speir never sent a blues musician to a record-company studio without personally hearing the man perform live, and he also distinguished between a good live performance and a performance that might translate well to a record. According to author Jeff Todd Titon, "Speir had no formal musical training; he simply relied on his musical taste. Unlike other scouts, he placed no weight on the prospective singer's popularity in his community. He observed that singers who were effective in person could lose their effectiveness on record." Regardless of what moved Speir to choose one musician over another, his system worked, and he was responsible for the first recordings of Charley Patton as well as just about every other blues great that came out of the Delta in the late 1920s and early 1930s including Tommy Johnson, Skip James, Ishmon Bracey, the Mississippi Sheiks, Bo Carter, Willie Brown, Son House, and Robert Johnson. Speir eventually left the music business and ended up selling real estate in Jackson. He died in 1972 with the significant role that he played in the evolution of American music in general and American blues music in particular still not widely recognized.[28]

In addition to receiving Patton's letter, there was always the chance that Speir first heard of the bluesman through other artists. By the time he met Patton, Speir had already dealt with several younger musicians from the Delta who would likely have mentioned Patton if questioned by Speir about other performers. Regardless, at some point during the spring of 1929 the talent scout gassed up his car and set out from Jackson driving north toward the Mississippi Delta to audition the man that would later be dubbed "King of the Delta Blues" by many around the world. When he first heard Patton sing, Speir knew that the course tone, or "gravel," in Patton's voice would carry on a phonograph record, and he was impressed with Patton's guitar playing. Other selling points were that Patton already had a catalog of his own songs ready to record. Speir also recognized Patton as a true original, someone who could compose, arrange, and sing his own songs or reworked traditional tunes with equal fervor and in a way that moved people. For the "white man from Jackson," individuality was a sign that an artist might do well on record, and in the marketplace, and Speir later identified Patton as the best blues singer that he ever heard. Speir was equally impressed with the bluesman's guitar playing. Whereas some of the lesser blues performers that Speir heard through the years sang different words but used the same basic rhythms on all of their songs, Patton did not. "Charley was good with that guitar; I mean he could handle a guitar out of this world," Speir once told an interviewer. "He just had method—he could play a guitar different on anything he'd sing."[29]

Speir sent Patton north to record for Paramount Records, a leading player in the race-music market. At the time, Paramount was constructing its own recording facility in Grafton, Wisconsin, and had contracted for the use of a studio in Richmond, Indiana, owned by Gennett Records, another label specializing in African American music. As a result, Patton boarded a train headed for Richmond in June of 1929. The Richmond studio was a large structure resembling a barn or a warehouse that was located next to some railroad tracks, which meant that all recording ceased whenever a train passed by. In addition to a recording facility, the building housed a new record-pressing plant that allowed music to be recorded and then mass produced with relative ease. Patton made his first recordings on June 14, performing some of the songs that for years had made him famous in the Delta. In all Patton recorded fourteen sides that day, including "Pony Blues," "Down the Dirt Road Blues," "Banty Rooster Blues," and "Tom Rushen Blues."[30]

During his first session for Paramount, Patton also proved his versatility as a musician and his ability to bring together the secular and sacred sides of African American music. He recorded mostly the dancing and drinking tunes that had made him a favorite in the barrelhouses, but he also recorded four spiritual numbers that proved he might have been a very effective preacher had he chosen another course for his life. "Prayer of Death, Part 1," "Prayer of Death, Part 2," "Lord I'm Discouraged," and "I'm Goin' Home" were Patton numbers that all spoke to themes of death, redemption, and faith. In subject they seemed to be a total departure from any of the fast, wild blues rants that got audiences dancing in the Delta, but in many ways these songs were consistent with the traditional blues theme of the human struggle between good and evil, sin and righteousness, God and the devil. In "Prayer of Death, Part 2," Patton's delivery proved to be more of a lyrical sermon:

> Yes, the wages of sin are death,
> The gift of God, eternal life. . . .
> Oh, hold to God's unchanging hand
> Hold to God's unchanging hand
> Build your hopes on things eternal
> Hold to God's unchanging hand.

Despite his singing religious music at his first recording session, Patton returned to the Delta once the session ended and fell back into his old familiar

patterns of life, although something had changed. He had gone north to record as a very popular live performer but had come back home as something
of a true celebrity, at least in the Delta's African American community. Patton had been paid seventy-five dollars per recorded song in Richmond, meaning that he had returned home with around a thousand dollars in his pocket.
While this might be a tawdry sum compared to the figures in modern recording contracts, it was a staggering amount of money for an African American
in the Mississippi Delta during the period. Patton used some of the money to
promote his live performances, paying to have flyers printed up with his face
on them. Stretching the truth a bit, Paramount marketed Patton nationally
as "one of the best known singers and guitar players in the South," and his
records began circulating in the Delta and elsewhere. More barrelhouse and
juke joint owners pursued Patton to play in their clubs, and larger crowds attended wherever he played. "Within the more insular world of the Delta," Ted
Gioia wrote, "he was now a celebrity of sorts, enjoying prerogatives—women,
money, a certain degree of freedom—that few other African American of his
time and place could claim."[31]

Patton's first recording session was also a landmark event in the history
of Delta blues, with many arguing that it represented the flashpoint of a process that would eventually bring the music to prominence. It produced fourteen classic recordings that sold well enough—some estimate in the tens of
thousands—to draw attention to the region and the region's musicians. It also
generated interest and ambition among younger performers in the talent-
rich Delta who saw Patton's celebrity status as a goal to pursue. Patton set a
standard for younger musicians, and as his records circulated among African
Americans in large cities in the North, they spread the influence of Delta blues
geographically. In reference to Patton's first session with Paramount, Gioia
noted that "only a handful of events, such as Robert Johnson's San Antonio and
Dallas sessions (1936 and 1937 respectively) or Patton's later recordings with
Son House, rival this momentous debut in the history of Delta Blues."[32]

While Paramount marketed Patton as an established artist, the label also
used promotional tricks design to sell the records that he produced. One was
released by the company credited not to Patton but to an unknown artist called
simply "The Masked Marvel." Paramount then ran a contest, complete with
advertisements in black-owned newspapers, challenging the record-buying
public to guess the true identity of the performer. The company also marketed
some of Patton's spiritual tunes as being written not by the bluesman with a

penchant for singing about women and whiskey, but by a fictitious preacher, Elder J. J. Hadley. The label created the alias believing that African American consumers who bought gospel music would shy away from tunes written by a bluesman with questionable morals. Giving an alias to a performer was not an unusual practice at the time, and in this case it was used to distinguish Patton's blues repertoire from his religious music in the marketplace.[33]

Back in the Delta, Patton continued moving around, living for a time in the city of Clarksdale and the small town of Lula. He continued playing at local events and on his usual circuits, and it was around this time that he met Henry "Son" Sims, a fiddler from Clarksdale who would later work with Muddy Waters. Sims was a talented instrumentalist who impressed Patton to the point that the bluesman recruited him as an accompanist. Patton and Sims toured the Delta together until Henry Speir contacted Patton to let him know that Paramount was ready for another recording session. Toward the end of 1929, Patton and Sims traveled to Paramount's newly constructed studio in Grafton, Wisconsin, where Patton recorded thirteen songs with Sims playing along, and at least a dozen others without the fiddler. Among the more notable Patton classics recorded at this session were his odes to the 1927 Mississippi River flood, "High Water Everywhere, Part 1," and "High Water Everywhere, Part 2," along with "Rattlesnake Blues," "Elder Greene Blues," and "Going to Move to Alabama." Though not really a singer, Sims recorded four solo numbers himself during the trip, which were quickly forgotten.[34]

Returning from this second session, Patton's personal life became more complicated. He moved to a plantation near Lula where he lived with a woman named Bertha Lee Pate, who would become his last "wife." She was a blues singer in her own right although she held a day job cooking for white families in area. She remained with Patton for the rest of his life and performed with him occasionally. As was characteristic with any romantic venture involving Patton, the relationship was tumultuous. At the same time Patton was moving in with Bertha Lee, he apparently became enamored with another woman, Louise Johnson, a favorite on the local barrelhouse circuit who played piano and sang songs about sex from a female perspective that endeared her to Delta audiences. Patton and Johnson began a stormy affair that eventually ended in an automobile on the way to a recording session.[35]

Around this time Patton met talented musician Son House, who also became a performing partner. About ten years Patton's junior, House was a failed preacher who had done time in Mississippi's Parchman penitentiary for killing a man at a Delta party. House likely picked up a good many things from Patton, but he was initially influenced by other older singers and guitarists in the area. By the time he met the Delta's most famous bluesman, House was already a solid guitar player with a gifted, natural voice. Patton and House performed together in the Delta, and Patton apparently respected the younger man's talents to the point that he was willing to recommend House to Paramount. Years later, as blues music became more popular among whites in the United States, House would also be considered one of the most important musical figures of the period to emerge from the Mississippi Delta.

In 1930 a Paramount representative named Art Laibley ventured into the Delta on his way to Texas in hopes of talking to Patton and arranging another recording session. Once the two found each other at the Lula, Mississippi railroad depot, Laibley told Patton that the label wanted him back in Grafton, and that he hoped Patton could bring with him other talented performers from the area. Patton recommended his old partner Willie Brown, his new friend Son House, and his part-time girlfriend Louise Johnson who, according to House, "didn't do nothing but drink and play music. . . . she could eat a piano up." Before leaving, Laibley gave Patton a hundred dollars in cash and arranged for a local man, Wheeler Ford, to drive the group in his Buick to the Grafton facility. This visit to Grafton was not very productive when compared to other Patton sessions—producing only four new Patton songs—but the trip itself became part of Delta blues folklore. Supposedly, Patton had recommended Johnson to Paramount in large part because he wanted a constant bedmate on the trip to Wisconsin, but the dynamics of having only one female in a car with a group of bluesmen known for womanizing eventually created friction. Somewhere just north of Memphis the group acquired some homemade moonshine, and the musicians proceeded to get drunk. As the story goes, Patton and Johnson, who were both sitting in the front seat, got into an argument, and Patton supposedly slapped his girlfriend across the face. At that point, Johnson apparently swore off Patton and climbed into the back seat of the car to be with House, and for the rest of the trip Johnson was House's paramour, sharing a hotel room with him once the car reached its destination. House later told an interviewer that he thought that he and Patton might come to blows over the incident, but instead Patton claimed that he had wanted to get rid of Johnson for some time, and that House was welcome to her. "Oh come here nigger. I ain't thinking about that old tight-haired woman" House claimed Patton told him. "I didn't want her in the first place. Now you keep her now and I'll treat you as good as I ever did. Go on and just act like there ain't nothing happening."[36] In various incarnations this story circulated in the Delta for years, and Patton may have been thinking of his relationship with Johnson at the second Grafton session when he recorded "Bird Nest Bound," which included the lyrics:

> Sometime I say I need you, then again I don't
> Sometime I say I need you, then again I don't
> (spoken: You know it's true, baby)
> Some time I think I'll quit you, then again I won't
> Oh I remember one mornin', standin' in my baby's door
> Oh I remember one mornin', standin' in my baby's door
> (spoken: Boy you know what she told me?)
> Looka here, Papa Charley, I don't want you no more.

After his trip to Grafton with House, Johnson, and Brown, Charley Patton's fortunes began to decline. He returned to the Mississippi Delta and continued his relationship with Bertha Lee, living for a time in Robinsonville, Cleveland, and finally moving with her onto a plantation near Holly Ridge, in Sunflower County. He developed a variety of health issues related to his heart and his lifestyle, but still managed to play on street corners during the day and in local joints on weekend nights. Despite complaining of constant pain in his back, shortness of breath, and various other ailments, Patton kept drinking whiskey, chain-smoking, and womanizing. In 1933 he reportedly had his throat slit by a jealous husband, but recovered. One version of that story held that it was actually Bertha Lee who tried to kill Patton after another confrontation with the bluesman over his infidelities. Regardless of who used the knife on Patton, the wound altered his voice somewhat, making it even more deep and gravely, and sometimes difficult to understand. The Great Depression severely affected record sales in the African American community and, as a result, the bluesman's record sales decreased sharply. Paramount began marketing new, younger blues artists, and Patton would not record for the label again.

By January of 1934 Patton was ailing and past his prime when William R. Calaway, a talent scout for the American Record Corporation (ARC), headquartered in New York City, sought out the bluesman for a recording session.

ARC was organized in 1929 as a consolidation of a number small record companies that had fallen on hard financial times. During the Great Depression, ARC continued to purchase failing labels, exploiting their catalogs and selling records at a cheap rate. Like other scouts of the period, Calaway was always on the lookout for talent that could make money for the company, and in addition to promoting blues players he worked with a variety of country performers. After scouring the Delta for Patton with no success, Calaway finally found him in a Belzoni, Mississippi, jail with Bertha Lee. The two had been arrested after getting into a drunken argument at a local party where they both were performing. After bailing the couple out, the talent scout asked them if they would like to come to New York and make some records. The couple was in New York for three days, during which time Patton recorded twenty-six titles, most solo and some with Bertha Lee, that proved to be his swan songs.[37] Among the most poignant were "Poor Me" and "Oh Death." "Poor Me" was probably written prior to the New York session during one of the many estrangements that Patton and Bertha Lee experienced, but considering that Patton was near death, he may have sung it as a tribute to his final "wife," who had also become his nurse as his health declined:

> Don't the moon look pretty shinin' down through the tree?
> Oh, I can see Bertha Lee, Lord but she can't see me.
> You may go, you may stay, but she'll come back some sweet day,
> By and by, sweet mama, baby won't you, by and by?

In "Oh Death" Patton and Bertha Lee sang together in a traditional "call and response" style that was sometimes a bit garbled. Ironically, and sadly, the end was coming closer for Patton as he sang during the session, "Lord I know, Lord I know my time ain't long" and "It was soon one mornin', Oh Lordy, when death come in the room." As if the song were a prophecy, Patton returned to the Delta once the recording session ended and just three months later he passed away. After the bluesman died, many stories circulated around the Delta as to the details of the colorful but troubled singer's demise. Some said that a jealous husband killed Patton either with a knife or a gun. Others claimed that Patton was poisoned, either by a jealous husband or a jealous lover. Still other believed that, if anyone killed Patton, it was Bertha Lee, either in a fit of rage or an attempt at self-preservation. In truth, the events surrounding Patton's death were far less dramatic. He reportedly played a dance near Greenwood on April 8, 1934, that was disrupted when a woman killed a man during a drunken argument. Many believe that this was Patton's last public performance. The following week he had great difficulty catching his breath and voluntarily visited a physician for one of the few times in his life. The doctor told Patton that his condition was serious, and the bluesman left the doctor's office knowing that he was in trouble. From there, two versions of the final week of Patton's life developed. According to one, Patton left the doctor's office and retreated to the shack where he lived with Bertha Lee near Indianola and Holly Ridge, on the Heathman-Dedham plantation. There he died, reportedly in Bertha Lee's arms, on April 28, 1934. Another account, drawn from his official death certificate, stated that Patton died on April 28, 1934, in the town of Indianola in a house located at 350 Heathman Street, where he may have taken up residence with a woman other than Bertha Lee. Patton's death certificate also lists the cause of death as a mitral valve disorder with most researchers believing that he died as a result of some form of heart disease. Regardless of the exact location of Patton's death, the bluesman's body was taken to Holly Ridge and buried in a local cemetery in a grave that remained poorly marked for many years. Patton's death was not reported in the newspapers and, while his music would live on, life in the Delta quickly moved on without him. The barrelhouse crowds that loved him had short memories, and most had already turned their attentions to younger performers. It would be decades before anyone outside the Delta took notice of Patton's death and, ironically, it would be whites more than blacks who ultimately rescued Patton's name from obscurity and his legacy from the dark mists of time.[38]

As Charley Patton was drawing large barrelhouse crowds in the Delta during the mid-1920s, paving the way for his brief but important recording career, it seemed that his fellow Mississippian Jimmie Rodgers had reached a dead end. Sick and unable to hold a permanent job, life was quickly passing Rodgers by. It would be an overstatement to say that music was the only thing keeping the future "Father of Country Music" going during the period, but it did seem to be the only part of his existence that remained consistent. Regardless of what else was going on, Rodgers always believed in himself as a musician. Though just about every other indicator that society used to judge success and failure found the singer wanting, Rodgers always held fast to the value of his talents, and to his dreams. As early as 1924, while he was traveling with the railroad, Rodgers was giving his mailing address to other musicians he met along the way as the offices of *Billboard* magazine in Cincinnati. At the time *Billboard*, the bible of the entertainment industry, offered a free mail-forwarding service to anyone claiming to be an entertainer. Each week the magazine would include in a separate section a list of the names of every person who received correspondence at its office. In turn, anyone on the list could send *Billboard* a self-addressed envelope to receive their mail. The fact that the unknown Rodgers chose to give those he met in his travels *Billboard* magazine as his mailing address indicated that, despite a reputation for lacking ambition, he always had high hopes for his music.[39]

Doctors advised Rodgers that because of his tuberculosis he should leave the hot, humid Mississippi climate and move to a place where the air was dryer. After a couple of unsuccessful attempts to relocate to Texas and Arizona, Rodgers in 1927 decided to move to Asheville, North Carolina, at the time a bustling mountain resort community with a population approaching fifty thousand. He believed that he might find work there and that the cooler and less humid weather—at least compared to Mississippi—would be better for his health. Desperate for work, Rodgers took jobs in Asheville as a taxi driver and as a runner for the local police department to make ends meet, finally saving enough money to send for his family. He also began introducing himself to members of the local music community. Rodgers arrived in Asheville in early 1927, the same year that advancing technology dramatically expanded the city's entertainment options.[40]

In 1927 many people viewed radio as a miracle. The new technology, for the first time in history, allowed individuals to instantly experience first-hand events happening in far-flung locales out of earshot and eyesight. The technology provided for mass communication of the spoken word at a staggering level. Radio brought the world into American homes, revolutionizing entertainment, advertising, and the distribution of news and other information. The first commercial radio station began broadcasting in 1920 and over the next decade the number of radio sets sold in the United States, and the number of stations broadcasting around the country, increased dramatically. By 1927 there were more than seven hundred stations broadcasting in the United States. Although churches and educational institutions owned many of the first radio stations, the potential for making money through advertising quickly brought entrepreneurs into the field. The new technology rocked the entertainment industry, mortally wounding vaudeville, the traveling theater troupe, and the old-time medicine show, all of which went into decline over the next twenty years. With the advent of radio a family could flip a switch and turn a dial and instantly find all different types of entertainment without having to leave their homes or pay an admission fee. During the 1920s radio threatened all other forms of popular entertainment in the same way that television would send shock waves through the entertainment industry thirty years later.[41]

Radio came to Asheville the same year Rodgers chose to take up residence in the city. Chartered as WWNC—Wonderful Western North Carolina—Asheville's first radio station naturally generated a great deal of excitement in the region. Many residents viewed the opening of a local radio station as a message to the outside world that the once-small town had arrived to take its place as an emerging, modern southern city. As was the case with most new stations, the anticipation of WWNC's first broadcast was a collective event in the city with excitement building daily among Asheville's population. After several delays, WWNC's heavily advertised first broadcast took place on the evening of February 27, 1927. In keeping with the idea that the broadcast represented Asheville's emergence as a sophisticated municipality, WWNC signed on with a rather tame musical performances from the Vanderbilt Hotel and speeches by local dignitaries. Marketing their programming to the local gentry who presumably had more money to spend with the station's advertisers, WWNC leaned toward broadcasting more highbrow material at first, but spent a good deal of time experimenting with its programming just to see what would or would not work in terms of selling more advertising.[42]

When Rodgers first heard a broadcast from WWNC is unknown, but he immediately recognized what radio might do for him. He understood that performers armed with only their unamplified instruments and voices might be able to reach an audience of, at the most, a few hundred at any given time, but with radio a performer could reach hundreds of thousands (and later millions) of listeners instantly. Were he able to land a spot playing and singing on WWNC, Rodgers would not just be entertaining the population of Asheville. Because of the station's broadcast power he would also be entertaining listeners in other parts of North Carolina and in Georgia, Virginia, Tennessee, and beyond. In a ten-minute span radio could give him more immediate exposure than a lifetime of nickel-and-dime gigs in Meridian or in run-down taverns up and down the rail lines. Since arriving in Asheville, Rodgers had been playing informally with a number of local musicians, and he eventually put together an act with a partner, Asheville native Otis Kuykendall, and finagled an audition at the station. The team landed a thirty-minute spot playing mostly popular standards of the day and appeared on WWNC at least three times in April and May of 1927. The appearances garnered little attention for Rodgers, but they did allow him to think of himself as not just a musician, but as a radio personality as well.

At around the same time Rodgers met a trio of musicians—Claude Grant and his brother Jack, who were both veterans of the medicine show circuit, and Jack Pierce, an experienced fiddler—who performed as the "Tenneva Ramblers." The Grant brothers were natives of Bristol, Tennessee, while Pierce was a Virginian, giving rise to the name "Tenneva" as a combination of both states. Rodgers reportedly charmed the Ramblers and impressed them by exaggerating his status as a "radio performer" to the point that they were willing to join up with him and rechristen the new group the "Jimmie Rodgers Entertainers." Basically a string band that played standards and dance tunes, the Entertainers appeared several times on WWNC and at local events in the Asheville region. Claude Grant later recalled of one lengthy engagement: "We were at the North Fork Mountain resort. We played there, oh, five, six weeks playing every night on the veranda; the resort had a screened-in veranda all the way around the dining room. Nice place. Big parties would come out from Asheville for supper. . . . We'd play songs, you know, that were popular at the time. After they'd eat, they'd usually dance—round dancing. They never square danced. I could double some on tenor banjo; Jimmie, of course, played guitar; Jack, my brother, played mandolin; and Jack Pierce, fiddle."[43] As they made the rounds, word reached the group, either by word of mouth or through newspaper advertisements, that representatives from the Victor Talking Machine Company were auditioning local acts in Bristol, Tennessee, about sixty miles from Asheville. As they understood it, those acts that passed muster would have the opportunity to make a record.[44]

Just as there were similarities in the rise of southern country and blues music, the early country and blues recording industries developed in much the same manner. Like "race" records made around the same time, what record producers initially labeled "hillbilly" music developed as the first generation of record-company executives struggled to find new markets for their products. The companies viewed both genres as a means to sell unsophisticated music to people they perceived as unsophisticated. They marketed blues to blacks in the South and in northern cities, and country music to rural southern whites as well as whites who had moved to the more industrialized North in search of work. Both genres seemed uncomplicated in presentation but were in fact the product of a complex mix of their times and the places where they developed. While they may have been literally as different as black and white to the naked eye, blues and country music had a host of similarities in form and content. They were both music of the masses that expressed a range of human emotions that could not be separated by race. Writing about blues and country music of the 1920s, Greil Marcus asserted that "For the first time, people from isolated, scorned, forgotten, disdained communities and cultures had the opportunity to speak to each other and to the nation at large. A great uproar of voices that were at once old and new was heard." Both blues and country had rural roots affected by poverty, deprivation, and desperate hopes, and both forms of music in presentation were raw and direct. Blues and country in their original forms were not the music of the elite, the comfortable, or the financially secure. When Jimmie Rodgers in "Jimmie's Mean Mama Blues" sang "I got no money in my pocket, I'm roving around so flat," and Charley Patton sang in "Dry Well Blues" "I ain't got no money, and I sure ain't got no hope," both men were projecting a reality that only those of a certain economic class in the South, regardless of race, could relate to and understand.[45]

Just as legal segregation in the South could not completely segregate different forms of culture, or eliminate the cross-pollination of blues and country, marketing practices of the larger record companies during the early twentieth century could not completely define black and white music or musicians, although they tried. While early record companies drew sharp distinctions between their race (blues) and hillbilly (country) catalogs, both classifications had songs in common, with the blues catalogs sometimes containing what sounded more like rural ballads and country catalogs containing some songs that seemed more like blues. Furthermore, there were a number of instances where individual musicians or bands were racially misclassified. For instance, the Chatmon brothers of Mississippi, who had connections with Charley Patton—possibly blood connections in addition to musical ones—and who performed as the Mississippi Sheiks, appeared multiple times in the hillbilly or "old time" listings of Columbia Records. More famously, in 1927 Columbia listed in their "race" catalogue a rendition of "Salty Dog Blues" by Austin and Lee Allen, two white siblings who performed for years as the Allen Brothers. The Allens, in turn, threatened a lawsuit claiming that the classification made it more difficult for them to get live bookings in white venues. While the listing was confusing to some, the song itself was actually an example of the often symbiotic relationship between early blues and country music. The origins of the tune were somewhat murky, though many versions were recorded over the years by artists in multiple genres including blues, jazz, traditional country, and bluegrass, dating back to 1924. Blues legends Blind Willie McTell and Mississippi John Hurt recorded versions, as did bluegrass icons Lester Flatt and Earl Scruggs and, later, country star Johnny Cash. As far as what the song was actually about, Lee Allen once told an interviewer that "a salty dog was somebody that was just a little low down, not too much. They just wanted to have a good time. . . . they were drinkin' people and that's about all they had on their minds." Allen's interpretation described a state of mind that knew no race. It was a state that certainly applied to a good many patrons of both the black juke joint and the white country beer joint, patrons who enjoyed the music of both Charley Patton and Jimmie Rodgers.[46]

Common themes related directly to sex were also well represented in the work of Rodgers and Patton, and both men exhibited a talent for getting their points across through innuendo without being graphically obscene. To a significant segment of the record-buying public, songs with veiled sexual imagery were more exciting, they were certainly more fun, and they tended to sell well. Both Rodgers and Patton knew that during stage shows songs of a prurient nature received more lively responses from audiences, and there was no reason to doubt that recorded versions of the same songs would be popular as well. The idea of using sex as a marketing tool knew no race, and the concept thrives up to the present day in all forms of media. While record-company executives of the more restrained era certainly recognized the lustful nature of some Patton and Rodgers recordings, they usually turned a blind eye as long as the recordings sold well and no blatantly obscene words were used in the lyrics. This was particularly true of Patton's work as white record-company officials seemed less concerned with offending African American blues consumers. Although the words to the racier songs of Patton and Rodgers were not necessarily "dirty," in the traditional sense, the images that they represented sometimes seemed to be. For instance, the word "rider" was used in songs by both men—and in many early blues and country recordings in general—as a replacement for girlfriend or sexual partner, with riding a horse or a mule being used as a metaphor for sex.[47] Patton recorded the song "Banty Rooster Blues," with lines like:

> My hook's in the water, and my cork's on top
> My hook's in the water, and my cork's on top
> How can I lose, Lord, with the help I got
>
> I know my dog anywhere I hear him bark
> I know my dog anywhere I hear him bark
> I can tell my rider, if I feel her in the dark.

Likewise, Rodgers in 1933 recorded "Blue Yodel No. 11 (I've Got a Gal)," a song that included similarly suggestive lines:

> I believe to my soul, somebody's been ridin' my mule,
> I believe to my soul, somebody's been ridin' my mule,
> 'Cause every time I want to ride her
> She acts a doggone fool.
> You may call yourself the meanest gal in town,
> You may call yourself the meanest gal in town,
> Now let me tell you one thing baby,
> I'm gonna turn your damper down.[48]

The link between the development of blues and country as commercial commodities was personified in Ralph Peer. Arguably the most important man in the first thirty years of the country-music industry, Peer also recorded a host of blues artists during his career. The son of a store owner, Peer was born in Kansas City, Missouri, in 1892. At the age of eighteen he went to work for the Columbia Recording Company and later became a producer for Okeh Records. There he helped supervise the recording of "Crazy Blues" by Mamie Smith, which some consider the first blues record. A pioneer in the emergence of "race" recordings, Peer eventually became a talent scout for Victor

Records, and in that position he scoured the South looking for black talent. In 1923, while Peer was in Atlanta, a record-store owner convinced him to record a white performer from north Georgia known as "Fiddlin'" John Carson. A fifty-five-year-old part-time moonshiner, Carson had a small following and performed occasionally on local radio. Though initially not impressed with Carson, Peer set up a recording studio in an empty building in Atlanta and in mid-June of 1923 Carson recorded "The Little Old Log Cabin in the Lane," which many country-music authorities claim was the first country recording. Peer had five hundred copies pressed and, to his surprise, they sold briskly. Suddenly Victor was in the country-music business, and in his travels looking for southern blues artists Peer also began searching for country talent. Peer invited Carson to New York to record more songs at the Victor studios, along with a group of musicians he found called the "Hill Billies" who eventually gave their name to the entire genre of rural music aimed at white audiences. Another performer who had early success with Victor was Vernon Dalhart. A Texan born in 1883, Dalhart had a classically trained voice and sang opera before turning to hillbilly music and recording a hit song, "The Wreck of the Old 97," in 1924. As hillbilly records sold for Victor, other labels became interested in the rural white market and began searching for their own country artists. Peer's strategy for locating talent—be they country "hillbillies" or African American bluesmen—was simple and effective. He traveled to isolated areas in hopes of finding traditional folk music that was as closely linked as possible to its original sources. He sought out artists who were "pure," in that they had not yet been corrupted by the clutter that accompanied modernization. It was this ongoing quest for new talent that brought Peer to Bristol, Tennessee, where in August of 1927 he found country music's first transcendent star.[49]

At the time Peer arrived in Bristol it was a bustling regional center similar to Asheville, with a population in the town and surrounding county of about fifty-two thousand. Bristol was also conveniently located at the terminal point of two railroads and near the spot where three states—Tennessee, Virginia, and North Carolina—came together. The town boasted two newspapers and numerous shops and stores. All this made Bristol one of Appalachia's more significant population centers and a central location where musicians could meet. Peer had high hopes for his two-week stay in Bristol, telling a local reporter that "in no section of the South have the pre-war melodies and old mountaineer songs been better preserved than in the mountains of East Tennessee and

Southwest Virginia." Peer already had a few acts lined up, but he was hoping to find even more new talent when he invited the editor of the local paper to the sessions. The result was more news coverage about what Peer was up to, and a flood of musicians descended on the town looking to audition. Peer rented an abandoned warehouse that had once housed a hat factory and outfitted it with good equipment, creating a crude but effective recording studio.[50]

Peer's efforts created what many people continue to refer to as the "big bang" of country music, or as country-music scholar Charles K. Wolfe put it, "the event that in one dramatic two-week period at once established the music's aesthetic and commercial validity." The basis for this description of Peer's 1927 Bristol recording sessions lies in the fact that, while most of the entertainers he heard during his stay in the town were never heard from again, Peer did discover two acts, Jimmie Rodgers and the Carter Family, that would both cast long shadows over decades of country music. Johnny Cash, who married into the Carter Family during the 1960s, later maintained, "These recordings in Bristol in 1927 are the single most important event in the history of country music." While the actual genre had existed before Jimmie Rodgers made his first record, the part-time railroad man from Mississippi became so popular that record companies began, in a very serious way, considering country a major commercial entity. In short, while Jimmie Rodgers did not create country music, a good argument can be made that his popularity created commercial country music and the commercial country-music industry, and in effect opened the door for every other country recording artist who followed him. In another parallel with blues or "race" music, record-company executives began to take "hillbilly" music seriously once they began to view it as commodity that could generate profits. At that point what would eventually become the billion-dollar country-music industry began to develop.[51]

Of his first contact with Jimmie Rodgers, Peer—who later was quick to take any credit offered for discovering country music's first star—said in an interview that the singer telephoned him about an audition for the Jimmie Rodgers Entertainers, having learned about Victor's recording activities in East Tennessee through an advertisement or story in the newspaper. Peer encouraged Rodgers and his band to make the trip over the mountains from Asheville to Bristol so that he could hear them. In late July the group arrived in Bristol with Rodgers's family in tow, but before they met with Peer and made arrangements to record, Rodgers and his "Entertainers" had an argument that quickly led to a falling out, reportedly over money and billing. "Jimmie stormed out of that boarding house," Claude Grant later recalled. "I remember after that argument, Jimmie said, 'all right George, I'll just sing one myself.' He called everyone George. And he left." As a result, Rodgers decided to go see Peer as a solo act while the rest of the band quickly regrouped as the Tenneva Ramblers. Peer recognized from the start that Rodgers had potential, later claiming, "When I was alone with Jimmie in our recording studio, I was elated when I first heard him perform. It seemed that he had his own personal and peculiar style, and I thought that his yodel alone might spell success."[52]

Jimmie Rodgers made his first recordings for Ralph Peer between 2:00 and 4:20 p.m. on August 4, 1927, the day before Peer shut down his Bristol operation. The session produced two recordings, "Sleep Baby Sleep," a reworked version of a traditional lullaby, and an original composition, "The Soldier's Sweetheart," for which Peer paid Rodgers one hundred dollars. The following October, Victor released Rodgers's work, which sold modestly but enough to allow Rodgers to press Peer for another recording session. Peer scheduled the session at the Victor recording studio at 114 North Fifth Street in Camden, New Jersey.[53] The studio was actually an old church that the company converted into a studio large enough to record orchestras. A number of notable musicians from Ferdinand "Jelly Roll" Morton to Enrico Caruso had already recorded there. It was in this converted church, on November 30, 1927, that musical lighting struck as Rodgers recorded the song that made him a star, the blues-based "T for Texas," which Victor released under the title "Blue Yodel" (sometimes referred to as "T for Texas" or "Blue Yodel No. 1") to market Rodgers's yodeling abilities. The first three lines would echo through decades of country, blues, and rock and roll music:

> T for Texas, T for Tennessee
> T for Texas, T for Tennessee
> T for Thelma, that gal that made a wreck out of me.[54]

In the song, Rodgers sang several stanzas, some old reworked blues couplets about a cuckold husband, a cheating wife, and the desire of the husband for revenge. He punctuated each stanza with his trademark yodel, which caught on instantly with the general public both white and black. While Rodgers's yodeling spawned a number of white country imitators—some of whom, like Ernest Tubb and Gene Autrey, would become famous—his overall style also caught on with some blues artists. For instance, in 1930 the Mississippi Sheiks imitated his yodel on "Yodelin' Fiddlin' Blues," and four years later Tampa Red used the Rodgers yodeling style in "Worried Devil Blues." Still later, blues legends like Muddy Waters and Howlin' Wolf would talk to interviewers about having listened to Rodgers records when they were young. As a result, while "Blue Yodel" launched Rodgers's career, selling almost a half-million copies in the next two years, it also set the stage for future debates over his status as a "white bluesman." Some scholars and music enthusiasts decades later would argue over Rodgers's position not as a country forefather, which was never up for debate, but as a pioneer in the realm of blues as well. Because Rodgers's music influenced some early blues performers, and many of his songs were bluesy at their core, some claimed that "white blues" was indeed a sub-genre of blues with Rodgers standing fast as a pioneer in the field. Others would say that such a thing was impossible because blues music was black music, period, and that Rodgers at most was a blues innovator of sorts, but not a true bluesman. "Country music borrowed incessantly from the blues, but certainly on a smaller scale the blues borrowed incessantly from country," Gerard Herzhaft wrote. "There is a southern culture and a southern music, whose black and white elements are at times differentiated, but for the most part they are so intertwined that it is often impossible to untie them."[55]

Commenting on Rodgers's style and musical choices, some referred to him as a "white man gone black," the same phrase used to describe Elvis Presley three decades later. Sam Phillips, who recorded Presley's early work and was himself a blues enthusiast, summed up Rodgers's musical and socio-economic kinship with the black community when he told an interviewer, "Jimmie Rodgers connected with you. He came from the same place as the black folks singing the blues."[56] Musician Cliff Carlisle, who knew Rodgers and recorded with him in 1931, expressed a similar sentiment: "Jimmie, he reminded me more of a colored person, or a negro, or whatever you want to call them . . . than anybody I ever saw, in a way. He had that old southern, long southern drawl, you know."[57] Despite the dangers of trying to dissect the structure and virtues of music that was made to be listened to and not written about, one thing was apparent after Rodgers had his first hit. In the commercial country-music industry, Jimmie Rodgers linked blues and country together forever. In summing up Rodgers's musical diversity, Mark Zwonitzer with Charles Hirshberg wrote, "He had enough Mississippi Catfish in his voice to read 'cracker' to any listener, but he was also bluesy enough to get with 'the race' and randy enough to put a blush on the twenties' most cynical café-society crowd."[58] Rodgers also composed many of his tunes in the three-line blues verse style, repeating the first two lines and using the third as a lyrical denouement of sorts. In "Blue Yodel No. 12 (Barefoot Blues)" for instance, Rodgers sings:

> Sorrow struck me at the break of day,
> Sorrow struck me at the break of day
> 'Cause a mean old man came and took my gal away.[59]

And in "Looking for a New Mama," he told the world:

> I want a brand new mama, I think I'll advertise,
> I want a brand new mama, I think I'll advertise,
> I want a woman who can cook, and one who won't tell me dirty lies.[60]

These same verses could have just as easily been sung by Charley Patton or any other traditional bluesman, and they could just as easily have come directly from the Mississippi Delta. In his study of the effects of race on the development of folk and pop music, Karl Hagstrom Miller maintained that Rodgers's music "continued to foster the interracial southern music culture out of which it had sprung," by featuring "his simple guitar, plucking out a steady, twelve-bar blues while the singer recited standard three-line blues verses, many of which had floated through the South for years."[61]

While Rodgers obviously was not a "white man gone black" in the literal since, there was a certain racial symmetry with regard to his music career. In assessing the power of music to smooth the rougher racial edges of social interaction, particularly in the Jim Crow South, B.B. King once told an interviewer, "We never would have had any segregation if people would've had enough music around." While King was overstating the concept, in Rodgers's particular case his love of music and his musicianship brought him in closer contact with African Americans, and in a more meaningful way, than most whites of his era. While as a human being Rodgers was not immune to racial prejudices like those that many whites in the South held during his lifetime, he tended to be comfortable interacting with African Americans.

From an early age he listened to and learned from African American musicians working in the railroad yards and, according to Miller, "as he honed his skills singing blues and common stock tunes, Rodgers found a receptive audience among the black railroad employees with whom he labored in the years leading up to 1920." The "Father of Country Music" wrote many of his songs in the twelve-bar black blues style, and lyrically he had much in common with African American blues musicians of the period. Conversely, Tommy Johnson, Skip James, Mississippi John Hurt, Muddy Waters, and Robert Johnson were among the blues stalwarts who used Rodgers songs in their stage act at one time or another. After he became famous, when he could pick and choose the performers that he wanted to record with, Rodgers enjoyed recording with African American artists like Louis Armstrong. From a political standpoint, Rodgers left behind few clues as to his leanings, but while in Texas he did support the political careers of James E. and Miriam Ferguson, known widely as "Pa and Ma" Ferguson, both of whom served as governor of Texas. The Fergusons had originally entered politics as an alternative to candidates backed by the Ku Klux Klan, which had experienced a resurgence during the 1920s. According to Rodgers's biographer Barry Mazor, while the colorful couple were populists with questionable ethics, they were also "tellingly anti–Ku Klux Klan at a time when the organization was at the height of its racist influence."[62]

While "Blue Yodel (T for Texas)" became Rodgers's first big hit, it also served as a shining example of the nature of early popular-music recording, a process that many times involved artists both black and white snatching untethered phrases and song fragments from the air and making them their own. It was an example of how popular music of the period could repeatedly cross the color line with ease. Many "new" songs of the early recording era borrowed from and built on the past, taking different musical elements and phrasings that had been around for decades in one form or another and crafting them into something worth hearing. Sometimes these new songs were innovative in their composition and style, and sometimes they were simply plagiarized in bits and pieces from other sources. In the case of "Blue Yodel (T for Texas)," the first line—in fact, the signature line of the song—"T for Texas, T for Tennessee" also appeared in "Nehi Mamma Blues," a song by Memphis bluesman Frank Stokes. Ralph Peer recorded the Stokes song, a race record, at about the same time that Rodgers recorded his hillbilly classic. The exact phrase "T for Texas" also appears in "Kansas City Blues," recorded in 1927 by Jim Jackson, another Memphian who was signed to Vocalion Records by Henry C. Speir, the man who played a major role in the career of Charley Patton. In turn, a variation of the line appeared in a similar recording, "Kansas City Blues," by blues and jazz pioneer Alonzo "Lonnie" Johnson. In his version, Johnson tells listeners "I got a gal in Texas, I got two in Tennessee."[63]

Other evidence that Patton and Rodgers were at times drawing lyrical drops of water from the same well is a comparison of the 1928 Rodgers recording of "Memphis Yodel" with the 1934 Patton offering "Revenue Man Blues." In the former, Rodgers sang:

> I woke up this morning the blues all 'round my bed,
> I woke up this morning the blues all 'round my bed,
> I didn't have nobody to hold my achin' head.[64]

While the Patton number includes the lyrics:

> I wakes up every mornin' now with the jinx all around my bed,
> I wakes up every mornin' with the jinx all around my bed,
> I have been a good provider, but I believe I've been misled.

In his wonderful study of the influence of Jimmie Rodgers, Barry Mazor referenced many blues-styled lyrics and songs that influenced the Rodgers repertoire as well as Rodgers lyrics that influenced later recordings by blues artists and others. For instance, Rodgers's "Muleskinner Blues" (1931) has phrasings in common with both "Southern Blues," recorded by the great blues queen Gertrude "Ma" Rainey in 1923, and "Section Gang Blues," recorded in 1927 by bluesmen Alger "Texas" Alexander and Lonnie Johnson. Arthur "Blind" Blake and the Memphis Jug Band both recorded versions of "In the Jailhouse Now" before Rodgers while in 1928 Willard "Ramblin'" Thomas recorded "Back Gnawing Blues," a song that had lyrics in common with the Rodgers tune, "I've Only Loved Three Women," released four years later. Conversely, Joshua Barnes "Peg Leg" Howell, a Georgia blues player who lost one of his legs to a gunshot wound, recorded songs with references to the Rodgers tune "Waiting for a Train," and Mississippi John Hurt recorded an adaptation of the song years after Rodgers's death. In 1931, Peetie Wheatstraw recorded "C & A Blues," which included lyrics from Rodgers's "Train Whistle Blues," and in 1932 Louis Armstrong recorded "Hobo You Can't Ride This Train" in an apparent homage to Rodgers as "the Singing Brakeman." Finally, Lead Belly recorded his own version of the Rodgers classic "Daddy and Home" in 1935, and he referenced Rodgers's lyrics in a number of other recordings.[65]

The success of "Blue Yodel (T for Texas)" led Ralph Peer and Victor to promote their new singing sensation as "America's Blue Yodeler," a nickname that Rodgers would carry for the rest of his life. The song also gave way to a dozen other tunes that Rodgers recorded as "Blue Yodel" songs. According to Ralph Peer, placing the term "Blue Yodel" in the title of these particular songs was a marketing gimmick that he came up with. "When we recorded the first blues I had to supply a title, and the name 'Blue Yodel' came out," Peer later remembered. "The other blue yodels made at the same time had titles suggested by the words, but when I witnessed the tremendous demand for the original, I decided to change these names to 'Blue Yodel No. 2,' 'Blue Yodel No. 3,' etc."[66] Besides the original "Blue Yodel (T for Texas)," probably the most memorable of Rodgers's so-called Blue Yodel songs were "Blue Yodel #8 (Mule Skinner Blues)," which would be covered over and over again by major country artists in the years to come, and "Blue Yodel #9 (Standin' on the Corner)," a song that featured a young Louis Armstrong on trumpet and included memorable lines about downtown Memphis, a blues mecca in its own right:

> Standing on the corner, I didn't mean no harm,
> When a big policeman grabbed me by the arm
> Now it was down in Memphis, Corner of Beale and Main,
> He said "Hey now, big boy, I'm gonna have to know your name."[67]

The significance of "Blue Yodel (T for Texas)" cannot be overstated. It changed the nature of the music business up to that time, opening the eyes of record-company executives who began to realize that there was money to be made in rural areas—a great deal of money—if their companies were willing to cater to country tastes rather than trying to shape country tastes. According to musician and writer Robert Coltman, who studied the Rodgers phenomenon, "Once Rodgers had recorded his first Blue Yodels, everything changed. His suave, rueful vernacular songs made him the first real people's popular singer, stylistically ten years ahead of his time."[68] While Rodgers used a blues form in his Blue Yodel songs, it was his delivery that kept him from being simply a white singer trying to copy the style of a black blues singer.

Rodgers made his blues tunes his own in the same way he made his reflective ballads his own, or his dance numbers, or his sad train songs. He could not be pinned down easily with regard to what type of music he wrote or played because the influences on his own musical style seemed to come from everywhere he had been, and they seemed to know no racial boundaries. His songs could be nostalgic or risqué, or anything in between. Over the course of his career Rodgers recorded dozens of songs that were not Blue Yodels, some he wrote himself or with his sister-in-law and some that he covered from other singers and songwriters. The session that produced "Blue Yodel (T for Texas)" was an early measure of Rodgers's lyrical and thematic range. In addition to the blues number, Rodgers recorded three other songs that day in Camden. "Ben Dewberry's Final Run" was a train song in the Casey Jones tradition that told the story of a brave engineer dying at the controls of a speeding locomotive. "Away Out on the Mountain" evoked grand images of the American West as a land of grizzly bears, buffalo, eagles, snakes and beavers, while "Mother Was a Lady" was a plaintive tune about the trials of a simple waitress in the big city. According to Nicholas Dawidoff, "He could deliver poignant sentiment, but Rodgers was not above singing about drinking, jailhouses, dice throwers, and a pretty woman's drop-stitch stocking."[69]

Rodgers's success also created a template that many future stars and their management would use in promotion and mass marketing. Once a song became a hit, the idea was to follow up quickly and try to give the star the maximum amount of exposure while his audience still recognized him. When "Blue Yodel (T for Texas)" became popular, Ralph Peer and Victor moved quickly to get their star booked for another recording session and a tour. In February and June of 1928 Rodgers recorded fifteen more songs, including "In the Jailhouse Now," which would be heavily covered in years to come with versions by other artists eventually being broadcast on television and included in movie scores. There were also numerous publicity photos. Reflecting again Rodgers's varied repertoire and attempts to appeal to as broad an audience as possible, Peer and Victor for publicity shots dressed Rodgers at various times in a tuxedo, a railroader's outfit, and even a cowboy costume. For the vast majority of his career he toured as one of two characters, the "Blue Yodeler" or the "Singing Brakeman."

In 1928 Rodgers made his first major public appearance as a well-known musical entity at the Earle Theater on Thirteenth Street in downtown Washington, DC. By that time he was developing a small circle of "show business" friends, among them Gene Austin. Austin was a popular jazz and pop crooner who had recently become famous after recording the pop standard "My Blue Heaven," which sold over five million copies for Victor. He and Rodgers got along because they had a lot in common. Their Victor recordings had made both men famous, and Austin was a Texan and therefore a fellow southerner. Austin had also run away and temporarily joined a vaudeville show at the age of fifteen, a story that appealed to the Mississippi singer. Austin encouraged Rodgers to play big rooms, and suggested the Earle Theater because he was friendly with the manager there. Rodgers got the booking and appeared briefly on August 4, 1928, as a "special attraction" among other previously booked acts. Rodgers reportedly sang only one song, his version of the risqué, traditional composition "Frankie and Johnny," a song about a woman who kills the man who is "doing her wrong" by cheating on her. According to one source the brief performance was well received and Rodgers took several curtain calls before going back to his hotel room exhausted.[70]

Unfortunately for Jimmie Rodgers, a heavy dose of notoriety could not cure tuberculosis. If anything, Rodgers's fame likely shortened his life. At a time when he should have been getting a great deal of rest each day, the singer was at the center of a whirlwind of public appearances and recording sessions. Everything he put on disc seemed to sell, and it was said that between the years 1927 and 1933 the most common request at any general store in the South was for "a pound of butter, a dozen eggs, and the latest Jimmie Rodgers record." On tour, Rodgers had good days when the effects of his disease were not perceptible, and bad days when he barely seemed to catch his breath and was unable to perform for any extended period of time. Every doctor he encountered told him to slow down, that he needed to rest. At the same time, the Victor company and promoters around the country were telling him how much money could be made if he appeared at one place or another. According to Ralph Peer, "The best doctors told him that he would not live because his tuberculosis was incurable. . . . He began to earn good money working in night spots, traveling shows, etc., but his bad state of health was a great handicap." Rodgers also continued drinking and reportedly chased women on the road despite the adverse effect that the rowdy lifestyle of a touring musician had on his constitution. Fueled by the adulation of his audiences, Rodgers never slowed down, and despite the risks to his health he began a series of major tours in 1928, the first on the Loew's circuit.[71]

Marcus Loew was an entertainment entrepreneur of the first order. Born in New York City in 1870, he was at the right place at the right time as motion picture technology first began to develop. Loew parlayed early investments in penny arcades and nickelodeons into one of the largest theater chains in the United States, and he would go on to help organize the entertainment conglomerate Metro-Goldwyn-Mayer (MGM). During the early twentieth century Loew promoted vaudeville shows in his theaters, sometimes as part of a twin billing that featured live entertainment followed by a motion picture. He developed a number of touring circuits, including the "Southern Time" circuit that took performers to Norfolk, Atlanta, Memphis, New Orleans, and Houston. Rodgers joined the Southern Time Loew's tour as a headliner and was well received wherever he went. "Jimmie Rodgers is a recording star who has the unique faculty of pleasing on stage to every bit a degree as he does on records and over the radio," one reviewer of the period wrote. "For purity of tone and finish in execution Jimmie Rodgers has no superior." While in Atlanta, Rodgers took the time to record four more songs, including "Waiting for a Train," a railroad ballad that would end up selling almost 400,000 copies, more than any other Rodgers record with the exception of "Blue Yodel (T for Texas)."[72]

While Rodgers wrote and arranged much of his own material, he also collaborated with other songwriters, most frequently with his sister-in-law, Elsie McWilliams. Rodgers always liked working with other musicians, but one of the main reasons he sought out collaborators was because along with fame came a great deal of pressure to produce not just more songs, but more hits. Rodgers had a number of good tunes that he had written over the years, but there was always a need for more. McWilliams was largely responsible for some of her brother-in-law's most famous sentimental songs, such as "I'm Lonely and Blue" and "Mississippi Moon." Other songwriters who furnished Rodgers with material included professional songwriter George Brown from New York who specialized in cowboy songs, and the colorful Raymond Hall, a Texas convict who sent Rodgers music through the mail. Among Hall's most notable compositions that became part of the Rodgers repertoire was the autobiographical "Moonlight and Skies," a song about a convicted criminal who longs for freedom.[73]

After touring on the Loew's circuit, Rodgers signed on with a successful tent-repertory company, the Paul English Players, that worked out of Mobile, Alabama. For two months he toured with great acclaim through Alabama and

Mississippi, including what for Rodgers must have been a very gratifying home-coming performance in Meridian in early February of 1929. "There is no posing about the work of Jimmie Rodgers," one newspaper crowed during the period. "He simply steps out there on stage with his guitar and begins to sing. In a few minutes he has the whole audience with him as he yodels and croons." Later in the year he performed on a tour sponsored by the Radio-Keith-Orpheum (RKO) theater chain playing mainly the Southwest and Great Plains states. He also found time to record a movie short in Camden titled "The Singing Brake-man," which promoted his railroad persona. By the end of the year he was earning two thousand dollars per month from recording royalties and public appearance, enough money to allow him build a large home for his family in Texas, where the drier climate was supposed to be better for his health. Rod-gers relocated with his wife and daughter to Kerrville, Texas, about eight miles north of San Antonio near a tuberculosis sanatorium. There, at 617 West Main Street, Rodgers built a large mansion for a reported fifty thousand dollars that he christened "The Blue Yodeler's Paradise."[74]

As he toured, Rodgers kept up a vigorous recording schedule with Ralph Peer setting up sessions in cities across the South and the West. Rodgers re-corded in Atlanta, Dallas, Louisville, San Antonio, and even Los Angeles. As he made more music he was more willing to experiment with new sounds, many of which would be used by other country performers in generations to come. At one point Rodgers fell in with a musician named Joe Kaipo, a Hawai-ian native who performed with a Hawaiian guitar—or as country musicians might put it, a steel guitar—in Dallas nightclubs. Rodgers recorded several songs with Kaipo's backing, introducing the steel guitar to millions of country fans who had never heard it before and cementing it as a mainstay of country recordings for generations. Another landmark session took place in July of 1930 when Rodgers entered a Los Angeles recording studio. There his backing band included a young Louis Armstrong on trumpet and Armstrong's wife Lil on piano. Ralph Peer was responsible for pairing the rising jazz great with the hillbilly star, but his exact reason for doing so remains unclear, and what Arm-strong biographers Max Jones and John Chilton call "one of jazz's unsolvable riddles." Peer had a previous relationship with Louis Armstrong, having origi-nally brought him to Okeh Records back in 1925, and Rodgers was a bluesy player who was familiar with jazz arrangements, so placing the two men to-gether in a studio really was not that odd a proposition. At the session, the

Armstrongs played on one of Rodgers's more famous blue yodel songs, "Blue Yodel No. 9 (Standin' on the Corner)," giving it a jazz flavor that was impossible to ignore. "Neither Armstrong is credited on the label of "Blue Yodel No. 9," Armstrong biographer Terry Teachout wrote of the session, "but their joint presence is unmistakable. Louis fires off a no-nonsense introduction, and Lil supports him in her best barrelhouse style. . . . The accent may be of a hillbilly from Mississippi, but the sensibility is straight out of Storyville." Many years later, in 1970, Armstrong recorded a country record that included a number of the genre's standards. When questioned about the seemingly strange decision to do so, an amused Armstrong quipped "No change for me, daddy, I was doing that same kind of work forty years ago."[75]

In early 1931 Rodgers got to fulfill yet another professional dream when he toured with Will Rogers, at the time one of America's favorite entertainers. Will Rogers was an Oklahoman by birth who had risen to great fame as a vaudevillian and eventually an actor, newspaper columnist, radio personality, lecturer, and humorist. His relaxed, down-home persona masked a sophisticated understanding of what audiences wanted, and his ability to produce brilliant one-liners for any occasion was legendary. By the 1930s he was one of the most admired men in the United States, and "America's Blue Yodeler" was one of his fans. Rogers organized a benefit tour through Oklahoma, Texas, and Arkansas in hopes of raising money for those in the Southwest suffering the effects of the Great Depression and the added misery of a recent draught. When Jimmie Rodgers heard about the tour, he wired Will Rogers, offering to donate his services, and the Oklahoman immediately invited the Mississippi musician to join the project. The two men became fast friends, and from all accounts the fifty-city tour was a great success, raising more than $220,000, although Jimmie missed a number of dates because of his health. Will Rogers Jr., who accompanied his father on the tour as a twenty-year-old, later recalled, "I had all of Jimmie's records and played them on an old crank Victrola. Dad, of course, was a great admirer of his so when they got together on the tour it was a natural mating. Sometimes Jimmie was too ill for the hard grind of daily touring, flying, driving, arranging, talking, in and out of small hotels, so he sat it out."[76]

It was around this time that Jimmie Rodgers, at a recording session in San Antonio, Texas, committed to disc what some believe was the most poignant, introspective, and singularly tragic song ever written by anyone, the autobiographical "T.B. Blues." At the time Rodgers knew that his strength was waning. He had begun avoiding doctors because they all told him the same thing, that he had at best a year or two to live. In this one song, a stark expression of fatalism also common in Charley Patton's music, he tried to relate to his audience what he had been going through, and what he expected to go through as the end came. At the beginning the lyrics seemed to lightly chide his wife, or perhaps one of the other women he had met in his travels, for trying to pretend that nothing was wrong:

> My good gal's trying to make a fool out of me
> Lord my gal's trying to make a fool out of me
> Trying to make me believe I ain't got that old TB.

From there the song seemed to express a range of emotions from self-pity ("When it rained down sorrow it rained all over me") to a stoic acceptance of his condition ("I've been fightin' like a lion, looks like I'm going to lose"). At the end of the song, Rodgers proved that he was indeed the master of expressing any emotion in his work, be it joy, sorrow, celebration, lamentation, or in this case the macabre:

> Gee but that graveyard is a lonesome place
> Lord but that graveyard is a lonesome place
> They put you on your back
> Throw that mud down in your face
> I've got the TB blues.[77]

Five months after he made "T.B. Blues," Rodgers was in Louisville, Kentucky, at a recording session arranged by Ralph Peer. At the time Peer wanted Rodgers, Victor's most successful solo artist, to record with the Carter Family, a popular act themselves whom Peer had initially recorded at the historic 1927 Bristol sessions. Native Virginians, the Carter Family consisted of Alvin Pleasant Delaney "A.P." Carter, his wife, Sara, and his sister-in-law Maybelle. Like Rodgers, they would have great influence through their recordings on future generations of country performers, with songs such as "Keep on the Sunny Side" and "Wildwood Flower" becoming enduring country classics. Always the innovative promoter, Peer hoped that pairing the two name acts might boost record sales for both, but he ultimately was disappointed. Although it had historical significance because of the parties involved, the Louisville session and the music produced there were decidedly unremarkable. Putting Rodgers and the Carters together was a concept that only looked good on paper. The musical styles of the two acts—Rodgers as a solo artist and the Carters as a trio—did not complement one another, and there were other tensions in the studio generated when Rodgers allegedly made unwanted advances toward Maybelle. In the end, the session produced two rather uninspired songs, "Jimmie Rodgers Visits the Carter Family" and "The Carter Family and Jimmie Rodgers in Texas."[78]

Through the early 1930s Rodgers's health declined dramatically, and his bad days began to significantly outnumber those that he considered good. Rodgers was still able to give performances and record in short bursts, but his career as the headliner of a major tour were over by the end of 1932. He could no longer keep up the pace of traveling from city to city, night after night, giving performance after performance for the crowds that loved him. He would appear occasionally, here or there, but even short performances sometimes left him completely exhausted. His declining health and the harsh economic climate in the United States began to dramatically eat away at his financial resources. Once the Great Depression hit in 1929, Rodgers's records continued to sell, but at a reduced rate that brought him fewer royalties. Doctor and hospital bills began taking an increasing percentage of his income, and through it all the singer spent extravagantly. By now he had the added financial burden of making child-support payments to his first wife, Stella, who in 1930 had filed an embarrassing paternity suit on behalf of Rodgers's daughter Kathryn. His perilous financial condition also forced Rodgers to do the unthinkable, sell his dream home, "The Blue Yodeler's Paradise," in Kerrville after living there for less than three years. Although Rodgers and his wife, Carrie, tried to put the best public face possible on the sale of their home, both were brought to tears in private at the thought of losing the house.[79]

Although his fortunes were in decline, Rodgers still enjoyed many of the perquisites of celebrity, and not everything was gloom and doom as he approached the end of his life. After moving to Texas, Rodgers became friendly with William W. Sterling, the state's adjutant general. Sterling was a colorful character who spent more than twenty years in the legendary Texas Rangers, rising from the rank of private to commander of the entire service. He later wrote a history of the Rangers that added to the mystique of the group. Sterling liked the limelight and enjoyed associating with celebrities. He was close to Tom Mix, the silent-era cowboy star, and liked the idea of a friendly association with the nation's most popular country singer. Sterling invited Rodgers to numerous public events, where the former Mississippi railroad man rubbed elbows with the governor and state legislators. He also bestowed on Rodgers one of the greatest, or at least most appreciated, honors that the singer ever received when he arranged to have Rodgers sworn in as an honorary Texas Ranger, complete with a shiny gold badge.[80] The incident apparently inspired the singer to pen "The Yodeling Ranger" in 1933, in which he sang:

> They call me the Yodeling Ranger,
> My badge is solid gold,
> I rove the land by the old Rio Grande
> And belong to that old ranger fold.[81]

When Rodgers left Kerrville he relocated to San Antonio, where he moved his wife and daughter into a duplex bungalow at 142 Montclair Street in the Alamo Heights section. Still in demand, he took a job appearing twice weekly on KMAC, a mainstay country station in the region that broadcast from the Blue Bonnet Hotel on North St. Mary's Street downtown. Rodgers's radio show included live performances and general homespun chatter in between tunes that was very popular with his fans. The radio program was the perfect vehicle for Rodgers at this point in his career. Unable to undertake serious tours because of his illness, the singer could still reach a large audience through the airwaves with relatively little physical exertion. Even when he was unable to appear in person because of out-of-town performances or hospital stays, the station still promoted his music by playing his records. As if he were in a complete state of denial about his health, Rodgers made plans for extensive tours not just of the South and West, but of the North and Canada as well, none of which would ever be realized. Ralph Peer later remembered, "In an effort to extend the Rodgers popularity to our Northern States, I booked him on the Radio-Keith-Orpheum Circuit. He was to appear as a single act in most of the leading vaudeville theaters. The salary, $1,000 weekly, was considered high at the time. Jimmie became ill, however, and we had to cancel the project."[82]

By the spring of 1933, Rodgers was physically spent. Sometimes he could barely breathe, and his hospital stays grew longer and more frequent. He could no longer ignore the fact that he was dying, although he seemed to make the attempt every day. Doctors continued to prescribe rest for the ailing singer, and Rodgers continued to ignore their advice. There were, however, some signs that he knew that the end might be near. At a significant expense he hired a private nurse who accompanied him everywhere. He also talked more frequently with his wife about business matters, something he had rarely done before, and things that would need to be done in the event that "something happened." Rodgers also seemed quietly desperate to organize more recording sessions that would generate more royalties for his family, even after he was gone. When Ralph Peer contacted him about coming to New York to record more songs and negotiate a new contract with Victor, Rodgers said yes without hesitation. Peer later recalled: "In the spring of 1933, Jimmie and I corresponded about the possibility of additional recordings. Victor had about a year's supply of material already on hand. The record business in general was not good, and they did not think it wise to be too far ahead of the market. Jimmie Rodgers by this time had become 'standard.' There were one or two masters to be remade because of technical defects. There was also the necessity to negotiate a new agreement between Victor and Rodgers. Working with all of these factors, I arranged matters so that Jimmie could come to New York for a series of recording work, and after the first two dates it seemed best to delay further activities."[83]

Rodgers and his private nurse arrived in New York on May 14, 1933, and took rooms in the singer's favorite hotel, the Taft, on the corner of Seventh Avenue and Fiftieth Street. Not aware of exactly how far Rodgers's disease had progressed, Ralph Peer was taken aback when first confronted with the singer's pale, gaunt, almost ghostly appearance. Peer scheduled two days' rest for Rodgers before recording began and assigned a man to be with the singer and his nurse to provide any help needed. On May 17, 1933, Rodgers attended his first recording session at the Victor studios on East Twenty-fourth Street. Peer had arranged for a cot and an easy chair to be brought in to make Rodgers as comfortable as possible between each exhausting take, and also provided the singer with whiskey to keep him going. According to Rodgers's wife, who tended to sugarcoat any discussion of the singer's drinking, "Because he'd found it was the one thing that would permit him to use his voice for a few moments at a time without the annoyance or embarrassment of that distressing cough, he would take a big swallow of good, bonded whiskey before singing."

Rodgers recorded nine songs between May 17 and May 20, including "Women Make a Fool Out of Me," which was later released under the title "Jimmie Rodgers' Last Blue Yodel," and then he took three days off. On May 24, America's Blue Yodeler went into the recording studio for the final time. Against all odds he was able to finish up his New York recording commitment by recording four more songs, the last of which was titled "Years Ago." He went back to his room at the Taft Hotel with plans to stay in New York to do some sightseeing and a little shopping in spite of his feeble condition. The next day he went with his nurse to Coney Island but suffered severe coughing spasms that landed him back in bed. He never recovered from the outing. Back at the hotel he lapsed into a coma and died in the early morning hours of May 26, 1933. Ralph Peer arranged for the body to be transported by train to Meridian for burial in a coffin draped with white lilies and blue ribbon on which was stenciled "America's Blue Yodeler." When the train pulled into the Meridian station the engineer blew the whistle several times in slow succession as a final salute to the former railroad worker who had become America's first country-music star.[84]

By the summer of 1934 both Charley Patton and Jimmie Rodgers were dead. Both lived hard lives and were acutely aware of their own mortality when the end came. In fact, both men had sung songs about their impending deaths. Patton and Rodgers did not live completely parallel lives as human beings, but their stories were similar in many respects. Told together, their stories paralleled the story of the American South, a region where racial divisions written into law could not completely restrain cultural interaction between blacks and whites. Both men were born in Mississippi, where rigid segregation was the law of the land during their lifetimes, but where many whites and blacks were equally poor and therefore suffering similar economic hardships. Neither man was satisfied with the conventional life patterns in which most southern blacks and whites of the early twentieth century toiled. They were both downtrodden. Patton was trapped in a permanent (at least during his lifetime) underclass that was never allowed to reach its full potential while Rodgers was poor and sick. Both men made their musical passions come alive, connecting with other human beings in a way that only a good musician can. From the standpoint of an emerging modern world, they were in the right place at the right time to capitalize on new and improving recording technology and new ways of marketing music to the masses. They were not the first to play their types of music, but they were among the best of their generation, and they sang and played in ways that set them apart. They synthesized what had come before and added something new, and they did so in ways that many in their audiences found unforgettable. Even when singing traditional material that they did not write themselves, both men could communicate feelings that their audiences related to, which is why their influence has endured.

★★★★ 4 ★★★★

HEIRLOOMS

Please myself. If I wanted to do that,
I would record some Charley Patton Songs.
—BOB DYLAN

I grew up with Blue Yodel #9.
—KEITH RICHARDS

I n 1903, when Charley Patton was twelve years old, most African Americans in his home state of Mississippi were languishing. The white power structure had taken their civil rights, and they risked physical harm if they complained too loudly about the inherent unfairness of their position in society. The glass ceiling of their hopes and dreams was actually more of an iron ceiling that was low, smothering, and painfully impenetrable. They struggled in a rigidly arranged society that had them on the outside looking in on the full privileges of American citizenship. "To be a poor man is hard," W. E. B. Dubois wrote, "but to be a poor race in a land of dollars is the very bottom of hardships." In Mississippi most African Americans could not vote, having been systematically excluded from the political process. They had no voice to influence policies that affected them directly and no true advocates in the state government. In communities across Mississippi, African Americans were not members of town or city councils, and even in counties where blacks outnumbered whites by large margins there were no local African American office holders. Patton was born into this environment, and as a young boy he had no reason to believe that anything about it would ever change. He certainly had no reason to believe that he would ever be noticed in a positive way by the white establishment. In his lifetime, the white politicians who governed his state did not recognize significant African American achievement, and did not reward African American achievement with plaques or medals. In 1903 Patton had no reason to believe that he would ever be anything but anonymous outside the confines of his family or his local neighborhood, no reason to believe that he would ever have a significant legacy.[1]

One hundred years later, in October of 2003, the state of Mississippi through an executive order issued by the governor's office created the Mississippi Blues Commission to promote the state's significant contributions to the birth of blues music. The commission's most visible project was the creation of the Mississippi Blues Trail, which to 2014 had placed interpretive markers at more than one hundred sites throughout the state to honor the people and places that "spawned the single most important root source of modern popular music." From the outset the program was a great success, drawing music fans, blues aficionados, and other tourists to the state in what could only be considered a kind of pilgrimage to see the stark, stirring sites that had spawned so many wonderful sounds. In 2006, when it came time for the commission to place along the trail the first of many markers honoring blues pioneers, the site chosen was the grave of Charley Patton in Holly Ridge. A number of dignitaries attended the ceremony, including Mississippi's governor, Haley Barbour, a white Deltan from Yazoo City, who personally unveiled the marker lauding Patton as a seminal figure in the history of American popular music. "This marker is the first of a long line to come," Barbour told the crowd witnessing the event. "People from around the country—indeed from around the world—will come to Mississippi to learn about and experience not only authentic Mississippi blues music but also the blues culture for years to come." The ceremony was certainly far removed from the world in which Charley Patton actually lived.[2]

The path from obscurity to high praise and respectability was long and twisted for Patton. His legacy became apparent in earnest only after the 1960s, when blues music experienced a worldwide surge that began pushing it steadily toward the mainstream. Before that time, blues in the United States was popular in the black community and with a relatively small number of whites, but few ever really took the time to understand or explore where the music came from. A number of factors came together in the 1950s and 1960s that spawned new generations of blues enthusiasts, many of whom were young and white. The emergence of blues-based rock and roll during the 1950s brought blues to the mass of white American teenagers and created a good deal of social tension as white parents were none too comfortable with the notion of their sons and especially their daughters listening to music that was black at its core. This tension affected politics in the South and elsewhere as the same authorities who fought in vain to silence this new music also fought unsuccessfully to nip the emergence of the civil rights movement in the bud. The simultaneity of the landmark Supreme Court case *Brown v. Board of Education of Topeka* (1954), ordering the desegregation of public schools, and the rise of rock and roll was not a coincidence. Both events would bring black and white young people closer together in new ways that, at the time, threatened the white establishment. "The emergence of rock and roll as a cultural phenomenon coincided with great ferment in the movement to grant civil rights to African Americans," Glenn C. Altschuler wrote in his study of how rock and roll changed the United States. "Enmeshed in the racial politics of the 1950s, rock and roll was credited with and criticized for promoting integration and economic opportunity for blacks while bringing to 'mainstream' culture black styles and values." Later, blues-based rock was the soundtrack for much of the social upheaval of the 1960s as the civil rights movement progressed and the war in Vietnam escalated. It fueled protests and celebrations and became a vehicle for social comment in ways that no other form of popular song ever had.[3]

As rock and roll reverberated from stereo speakers across America during this era of protest, and the genre's influence continued to grow, some began to study it in an attempt to discover the music's true essence by tracing its blues roots. The search for the blues origins of rock, and for the bluesmen associated with them, became something akin to the search for the Holy Grail for those caught up in the activity. Many of the researchers interested in tracing the history of the blues during this period were middle-class whites with ties to the counter-culture or academia. Some claimed to be searching idealistically for something pure and therefore not yet tainted by the darker elements of modern society. Others claimed to be searching for the original form of American protest music, a powerful form that sprang directly from the ranks of the enslaved. Were its source located, they believed, then the music might be translated into a more modern context and used against the politicians or corporate interests that some believed were enslaving the American people. "Blues focuses on autonomy and independence," Dick Weissman wrote, "and given the social conditions during the time the music began and flourished, one could make a good argument that the very existence of the music was a protest." Still others just enjoyed good music and were curious as to where it came from.[4]

By the end of the 1970s many aging Delta bluesmen who began their careers before and immediately after the Second World War had been "discovered" and were being hailed as founding fathers of a musical movement that for some was spiritual in nature. Muddy Waters, Howlin' Wolf, Son House, Big Bill Broonzy, and others became larger-than-life icons to the true believers who were moved by their music. At the same time, blues became big business. Record companies took advantage of the popularity of the music—again, mainly among whites—by promoting modern blues and rock artists. Blues music suddenly warranted its own section in record stores, and blues programming became common on mainstream radio stations across America that catered primarily to whites. Even the most decadent millionaire rock musicians regularly paid homage to the old blues masters and sometimes sought them out for recording sessions. Some of the most famous rock bands in the world produced covers of old blues tunes that were decades old. As the twentieth century came to a close, blues music was still gritty, rough, and honest, but it was also acceptable, which had not been the case decades earlier. It also had jumped the racial divide as whites began to look at blues as a truly respected art form.

It is difficult to discuss the family tree of any type of popular music in a biblical "this artist begat that artist, who begat this artist," sort of way. Music is not produced with that type of scrutiny in mind. Even the terms used to describe various genres—country, blues, jazz, pop, rhythm and blues, easy listening—are products of the marketplace more than of the actual music they are meant to describe. They are labels produced by music companies to describe a product, a commodity that is for sale. There is really no definitive answer to the question "What is blues music?" because it is different things to different people. There are some defining technical qualities to the music, but aside from that a definitive description is hard to pin down because the music is like a proverbial river that has many tributaries flowing into it. There are different styles of singing blues and playing blues guitar, and almost anything can become the subject of a blues song. Some blues tunes are mournful and sad, but others are upbeat and happy. Some describe fictional people and events while others relate to things that actually happened. "There are so many exceptions to almost any statement about the blues that it is impossible to arrive at a concise definition of the genre," David Evans wrote. "The term blues covers a broad range of formal, stylistic and textual traits, and whenever enough of these occur together in a single performance, it is called 'blues.'"[5]

A prime example of the complicated and convoluted nature of the relationship between blues, country, and rock was the popular 1950s song "Hound Dog." The song was written by Jerry Leiber and Mike Stoller, two Jewish songwriters enamored with blues music who would go on to write many classic early rock-and-roll hits. Leiber was born to Polish immigrants in Baltimore in 1933, and Stoller was born the same year in New York. They began their songwriting partnership in 1950 and, two years later, when both were only nineteen, they penned "Hound Dog," a twelve-bar blues song. Despite his own heritage as the son of Jewish immigrants from Poland, Leiber once told an interviewer "I felt black. I was [black] as far as I was concerned. And I wanted to be black for lots of reasons. They were better musicians, they were better athletes, they were not uptight about sex, and they knew how to enjoy life better than most people." Similarly, Stoller once said, "As would-be songwriters, our interest was in black music and black music only. We wanted to write songs for black voices." The two men wrote "Hound Dog" for the formidable African American singer Willie Mae "Big Mama" Thornton, a rough-and-tumble blues queen. Born in Alabama, Thornton was the daughter of a Baptist minister. For several years she toured the black theater circuit in the South with a variety show called Sammy Green's Hot Harlem Revue. She eventually settled in Houston, Texas, where she signed with Peacock Records and in 1953 recorded the Leiber and Stoller classic. Thornton's "Hound Dog" topped the Billboard rhythm-and-blues charts with the magazine describing it as "a wild and exciting rhumba blues."

Ironically, while blues audiences were quick to notice the song, so were country artists and producers. Not long after Thornton's record hit the airwaves and record stores, different, reworked versions of the song recorded by artists labeled as country began to appear. Charlie Gore and Louis Inness, Tommy Duncan, Jack Turner and His Granger County Gang, and Betsy Gay among others all recorded versions of the song. In 1956 "Hound Dog," the song written by two male Jews from the north for a powerfully voiced African American female blues singer from the South, and was then recorded by several white "hillbilly" acts, came full circle. That year Elvis Presley, the white kid from Mississippi who sang and moved on stage with the passion of an experienced, high-energy juke-joint blues performer, recorded the song and made it his own, creating forever after a place for "Hound Dog" in the annals of American popular culture. The song is one of the best examples of American popular music as music from the melting pot. The origins and history of "Hound Dog" speak to overlapping elements of race, ethnicity, and gender that all came together musically at a particular moment in time to create something that fascinated and excited large segments of the American public. The same can be said of rock music in general and of the foundations of American popular music in all of its manifestations.[6]

Regardless of the problems inherent in trying to define the blues, the generally accepted notion is that the music most people call blues today originated in the South, much of it in the Mississippi Delta. Though the influences on the early Delta sound are many and varied, and they have been romanticized somewhat through the years, Charley Patton continues to be a dominant figure who many still to refer to with reverence as the "Father of Delta Blues." His skills and reputation were such that he influenced a host of younger bluesmen who themselves would become larger-than-life figures in the years to come. In short, Patton was a prototype. He would not be as well known or as commercially successful as some who followed him, but because he had great influence on later generations of performers, their success in some ways could be considered his success as well, and his legacy. "If any performer can be said truly to reflect the sound of the birth of the blues it was Charley Patton," Bill Wyman, longtime bassist for the Rolling Stones, once wrote. "He was there at the start, absorbing and shaping the blues, besides creating opportunities for others to record. He may not have been the first country blues player to record, but he was definitely the greatest of the early Delta bluesmen." Similarly, Ted Gioia, in his outstanding study *Delta Blues*, summed up Patton's influence when he observed, "An important divide was crossed with Charley Patton. He was the first star of the Delta blues, his records travelling far and wide to locations he himself would never see. His music perhaps began as folk art, but it ended up as an influential style of commercial music."[7]

The list of performers Patton influenced is long and varied and includes Howlin' Wolf, Muddy Waters, Robert Johnson, Son House, Tommy Johnson, David "Honeyboy" Edwards, Big Joe Williams, Johnny Shines, and others. "Different ones from different places would come and try to learn like Uncle Charley," one of Patton's nieces later related. "They would hang on to him, trying to learn to play like he could play."[8] In his book *Deep Blues*, Robert Palmer described Patton as "never tied to a menial job or a plot of land for very long. He went where he pleased, stayed as long as he pleased, stayed intoxicated as he pleased, left when he wanted to, and had his pick of women wherever he went. He created an enduring body of American music, for he personally inspired just about every Delta bluesman of consequence, and blueswomen as well. Along with Louis Armstrong, Elvis Presley, and a few others who created not just styles but dynasties, he is among the most important musician of the twentieth century America has produced."[9]

Although Patton would be hailed as a Delta blues pioneer, blues would not enter the mainstream of American popular music until decades after his death, and the route to respectability that the music took was long and arduous. Patton's form of blues first escaped the Delta as a result of the Great Migration that brought millions of African Americans from southern cotton fields to northern cities, where they took factory jobs or other types of employment. The migration took place in two waves that corresponded with a surge in available jobs caused by America's involvement in the two world wars. Between 1900 and 1930 around 1.6 million African Americans moved north, followed by about 5 million who relocated between 1940 and 1970. Chicago in particular drew African Americans to its south side, which became known to many as "little Mississippi" because of the large number of former residents of that state who congregated there. From the onset of the Second World War to the end of the 1950s, the black population of Chicago blossomed from just under 300,000 to just over 800,000. As a result of these demographic changes, a vibrant entertainment community developed in Chicago that catered to the black population. By the 1920s blues and jazz performers such as William Lee Conley "Big Bill" Broonzy, Thomas Andrew "Georgia Tom" Dorsey, and Tampa Red had established themselves in Chicago, and a generation later a second wave of southern musicians, many of whom were Patton devotees from the Mississippi Delta, moved to the city, quickly modifying their music to suit their new, urban surroundings. In Chicago, Delta blues "plugged in" as blues artists used electric instruments to reach their audiences in loud, crowded nightclubs. This electrically amplified music was still raw at its foundation, but it was somehow more raucous, more modern. It improved upon the old Delta sound without rendering the old sound obsolete. Electric blues became popular in Chicago nightclubs, and a market for "urban" blues records began to grow.[10]

Major record companies were slow to capitalize on these new sounds, but smaller, independent record labels were quick to recognize an opportunity. Chess Records in Chicago was the most notable blues label of the period. Founded in 1950 by brothers Phil and Leonard Chess, Polish immigrants who had started out in the liquor business, Chess recorded all of the early Chicago bluesmen, including Muddy Waters, Sonny Boy Williamson, Jimmy Reed, and Elmore James. These men, in turn, influenced rock musicians of the 1960s who would bring, in one form or another, blues music to the masses and make it a global commercial entity. According to one writer, "The blues that made the trip north to Chicago and so, in the Darwinian sense, was fated to survive to pass on its DNA to rock & roll, was the blues of the Mississippi Delta." While many Delta musicians made it as far north as Chicago, others moved north but never left the South, congregating instead in Memphis, which some people still call "the capital of North Mississippi." Memphis, like Chicago, had been a mecca for African American musicians for more than two decades by the time Patton devotees began arriving there after World War II. Before he went to Chicago to record for Chess, Mississippi native and blues great Chester "Howlin' Wolf" Burnett recorded in Memphis, as did Deltan Ike Turner, another significant pioneer in the blues-to-rock saga. Without a doubt the most famous blues artist to record in Memphis during the 1950s was Delta native Riley B. King, who later became known worldwide as B.B. King. Sam Phillips, the entrepreneur and blues enthusiast who first recorded Elvis Presley, produced early recordings for King, Turner, Howlin' Wolf, and others in his tiny studio on Union Avenue that Presley would one day make famous.[11]

Ironically, when rock and roll first hit during the 1950s it devastated the blues market from a commercial standpoint by taking up a large percentage of the market share. For the first time in American history, merchants who sold music began looking at teenagers as true consumers, and they began to carry records in their stores aimed specifically at the youth market. Rock and roll overwhelmed almost all other forms of musical entertainment during the period, appealing to both black and white teenagers. Little Richard, Bo Diddley, Fats Domino, Jerry Lee Lewis, and, of course, Elvis Presley were among the most popular entertainers of the era. Chess Records became the label of Chuck Berry, a black man who made legendary rock and roll with a country flavor that many whites loved and some blacks shunned, while Sun Records, Sam Phillips's outfit in Memphis, became forever associated with Presley, the "white man gone black." While many blues pioneers still made a decent living in the African American nightclubs of cities like Chicago and Memphis, their records stopped selling in significant numbers. "The rock and roll, this hurt the blues pretty bad," Muddy Waters later remembered. "We still hustled around and made it and kept going, but we were only playing for black people when rock and roll came along." In the 1950s radio stations began catering to the lucrative white teenage market by developing formats highlighting rock records, and the new medium of television began devoting significant air time to programs that appealed to young music fans, such as *American Bandstand,* which premiered in 1957. Between 1954 and 1960, sales of records in the United States increased from $182 million to $521 million due primarily to the expanded market for records among the nation's youth. Major record companies began massive and very successful promotional campaigns aimed at selling music with a black foundation to white teenagers all over America. It would take a while, however, for the white rock fans to realize the true origins of the music that they loved, and for blues musicians to regain their footing in the marketplace. But even as many blues musicians languished in the shadows of early rock and roll, circumstances were already coming together that would place these bluesmen on a pedestal.[12]

As rock and roll began to dominate the musical marketplace in America during the 1950s, another movement developed that was akin to rock and roll but at the same time something completely different. The American folk-music revival began in earnest during the period as an effort by some to explore their cultural heritage by preserving what was believed to be the purer, more sincere "folk music" of the past. The folk revival was in large part a sort of intellectual backlash led by college students who questioned the suburban commercialism of the 1950s and idealized the old folk tunes as artistic remnants of a bygone but superior environment. There were different definitions for folk music, but in the general context of the 1950s it was music that came from traditional, primitive sources. African American blues music was linked to it as was the music of Appalachia. The music was viewed by many as a spontaneous, foundational type of music unsullied by the influences of modern record companies and radio stations that were on a constant quest for profits. It was simple music usually produced by a lone singer with a guitar. To many it was also viewed as music of the poor and oppressed, songs that reflected the human condition at its most basic level. As folk artists of the period began to move away from traditional material to explore more politically sensitive themes, the folk movement came to be associated with radical activity. With the Red Scare of the 1950s in full swing, many folk artists found themselves branded as subversives. Performers such as Woody Guthrie, Pete Seeger, Josh White, and others were rarely heard on the radio, but eventually folk musicians developed a circuit of coffee houses, college campuses, and other venues that kept their music alive. Surviving the oppressive 1950s, the folk phenomenon surged in the early 1960s as younger artists such as Bob Dylan and Joan Baez entered the fray. While the larger record companies were interested in signing singers with a younger, more modern folk sound, smaller labels took advantage of the folk craze by reissuing older recordings of the simpler traditional music from which folk enthusiasts drew their original inspiration. In turn, this created a musical environment where there was a greater appreciation for things that had come before. Long forgotten "hillbilly" and "race" recordings from the 1920s and 1930s were resurrected, some as anthems with universal themes still relevant in the modern age. Old, scratchy 78-rpm records became priceless artifacts when, during the 1960s and beyond, people of varied musical tastes from blues to country to rock and roll would deem it important to recognize and preserve the origins of the music that they loved. This move to preserve "roots music" would lead many to discover the music of both Charley Patton and Jimmie Rodgers.[13]

As folk music became popular in the United States during the 1950s and early 1960s, another music phenomenon was taking place in England that would have huge repercussions on blues music and American popular culture in general. Many English music lovers had been familiar with African American jazz and blues for some time, though relatively few American records made it into England because of restrictions on imports. Most jazz and blues discs were either brought in by British sailors who made frequent trips to American port cities or by African American soldiers serving in England during World War II or afterwards during the Cold War. Profiteers smuggled in some American records and made them available on the black market to anyone who was interested. While jazz and blues were slow to catch on nationwide, a fan base began to develop after the Second World War and many English musicians began playing their own versions of traditional American music, including music in the country blues style of the Mississippi Delta. During the mid-1950s "skiffle" music became popular with many British teenagers. Skiffle was an attempt by British musicians to pay homage to traditional American folk music in a more modern setting. The most significant skiffle performer of the period was a banjo player named Lonnie Donegan who scored a hit with an uptempo version of the 1930s American folk classic "Rock Island Line" in 1956. Donegan went on to cover Jimmie Rodgers's "Muleskinner Blues" two years later. Teenagers across Britain formed skiffle bands in large part because the style did not require one to be too proficient on a musical instrument. Sales of guitars skyrocketed, and if a teenager could not play that instrument, he could still be part of a skiffle group by playing a one-string washtub bass, by scratching on an old washboard, or by simply blowing into a large jug. It was primitive music that needed no complicated arrangements, and it gave many British teenagers their first exposure to traditional American folk and blues music. John Lennon's first musical endeavor was with a skiffle group, and other musicians from the British Isles who would later become famous such as Jimmy Page, Roger Daltrey, Graham Nash, Van Morrison, and Ronnie Wood were all drawn to the craze.[14]

As the skiffle craze subsided in the late 1950s, blues clubs began to spring up in British urban centers, especially London, and more and more British young people began listening to and performing traditional American jazz and blues. Ironically, it would be British performers who eventually brought American blues back to the United States and created a market for American blues records. Savvy promoters soon began bringing African American blues artists into Britain to tour. The first country blues performer to tour Europe was William Lee Conley "Big Bill" Broonzy, who gave well-received acoustic-based performances in Britain and France and appeared on British television. Broonzy's visit generated more interest in blues music in Britain, paving the way for other artists like Muddy Waters, whose 1958 tour rocked the European continent literally and figuratively. Waters's electric blues shocked British audiences—accustomed primarily to the acoustic country blues style of Broonzy—as it poured out of his high-volume amplifiers. "We opened up in Leeds, England. I was definitely too loud for them," Waters recalled. "The next morning we were in the headline of the paper—'Screamin' Guitar and Howlin' Piano. That was when they were into the folk thing before the Rolling Stones." At a time when sales of blues music were declining in the United States, the demand for blues records in Britain began to grow, as did a general excitement about the power of blues. Though the music itself was old, it was new to most white audiences of the period, offering them something both exotic and exciting. It connected and generated heat between audience and entertainer in the same manner as when it was originally produced a half-century earlier. By the time Waters went back to England in the early 1960s, audiences were ready to embrace his brand of electric blues in addition to all the other forms. [15]

If there was a ground zero for the explosion of British blues that took place in the late 1950s and eventual brought blues back to America, it may have been the London Blues and Barrelhouse Club, founded during the period by Alexis Korner, who had started out playing jazz before becoming completely obsessed with blues music, and Cyril Davies, an outstanding blues harmonica player. The club hosted local blues musicians and enthusiasts as well as visiting American artists before it was closed down in its third year after neighborhood complaints that the music pouring out of the club was too loud. With Davies, Korner formed the band Blues Incorporated in 1962, with whom some of the most famous rock musicians of the 1960s performed as they were just starting out. At one time or another Mick Jagger, Charlie Watts, Rod Stewart, Brian Jones, Jimmy Page, Keith Richards, Ginger Baker, and Jack Bruce either played with or sat in with Blues Incorporated and received their education in the nuances of performing American-based blues music. "Alexis played acoustic guitar and Cyril was an amazing electric harmonica player," Jimmy Page later recalled, "and back in the early sixties they would host these regular blues jam sessions on Thursday nights. It was the only thing like that in London at the time. The Rolling Stones played there before they became famous, Clapton would be in the audience and I would regularly participate." In addition to Blues Incorporated, the other great English blues band of the period that served as a springboard for some of Britain's premier rock talent was John Mayall's Bluesbreakers. Formed in 1963 by guitarist and songwriter John Mayall with encouragement from Alexis Korner and others, the band quickly became very popular among British blues fans. Among the band's famous rock alumni were Eric Clapton, Mick Taylor, Mick Fleetwood, Jack Bruce, Peter Green, and John McVie. [16]

Through Britain, the blues came back to the United States in a big way beginning in 1964 when the Beatles launched the so-called "British Invasion," overwhelming the American music scene in a phenomenon that the American press dubbed "Beatlemania." The popularity of the Beatles opened the door for other British bands, many with deep blues roots, to enter the United States and spread their musical message. Groups like the Rolling Stones, the Animals, the Kinks and the Who entered the country with a greater knowledge of

American music than most of the Americans in their audiences. When American journalists interviewed band members and asked them to name their primary musical influences, the musicians routinely answered with the names of older American blues artists such as Muddy Waters, Howlin' Wolf, Big Bill Broonzy, Jimmy Reed, and others, most of whom the puzzled journalists had never heard of. In turn, many of the British musicians were puzzled that the American media were so unfamiliar with American music. "Don't you know who your own famous people are over here?" an amazed Paul McCartney once asked a reporter who was obviously clueless about the influence of American blues overseas.[17] British musicians soon began to make a point of promoting their blues idols, and suddenly white teenagers who were purchasing the bulk of rock and roll records in the United States became curious as to how the young, hip, and mostly white rock gods of their generation could draw inspiration from a group of middle-aged black men. This was the first stage of a process that would soon find millions of white kids discovering black music, and in some cases very old black music. It was near this point in history that, according to Francis Davis, guardianship of the blues "passed from the black community to white bohemia."[18] In the 1970s, years after the original British invasion, blues icon Muddy Waters summed up the situation:

> Before the Rolling Stones, people over here [in the United States] didn't know nothing and didn't want to know nothing about me. I was making race records, and I'm gonna tell it to you the way the older [white] people told it to the kids. If they'd buy my records, their parents would say, 'what the hell is this? Get this nigger record out of my house!' But then the Rolling Stones and those other groups come over here from England, playing this music, and now, today, the kids buy a record of mine and they listen to it. Fifteen years ago . . . at some of my gigs I might have a few kids from the university, but if it wasn't a school date I was playing, if it was just a club in Chicago, it would be maybe one percent, two percent white. I play in places now that don't have no black faces in there but our black faces.[19]

As white teenagers became more familiar with blues, the names of the old bluesmen became much better known. Muddy Waters, Robert Johnson, Howlin' Wolf, Son House, and others became topics of conversation among rock fans, and blues enthusiasts began collecting their old records. Some of the older bluesmen who were still alive during the 1960s and 1970s began producing new music and appearing onstage before young, white audiences who thought that they were watching and listening to the first generation of blues pioneers when, in fact, they were hearing the second generation. Whether it was a Robert Johnson record or a Muddy Waters live performance, these audiences stood in awe of a long and varied list of entertainers who were the product of an environment that Charley Patton helped create.

While the British Invasion groups may have helped Muddy Waters gain notoriety, his music had Charley Patton's fingerprints all over it. Patton was already a well-known figure in the Delta's barrelhouses and juke joints by the time Muddy Waters was born in Rolling Fork, Mississippi, in 1915, and Waters grew up listening to Patton's records. As a teenager and fledgling musician, Waters also drew inspiration from the older man's flamboyant live performances. "I saw Patton in my younger life days," Waters once told an interviewer. "What got to me about Patton was that he was such a clown man with the guitar. Pattin' it and beatin' on it and puttin' it behind his neck and turnin' it over. . . . I loved that." Waters was one of many young blues artists in the Delta during the 1930s who aspired to have the notoriety of Charley Patton and who copied Patton's guitar style and delivery. In the world of the Delta's black community, the world in which Waters grew up, Patton was famous and impossible to ignore. As he came of age as a musical talent, Waters also learned a great deal from another blues legend, Eddie James "Son" House. A decade younger than Patton, House was also influenced by the older bluesman's records and performed with him from time to time. While House influenced Waters and put his own stamp on future generations of bluesmen, he may have never had the opportunity to do so had Patton not arranged for him to make his first record for Paramount in 1930.[20]

One Delta artist who has also been called "the Father of Blues" is Robert Johnson, whose name today is still more familiar than Patton's to many blues fans. Born in Mississippi in 1911, Johnson may be the most legendary and mysterious blues performer of the early twentieth century. A street corner and barrelhouse performer in the Patton mold, Johnson also recorded with Henry C. Speir in 1936 and 1937, creating influential music that had a great impact on the rock scene beginning in the 1960s. Some of rock's biggest names would cover Johnson's songs and hail him as a master, with Eric Clapton once calling him the most important blues player in history. Despite Johnson's heady posthumous reputation as a musician, his notoriety was also fueled by a famous myth that grew up around him. As the story goes, Johnson supposedly met the devil one night at a Delta crossroads and bargained away his soul in exchange for musical prowess. While the Faustian story of a musician "selling his soul to the devil" had been told before, it became associated with Johnson and added to his legend as yet another mysterious element of the mysterious music that became the foundation of rock and roll. Johnson also benefited from his records being of better technical quality than many of the older artists, and more of them survived over time to be played by future generations.

Still, Johnson was a musical contemporary of Muddy Waters, about a generation removed from Charley Patton, who was twenty years old when Johnson was born. As Johnson grew up in the Delta, Patton was already making the rounds, already making his imprint on the music that would eventually exit the Delta and waft around the world. More Patton fingerprints can be found on Johnson's work. "Robert Johnson's name may be more familiar," one noted blues researcher has asserted, "but Patton came first and Johnson used his recordings as a kind of source book. Patton's 'Down the Dirt Road Blues' and 'Tom Rushen Blues' became Johnson's 'Crossroads Blues' and 'From Four Till Late,' respectively."[21] While many claim Johnson was the father of Delta Blues, it would be more accurate to say that he successfully synthesized blues traditions that were already beginning to flower by the time he picked up his first guitar. One biographer summed up Johnson by writing, "The early Mississippi masters—Charley Patton . . . and a handful of others, are among the greatest musicians this country has produced, and Johnson's work can be seen as summing up their tradition." According to the national Blues Foundation Hall of Fame, whose inductees include both Patton and Johnson, "While Robert Johnson may be the artist most associated today with the title 'King of the Delta Blues,' if such a title had been bestowed back when the music was first being recorded, the premier royal figure would by nearly all historical accounts have been Charley Patton."[22]

Many blues artists who were in the spotlight as a result of the blues revival of the 1960s were quick to mention Patton when asked about the music of the Mississippi Delta. Booker T. "Bukka" White, a country blues artist with a distinctive style that influenced his younger cousin B.B. King as well as Bob Dylan, dreamed as a young man of one day being Charley Patton. White later remembered that immediately after a Patton record came out it was almost impossible to see the bluesman in the local Delta clubs because of the large crowds. White was awestruck at the performer's musical abilities and fascinated by his lifestyle. "I wants to become a great man like Charley Patton," was White's usual refrain when anyone asked him about his future. David "Honeyboy" Edwards, another Delta blues master whose career spanned decades, also grew up immersed in the Patton legacy. "I had been hearing about Charley Patton for a long time," Edwards once told an interviewer. "Charley was the leading musicianer in Mississippi at that time. . . . I went to Dockery's a few times and saw him there. I wanted to see him and learn what he was doing. . . . Charley had recorded and had a big name for himself out in the Delta. . . . I was lucky to come up in time to know him."[23]

If there was a single person who may have served as a direct link, a human bridge, between Charley Patton and modern rock and roll, it was probably Chester Arthur Burnett, a true Patton disciple who later became known worldwide by his stage name, "Howlin' Wolf." Born in 1910 near the town of West Point in eastern Mississippi, Burnett moved to the Delta in 1923 with his father after his parents split up. At the time, Charley Patton was making a name for himself in the region, playing at local nightclubs, picnics, and house parties, and he just happened to live near Burnett's father. Burnett was enamored with Patton, reportedly following the bluesman around wherever he went and listening to him first as a youngster through the open windows of nightclubs and later in the clubs themselves. Burnett eventually played with Patton onstage with the younger man's gruff, throaty singing voice sounded a great deal like his mentor's. "He showed me things on the guitar," Burnett later remembered, "because after we got through picking cotton at night, we'd go hang around him, listen to him play. He took a liking to me, and I asked him would he learn me, and at night, after I'd get off work, I'd go and hang around. . . . You asking me for my all time favorite singer? That was Charley Patton."[24]

Forty years later, Howlin' Wolf would have his own disciples, but they were not black and they were not from the Mississippi Delta. They were not even from the United States. They were members of a fledgling, blues-based rock band in England who called themselves the Rolling Stones. They revered men like Howlin' Wolf and Muddy Waters—actually naming themselves the Rolling Stones after a Muddy Waters song—and were infatuated with the Delta sound. "When we first started playing together," Brian Jones, one of the founders of the band, once told an interviewer, "we started playing because we wanted to play the blues, and Howlin' Wolf was one of our greatest idols." In 1964 the Stones recorded a version of "Little Red Rooster," a song written by Willie Dixon but recorded by Howlin' Wolf three years earlier. The band's version of the Wolf classic hit the top of the British pop charts—the first time an American blues song had ever done so in Britain—and helped increase the popularity of the Stones in their own country and in America. That same year the group helped lead the so-called "British Invasion" of English bands in the United States. The Stones performed "Little Red Rooster" several times on American television, which eventually led them to a famous appearance with their idol Howlin' Wolf on the popular variety program "Shindig!"[25]

During the mid-1960s "Shindig!" aired in prime time on ABC and showcased musical acts that appealed specifically to teenagers. By the end of the show's run, everyone from the Righteous Brothers and Chuck Berry to the Beatles and the Beach Boys had made appearances. Los Angeles disc jockey Jimmy O'Neill hosted the show, and the house band included keyboard master Billy Preston and future country star Glen Campbell. Once the British Invasion took place, the program regularly featured British groups, with some shows taped in England. With the Rolling Stones booked to appear on "Shindig!" in 1965, one of the show's producers thought it would be a great idea to also feature the artist who had originally recorded the Stones' hit "Little Red Rooster," so he had Howlin' Wolf booked. According to some sources, network executives, who were completely ignorant of the significance of pairing Howlin' Wolf with the Stones, resisted the notion that a fifty-five-year-old black blues singer should appear on a show designed to appeal to white teenagers. The Stones, in turn, reportedly issued an ultimatum that, if the network rescinded the offer for their idol to appear, the band would not appear either. "I knew this was a very rare thing," Stones guitarist Keith Richards later said of the incident. "That *Shindig!* was a high-rated TV pop show and the fact that we'd got Howlin' Wolf on it was a triumph for us, one of our first triumphs." The Rolling Stones introduced Howlin' Wolf and literally sat at his feet with other audience members, nodding with the music, as one of the Mississippi Delta's finest sang "How Many More Years." The show aired on May 26, 1965, and did much to expose America's white teenagers to a type of blues music that they would have otherwise never known about, a type of music that Howlin' Wolf learned directly from Charley Patton. The Rolling Stones putting their stamp of approval on blues helped popularize the genre and, of course, the young men who sat at Howlin' Wolf's feet on "Shindig!" went on to become a global phenomenon and one of the most popular, influential, and long-lasting bands in the history of popular entertainment. Decades after the television appearance with their idol, the twenty-first-century Rolling Stones were still performing "Little Red Rooster" in concert. One could therefore make an argument that, with regard to raw, Mississippi Delta blues there was at least one direct musical strand of descent from Charley Patton, to Howlin' Wolf, to the Rolling Stones, to the world.[26]

The Rolling Stones were not the only up-and-coming rock stars of the 1960s and beyond to recognize the power of blues music. Once the rock scene in America began to blossom, the names of the old blues masters circulated at the highest levels, and blues became the driving force behind much of the popular music that followed. As the enormity of the cultural imprint that blues music made on the United States became more apparent during the modern era, more and more people became interested in the origins of the blues, and as a result the music became a subject of academic study. Serious people devoted and continue to devote a significant amount of time and energy to researching the blues. Most agree that Patton is a seminal figure who had an extraordinary influence on many of the bluesmen who followed him, not only with regard to his music, but his seemingly carefree lifestyle as well. About Patton's ongoing influence on modern music, David Evans wrote, "It is probably fair to say that Charley Patton is the only black person of his generation to live virtually his entire life in Mississippi who still has a national and international impact and whose name and accomplishments are known to many outside his immediate family and community over a century after his birth and almost seventy years after his death." James C. Cobb highlighted Patton in his book *The Most Southern Place on Earth* as a force to be reckoned with despite his vices. "In the process of drinking, fighting, abusing and exploiting women, and avoiding insofar as possible having to work for whites himself," Cobb wrote, "Patton also earned a lasting place in the history of American popular music through his influence on a host of bluesmen whose work in turn left a major imprint on several distinct musical forms." According to southern historian J. William Harris, "Charley Patton in all likelihood did not 'invent' the blues, but he brought it to a new kind of perfection. With guitar playing that was extraordinary—he could indeed make it 'sing' and 'talk' and 'cuss'—and a raw voice that Patton used as another instrument. . . . Patton's influence was felt directly by many of the early blues singers who played with him at Dockery's and elsewhere."[27]

If Charley Patton was indeed playing the devil's music, as some always claimed, it seemed that as the twentieth century drew to a close more and more people were willing to give the devil his due. As blues became more popular, Patton's music and influence began to garner posthumous recognition by a number of organizations dedicated to preserving blues and American popular culture in general. In 1980 he was among the first group of inductees to the Blues Foundation Hall of Fame, a national organization headquartered in Memphis, just north of the Mississippi Delta where Patton plied his trade. In 1991 the selection committee for the American Folklife Center of the Library of Congress recognized the bluesman's music and Patton himself as "the most prominent musician of his time in the central Mississippi Delta, [who] shaped generations of blues musicians as teacher, mentor, and influence." In 2003 the governing board for the National Recording Registry of the Library of Congress selected Patton's "Pony Blues" for inclusion on the registry, which was designed to "maintain and preserve sound recordings and collections of sound recordings that are culturally, historically, or aesthetically significant." Probably the most public accolades that Patton ever received for his recorded work came at the 2003 Grammy Awards, held at Madison Square Garden in New York City. Two years prior to the awards ceremony, Revenant Records produced a massive, multi-CD boxed set of all of Patton's recordings along with recorded interviews about Patton and versions of the bluesman's songs performed by other artists. Titled *Screamin' and Hollerin' the Blues: The Worlds of Charley Patton*, the set won three Grammy Awards at the 2003 ceremony, including best historical album, best boxed or limited edition package, and best album notes. Down through the decades, Patton's music continues to persevere. While many of his original recordings are rough, scratchy, and at times difficult to listen to, and while he is still an obscure figure outside the universe of blues enthusiasts, the songs he sang still echo. Tunes like "Pony Blues," "Down the Dirt Road Blues," "Banty Rooster Blues," "A Spoonful Blues," and others have been covered in one form or another by generations of blues and rock performers. Bob Dylan paid tribute to Patton as an influence by dedicating the song "High Water (For Charley Patton)" to the bluesman on his 2001 album *Love and Theft*. According to successful musician and producer Jack White, who first gained notoriety with his band the White Stripes, "If a musician calls himself a musician and listens to Charley Patton and doesn't hear anything at all, I don't think they should call themselves musicians, because they're obviously just looking for fun and kicks and a good time out of it."[28]

In 1991 Patton's grave at Holly Ridge, Mississippi, which had been poorly marked for decades, finally got a headstone through the Mount Zion Memorial Fund, a nonprofit organization founded by blues fan and vintage guitar dealer Raymond "Skip" Henderson and dedicated to memorializing and marking the graves of early blues musicians. While many individuals and businesses contributed to this fund over the years, John Fogerty, founding member of the band Creedence Clearwater Revival and a successful solo artist, paid for Patton's headstone. Fogerty became involved in the project after a chance meeting with Henderson and a brief discussion of what Henderson's organization was doing. Among those in attendance at the ceremony marking Patton's grave were members of the bluesman's family, Fogerty, and seventy-six-year-old Roebuck "Pops" Staples, who grew up on Dockery's plantation and as a young man heard Patton perform many times. The artwork on Patton's granite monument included an image of Patton, his birth and death dates, and the simple inscription:

Charley Patton
"The Voice of the Delta"
The foremost performer of early Mississippi blues
whose songs became cornerstones of American Music

"That big event for Charley Patton, it was an anchor for me," Fogerty later said of the gathering. "One of the really cool things I've done in my life."[29] Charley Patton would have been amazed.

Equally amazing was the effect that frail, sickly Jimmie Rodgers would have on generations of musicians. Unlike Patton, whose reputation as a musician really did not escape the Mississippi Delta until after his death, Rodgers sold records in large numbers during his lifetime, especially in the South and West. One Rodgers biographer estimated in the 1970s that "Blue Yodel (T for Texas)," by far his most popular song, likely sold more than a million copies while his second-highest seller, "Waiting for a Train," may have sold more than 350,000. Rodgers was a celebrity, and his influence on country music—still called "hillbilly" music by many at the time of his death—was immediate and far reaching. By the time he died, scores of country musicians were already listening to his records and attempting to copy his style and delivery. He was revered like no other country artist of his day, and while his fans loved his music, record companies were even more in love with the potential profits from the sale of country records. After the Jimmie Rodgers phenomenon hit, nothing about country music, either as an art form or as a measured retail consumable, was ever the same. He opened the door for the country entertainers who followed him. "After Jimmie Rodgers," music historian Don Cusic wrote, "country artists found employment on radio stations, northern music publishers and record men saw the potential of country music, booking agents booked country talent into major theaters and other venues in major cities, and young southern boys bought guitars." Country music began to flower after the Great Depression and the Second World War, broadening its influence and appeal in different variations including "honky tonk" music, cowboy songs, and bluegrass. "Country emerged shortly after World War II," Benjamin Filene wrote, "drawing on Anglo-Celtic ballads, minstrel and medicine-show songs, blues, church tunes, tin pan alley and, most immediately, commercial hillbilly singing from earlier in the century." New stars emerged, many of whom were Rodgers devotees, who helped push country music toward the modern era and who created large fan bases of their own. Many radio stations in the South and West began broadcasting country formats, and the most famous country radio program ever, the "Grand Ole Opry" broadcasting from Nashville, helped spread the word, creating legions of new country fans in the process.[30]

Within the confines of country's family tree, the best-known first-generation musical descendent of Jimmie Rodgers, and one of the artists who most closely tried to emulate him, was Ernest Tubb. Tubb, who became a country giant in his own right, was best known for popularizing the "honky tonk" style. Born on a small farm in Crisp, Texas, in 1914, Tubb was in his teens when he first heard a Jimmie Rodgers record, and from that point on he idolized the older man, spending hours trying to play Rodgers's songs on a cheap guitar and trying to sing and yodel like his hero. Tubb also lived in San Antonio as a youngster and was able to hear Rodgers's performances on KMAC. At seventeen he apparently had the opportunity to see Rodgers in person but was too frightened to do so. "I was afraid to meet him," Tubb later told an interviewer. "I worshipped him so much, I was afraid he would say or do something that would upset the image I had of him. . . . I was just a kid, but I'm sure he would have been nice to me." Perhaps because he missed a chance to meet his idol, Tubb's worship of the man seemed to grow in intensity after Rodgers's death. He became completely obsessed with America's Blue Yodeler and remained an unwavering fan for the rest of his life. "I know you shouldn't worship anyone in this life," Tubb later said, "but I have to admit I worshipped Jimmie Rodgers, it was that bad. I worshipped him so much that for a time I was convinced that I wouldn't live past the age of thirty-five either."[31]

While Tubb never met Rodgers, he eventually developed a close relationship with Rodgers's widow, Carrie, who helped Tubb's career get off the ground. The two met as a result of Tubb contacting Mrs. Rodgers, hoping to get a large photograph of her husband, suitable for framing, to replace the tattered, wallet-sized photo that he carried around with him. Impressed with Tubb's sincere appreciation for her husband's music, Carrie Rodgers took the young singer under her wing, helped arrange a short tour for Tubb, and in 1936 pulled some strings to get him his first recording session with Bluebird Records, a hillbilly and race label owned by RCA Victor. According to Tubb, Rodgers's wife told him, "You do have feeling in your voice. The audience knows how you feel about the song you are singing, and Jimmie always thought that was the most important thing of all." Mrs. Rodgers also put Tubb in touch with her sister, Jimmie Rodgers's old song writing partner Elsie McWilliams, who provided Tubb with some songs. Carrie also lent Tubb the prized Martin guitar, her husband's favorite performing instrument, to use at his first recording session. Tubb's initial release was a tribute to Jimmie Rodgers written by McWilliams and titled "The Last Thoughts of Jimmie Rodgers."[32]

After a case of tonsillitis altered his voice, Tubb abandoned the idea of imitating Rodgers and developed his own style, scoring a monumental hit in 1941 with "I'm Walking the Floor over You." The song made him a star who would dominate the country scene for years. Tubb was credited with popularizing the "honky tonk" variation of country which, generally defined, blended the singing style, steel guitars, and pop sensibilities of a Jimmie Rodgers record with a healthy dose of Texas swing and a hint of New Orleans ragtime. As the name implies, it was music at home in the barroom that could be raucous and bawdy or, on occasion, lonely and sad, with songs that included colorful characters who drank, cheated, gambled, and had a host of regrets once their personal relationships turned sour. Tubb was also one of the first country singers to move away from acoustic performances and use electric guitars that could be heard over a boisterous beer joint crowd. Tubb's honky tonk style dominated country music from the 1950s forward, with Hank Williams being its most formidable practitioner. Even in the twenty-first century many of the tenets of honky tonk are still part of country-music culture even though in the modern era the lines between pop and country have blurred considerably. During a legendary career that lasted almost a half-century, Ernest Tubb created more musical progeny that could trace their heritage back to Jimmie Rodgers. Just as Rodgers influenced Tubb, Tubb influenced a host of other important artists such as Johnny Cash, George Jones, Hank Williams, and Willie Nelson, who once told an interviewer, "I would compare Ernest Tubb to Frank Sinatra in that both had distinctive styles that you couldn't confuse with anybody else." He was also a hero to a number of female country artists, including Loretta Lynn, who throughout her long career has been referred to as the "Queen of Country Music." "I was raised on Jimmie Rodgers and Ernest Tubb," Lynn once wrote, "[Ernest Tubb] is like a father to me. As far as I'm concerned, Ernest Tubb hung the moon." Through it all and until his death in 1984, Tubb never wavered in his devotion to Jimmie Rodgers, mentioning him by name at concerts, recording his songs, and appearing at functions that paid tribute to Rodgers as the founding father of the country-music industry.[33]

Another influential first-generation Rodgers disciple was Gene Autry. A rancher's son born in 1907, Autry, like Ernest Tubb, started off his career as a Jimmie Rodgers imitator, although Autry was particularly enamored with the special talent that gave America's Blue Yodeler his nickname. Autry would eventually mimic Rodgers's yodel on stage, on record, and in films, making a name for himself as a singing cowboy. During his early career he recorded more than twenty cover versions of Jimmie Rodgers songs, attempting to sound as much like Rodgers on record as possible. Known to many as the "Yodeling Cowboy," Autry parlayed his music career into a movie career that created the template for a generation of singing cowboy movies starring various singers and actors. His image as a western troubadour was almost completely caste from one of Jimmie Rodgers's western-themed personas that Victor had used to market their star in Texas. Autry eventually abandoned Hollywood for a career as an entrepreneur, becoming best known in the late twentieth century as the owner of the California Angels professional baseball team. Roy Rogers, another famous singing cowboy star from the 1950s and an Autry rival, crafted basically the same image for himself, recording Jimmie Rodgers songs during the early stages of his career and sometimes mimicking the Rodgers yodel on record and in films.[34]

Jimmie Rodgers also influenced the career of Bill Monroe, another important figure in country-music history who most people refer to as "the Father of Bluegrass." One of the bluegrass state's most famous native sons, Monroe was born in 1911 in Rosine, Kentucky. He was part of a large musical family and learned to play the guitar and mandolin at an early age. Like Rodgers, Monroe felt the influence of blues music as he was growing up. An African American guitarist and fiddler named Arnold Shultz, who had a day job as a coal miner, tutored Monroe for a time and introduced him to African American music. Monroe played and sang with his brothers until the late 1930s when he formed the original version of his famous band, the Blue Grass Boys. Like other young men of his generation in the South, Bill Monroe grew up in an era when Jimmie Rodgers songs filled the airwaves and left an imprint on all who heard them. In 1939 Monroe and his group auditioned for a regular spot on the Grand Ole Opry by performing the Rodgers classic "Muleskinner Blues" for Opry officials. Bill Monroe and the Blue Grass Boys passed the audition, winning a regular spot on the show and drawing the attention of RCA Victor. "Jimmie Rodgers, he was the first to come out with yodel numbers that I ever got to hear," Monroe later told an interviewer. "He could sing 'em so good; had a wonderful voice and he played a good guitar. I always liked his singing and playing, and I guess that's why I wanted to do "Muleskinner Blues." Monroe and his band followed up their successful audition for the Opry with their first major recording session for RCA Victor, producing a bluegrass cover version of "Muleskinner Blues" that put Monroe on the path to country-music immortality.[35]

Canadian-born Hank Snow, who had a string of major hits during the 1950s and 1960s, also began his career trying to imitate Jimmie Rodgers. Snow was born in Nova Scotia in 1914 and worked on fishing ships as a young man. After hearing Rodgers's music on the radio, Snow purchased a guitar and began taking it with him out to sea, entertaining other hands on the boat with Rodgers songs. He eventually found his own singing and playing style and performed in Canada for many years as "the Yodeling Ranger," a nickname derived directly from his worship of Rodgers. In 1936 a successful radio appearance led to a recording contract with RCA Victor in Canada, and several years later he began recording in the United States. His records sold well, and American radio stations began playing his music more frequently. In 1950 he was invited to play at the Grand Ole Opry, and that same year he recorded his first number-one hit, "I'm Moving On." A string of hits followed as Snow became one of the most successful country artists of the era. Never forgetting his roots, Snow recorded a Jimmie Rodgers tribute album in 1953, but it could never rival the accolade that he had paid his hero some years earlier by naming his only child "Jimmie Rodgers Snow."[36]

While country music may have borrowed more from blues music as it developed than blues borrowed from country, African American artists did not ignore commercial country as it developed side by side with early blues. While bits and pieces of blues lyrics appeared in country songs, snippets of traditional country songs also appeared on early blues records, a true testament to music's ability to break down barriers of race in the South years before the southern states legally removed those barriers. Rodgers was certainly one of the catalysts for this exchange, and he was highly regarded among many members of the blues community. According to one source, Tommy Johnson, a major figure in blues history and a contemporary of Charley Patton, "began his first session for Paramount Records by trying out two versions of a yodeling cowboy number, complete with Jimmie Rodgers–flavored guitar strumming." Bluesman Mississippi John Hurt was known to copy the Rodgers yodel on occasion, as was the talented blues singer and songwriter Skip James. Parts of the Rodgers song "Waiting for a Train" appeared in recordings by African American artists Frank Stokes and Furry Lewis. Robert Johnson, perhaps the most famous blues artist of them all, occasionally performed Rodgers songs on stage as part of a repertoire that included many standards of his day. "The country singer Jimmie Rodgers," Johnny Shines, one of Johnson's contemporaries and musical partners, later recalled, "me and Robert used to play a hell of a lot of his tunes, man, and I liked him. Robert played all that stuff." Just as he provided a direct musical link between Charley Patton and modern rock music, Patton disciple Howlin' Wolf may very well have provided a personal link, at least in musical influence, between Patton and Rodgers. In addition to learning from Patton, Howlin' Wolf once told an interviewer that he listened incessantly to Jimmie Rodgers records as a young man. "I was inspired by the records of Jimmie Rodgers," he said. "I took up that idea [of yodeling] and adapted it to my own abilities. I couldn't do no yodeling, so I turned to howlin' and it's done me just fine." B.B. King, one of the most commercially successful blues singers of all time, also sang along with Rodgers records as a youngster, later telling an interviewer, "Jimmie Rodgers was one of the first country singers to sing blues that black people liked."[37]

As country music continued to evolve, many talented performers came to the forefront, but no country entertainer of the post–World War II period was more dominant than Hank Williams. Born in Mount Olive, Alabama, in 1923, William eventually eclipsed Rodgers in name recognition and became one of the greatest songwriters in the history of American popular music. Ironically, Williams was one of the few country stars of his generation who claimed that he was not heavily influenced by Jimmie Rodgers, at least not directly. This may have been due to Williams being an original and not liking being compared to others even if the comparisons were favorable. However, through the years evidence has suggested that Williams did owe some musical debts to the Blue Yodeler. Williams, like Tubb, Autry, Monroe, and many others, initially walked into the music industry through a door that Jimmie Rodgers opened. Had Rodgers not proved that country music would sell, Hank Williams likely would have never gotten the opportunity to become a star. "Hank was a few years younger, just nine years old when Jimmie died," Williams biographer Colin Escott explained. "Rodgers brought the barroom culture to country music, and inasmuch as Hank's music came from the honky tonk, he was a Rodgers disciple." Williams also yodeled on a number of his songs, though he used the device in a different manner than Rodgers, hitting a high falsetto in the middle of many of his verses rather than yodeling at the end of a verse or treating the yodel as a separate stanza. In 1937 Williams named his backing band the Drifting Cowboys, which would seem to be an homage to the singing cowboy image that Jimmie Rodgers created and Gene Autry helped popularize.

While Williams did not cover any Rodgers songs on record or on stage, there were numerous accounts by his friends of informal, backstage jam sessions that routinely featured Rodgers tunes. A direct musical influence between the two may have been hard to discern, but there was no mistaking that the entertainment persona of Hank Williams mirrored that of Jimmie Rodgers. Both men were born in the poverty-stricken Deep South, both succeeded against the odds, and both lived difficult lives even in the face of success. Both were drinkers, and both died young (Williams in 1953 at age twenty-nine) under tragic circumstances. In short, if Jimmie Rodgers created the original tragic country hero in myth and image, Hank Williams mimicked it perfectly. According to Barry Mazor, "Hank's relationship with Jimmie Rodgers seems obvious on the face of it. In fact, what linked them was not so much any direct, acknowledged musical influence, but an inheritance of style, sensibility, and approach, of how you would carry yourself as a roots music star along the path that Jimmie had first designed and illuminated. And that was no small thing." Williams also contacted Carrie Rodgers on occasion, treating her as a confidante, and Mrs. Rodgers once commented to Ernest Tubb how the career of Hank Williams and the career of her husband paralleled one another.[38]

In 1947, fifteen years after his death, Jimmie Rodgers remained popular among the growing throng of country-music fans. His records continued to sell and a record collector founded a national fan club honoring the singer. Six years later *Billboard* magazine ran a tribute to the singer marking the twentieth anniversary of his death that, in effect, gave Rodgers credit for the careers of every country musician who followed him. Victor released Hank Snow's tribute album that same year and, with the help of country stars like Snow and Ernest Tubb, Meridian, Mississippi began an annual festival to commemorate the life and music of the city's favorite son. The first Jimmie Rodgers Memorial Festival was held during the last week of May in 1953, and some of the biggest country stars of the era attended along with thousands of fans. In addition to performances by Tubb and Snow, audiences heard Bill Monroe, Roy Acuff, Red Foley, Jimmie Davis, Minnie Pearl, Webb Pierce, Bill Bruner, Cowboy Copas, Jimmy Dickens and many others pay tribute to the man that was already being hailed by many as "the Father of Country Music." It was the beginning of an annual event that year after year drew major stars to Meridian to pay tribute their hero. In 1955, while still a regional star, Elvis Presley performed two songs at the event that he had recently recorded at Sun Studios in Memphis, and rode in a parade honoring Rodgers through downtown Meridian. Presley got his love of Jimmie Rodgers music from his mother Gladys, a Rodgers devotee. She played Rodgers' records frequently in her home when the future "King of Rock and Roll" was young, with "Jimmie's Mean Mama Blues" reportedly being her favorite Rodgers song.[39]

While native Mississippian Elvis Presley was exposed to Rodgers's music throughout his childhood, there were few bigger Jimmie Rodgers fans among the first generation of rock and rollers than Jerry Lee Lewis. Born in Ferriday, Louisiana, in 1935, Lewis exploded on the scene during the 1950s playing wild piano and singing songs such as "Whole Lotta Shakin' Goin' On" and "Great Balls of Fire." Lewis himself personified everything that was turbulently glorious and conflicted about southern music. He was a legendary sinner who had at one point studied for the ministry, and while he was heavily influenced by African American blues that he heard as a youngster, he also spent his formative years listening to his father's Jimmie Rodgers records. According to one biographer, Lewis's father, after one particularly successful cotton-planting season, bought an old hand-cranked Victrola and then "went out and bought just about every record that Jimmie Rodgers ever made, and he got good and drunk, and he sang along with them." Lewis routinely sang the tunes with his dad and many years later told interviewers that when he first started playing music he dreamed of one day being as popular as the Rodgers. "You'll never find anyone that Jerry Lee Lewis has ever taken from, brother," Lewis once said. "I'm a stylist. Just like Jimmie Rodgers—the late great Jimmie Rodgers." In the fall of 2010 Lewis celebrated his seventy-fifth birthday at a private party in Memphis where, surrounded by well-wishers, he watched a video tribute to his career that had been prepared specifically for the occasion by those who knew him well. The first image to appear on the screen that night was not ancient footage of Lewis, but an image of the icon's childhood hero Jimmie Rodgers singing "Waiting for a Train," a song that was among a number of Rodgers tunes that Lewis covered during his career.[40]

Johnny Cash also covered "Waiting for a Train" and several other Rodgers classics during his long and storied career. Born in 1932 in Arkansas, Cash came out of the rockabilly world of Lewis, Presley, Carl Perkins, and others who recorded with the Sun label in Memphis during the 1950s. Like Lewis, Cash revered Rodgers and listened to his records over and over again from the time that he was a child. As he was becoming famous in 1957, Cash, like Elvis before him, played the Jimmie Rodgers Memorial Festival in Meridian, where he entertained a crowd of around twenty thousand Rodgers fans. "Jimmie is terribly important to country music," Cash told the gathering between songs. "Not only did he revise and keep alive some old songs . . . but he wrote from a gut level, the life of the working men, the common men, the down and outers, the hobos, the men on the move, the men who built our country." Thirteen years later Cash was an international celebrity with a new variety program airing in the United States on the American Broadcasting Company (ABC) network. The weekly show featured a wide range of musical headliners from rock icons Bob Dylan and Joni Mitchell to country stalwarts the Statler Brothers and Grandpa Jones. In October of 1970 Cash's show featured jazz great Louis "Satchmo" Armstrong, who during a 1930s recording session had played trumpet on Jimmie Rodgers's original recording of "Blue Yodel No. 9 (Standing on the Corner)." "Jimmie said 'I feel like singing some blues,' you know," Armstrong told Cash during the show's taping, "and I said 'ok, daddy, I'm going to blow behind you.' And that's how the session got started." Not long afterwards, Armstrong and Cash recreated the session with a spirited rendition of the tune that had Cash playing and singing the Rodgers parts with Armstrong on trumpet. It was obvious that Cash relished playing the Rodgers song with Armstrong during a period when Cash later recalled that he was "obsessed with Jimmie Rodgers' music."[41]

The list of other artists who have covered Jimmie Rodgers songs through the years is long and varied. It includes many country performers and a host of pop and rock musicians as well. Merle Haggard recorded a well-received tribute album of Rodgers songs in 1969, and the next year Dolly Parton scored her first major hit single with yet another cover of the Rodgers classic "Muleskinner Blues." In addition to Parton's hit version and Bill Monroe's classic bluegrass interpretation, "Muleskinner Blues" has been a source of inspiration for many other musicians and remains one of Rodgers's most frequently covered numbers. British skiffle king Lonnie Donegan recorded a version in 1957, and five years later American singer Harry Bellefonte recorded his rendition for a best-selling album. Connie Francis and Hank Williams Jr. sang the song as a duet during the 1960s, and Van Morrison produced his rendition in 1997. Probably the most unusual version of the song ever committed to disc—and a version that Rodgers himself might have found a little hard to follow—was an interpretation by the punk group the Cramps, who put the song on one of their albums in the 1990s. Dozens of artists from multiple genres have also recorded "Waiting for a Train," one of Rodgers's most popular songs during his lifetime. In addition to Rodgers fanatics Johnny Cash, Jerry Lee Lewis, and Hank Snow, New Orleans blues, rock, and zydeco icon John "Dr. John" Rebennack produced a version of the record in 1983, and in 1997 Dickey Betts, guitarist and founding member of the Allman Brothers Band, recorded a version for one of his solo projects. Even though he never recorded the song with the Beatles or as a solo performer, George Harrison was profoundly affected by the tune as a child. "My dad bought a wind up gramophone in New York when he was a seaman," Harrison once said. "He'd also bought some records from America, including one by Jimmie Rodgers, 'the Singing Brakeman.' . . . The one my dad had was "Waiting for a Train." That led me to the guitar."[42] Other Rodgers tunes have been covered time and again by artists ranging from Fats Domino and George Jones to Emmylou Harris and Lynyrd Skynyrd. In 2000, "In the Jailhouse Now," a song with vaudeville roots that Rodgers reinvented and popularized, was included on the best-selling soundtrack to the popular motion picture *O Brother, Where Art Thou?*

As was the case with Charley Patton, in the waning decades of the twentieth century Jimmie Rodgers and his legacy began attracting the attention of academics and authors studying music and popular culture. Their interest in American roots music and its relationship to modern popular culture in the decades after Rodgers's death fueled a number of studies of what one author referred to as "Country Music Culture."[43] Just as there is no single, definitive starting point for blues—or most types of music, for that matter—country music emerged from an organic blending of ancient sounds and rhythms that are difficult to completely trace. Ballads brought from Europe that were later peppered with a host of other influences, blues prominent among them, somehow gelled to create a type of music that American record companies eventually affixed with the label "hillbilly" and later "country." Still, in all the books, articles, and documentaries related to the history and importance of country music, Jimmie Rodgers is always a central figure. While the type of music that Rodgers played existed before his career began, his popularity is universally cited as the launching point for the modern country industry and particularly the commercial aspects of country as a form of popular entertainment. "Rodgers single handedly originated a new tradition in country music," Bill Malone wrote. "[He] inspired a host of followers, most of whom only heard him on records, to become country musicians. The center of country music activity shifted . . . and a new generation of hillbilly entertainers, captivated by Rodgers' blue yodels, his unorthodox guitar style, and his intriguing songs, began to dominate the country music scene."

Rodgers's music met emerging entertainment technology head on. As Nolan Porterfield pointed out, "In the entertainment world, his life spanned the rise of the phonograph, the flowering of motion picture and radio, the decline and fall of live entertainment in the United States. More than any other entertainer, Rodgers was actively involved in all of it from the grass-roots level. . . .

No one who had been touched by his spell ever forgot." Journalist and southern commentator Paul Hemphill related that Rodgers's lifestyle and notoriety served as an inspiration to generations of country musicians who dreamed of success and the ability to make a good living playing and singing. He was a model that others followed closely. "From the day Rodgers died," Hemphill wrote, "they started coming out of the woods: country boys, many of them trying to emulate Rodgers' blue yodels, seeking out recording executives and straining for the brass ring. The record companies began taking closer note of what would sell and what wouldn't sell, helping create a whole new type of 'country music.'"[44]

In 1958 a large group of country-music performers, record executives, talent and booking agents, songwriters, and broadcasting executives came together to form the Country Music Association (CMA), an organization dedicated to promoting country in the United States and around the world. Three years later, the group created the Country Music Hall of Fame in Nashville to recognize individuals who made major contributions to the development and popularity of the music as an art form. On November 3, 1961, CMA officials announced the first inductees to the Hall of Fame at a banquet held at a Nashville hotel with leading members of the country-music community in attendance. When it came time to announce the first inductee, few were surprised when officials uttered the name "James Charles 'Jimmie' Rodgers," who they credited as "the man who started it all." Also inducted that night were Hank Williams, who had taken country music and the Rodgers legacy to new heights, and music publishing executive Fred Rose.[45] Plaques recognizing the three men went on display at the Grand Ole Opry and the Tennessee State Museum until 1967 when construction was completed on a large building designed specifically to house the Hall of Fame in Nashville. The plaque honoring Rodgers, which was originally unveiled by Rodgers disciple Ernest Tubb, included a bas-relief image of the man, his birth and death dates, and the following inscription:

> Jimmie Rodgers' name stands foremost in the country music
> field as "the man who started it all." His songs told the great stories
> of the singing rails, the powerful steam locomotives and the wonderful
> railroad people that he loved so well. Although small in stature, he was a
> giant among men, starting a trend in the musical taste of millions.

Phenomenally successful, the CMA for decades oversaw the expansion of the country industry to the point that, by the early years of the twenty-first century, country music enjoyed worldwide popularity with more than twenty-three hundred country radio stations in North America alone. If Jimmie Rodgers was indeed "the man who started it all," then the work of the CMA and the worldwide popularity of country music as a multi-billion-dollar concern serve his legacy well. Induction into the Country Music Hall of Fame was one of many posthumous honors Rodgers received as his influence on the music industry as a whole became more widely recognized. In 1970 he was among the first group of songwriters inducted into the national Songwriter's Hall of Fame alongside Irving Berlin, Woody Guthrie, Cole Porter, George Gershwin, W. C. Handy, and Stephen Foster. That same year Rodgers became a charter member of the Nashville Songwriters Hall of Fame, an organization created to specifically honor country songwriters. In 1978 the U.S. Postal Service made Rodgers the first country artist whose likeness was ever reproduced on a postage stamp, and the first in its long-running "performing arts" series. In 1985 the Rodgers classic "Blue Yodel (T for Texas)" received a Grammy Hall of Fame Award, and in 2004 the song joined Charley Patton's "Pony Blues" on the National Recording Registry of the Library of Congress.[46]

While Rodgers was most closely associated with country music, he has also been recognized as a performer whose work affected other genres, most notably blues and rock and roll. As Jocelyn R. Neal stated, "His songs hold the secret of country's relationship to black blues, vaudeville, pop, rock, and, most of all, the concept of the song as a commercial commodity." In Rodgers's home state the relationship between blues and country became evident on May 3, 2007, when the Mississippi Blues Commission unveiled in Meridian the eleventh in a series of markers along the Mississippi Blues Trail. The trail had been commissioned four years earlier to celebrate Mississippi's place as the cradle of the blues and mark important sites in the history of blues music. Since placing the first trail marker at the grave of Charley Patton, the commission had recognized nine other spots in the Mississippi Delta. The new marker honored Jimmie Rodgers, and it was both the first marker placed outside the Delta region and the first paying homage to a white artist. The marker credited Rodgers for establishing "blues as a foundation of country music" and pointed out that as many as a third of Rodgers's songs were recorded in a blues style. Building on the success of the Blues Trail as a tourist attraction, the state

sanctioned the creation of the Mississippi Country Music Trail in 2010, with
the first marker of this project also being placed in Meridian to honor Rodgers
as the "father of country music." In addition to markers on the blues and country trails, Meridian also boasts a Jimmie Rodgers museum that houses many
artifacts celebrating the singer's life and career.[47]

Like rock and roll itself, much of Jimmie Rodgers's music sprang from an
amalgamation of country, blues, and pop rhythms and words. While many
country artists have covered Rodgers's material, a host of veteran rock performers have also recorded his tunes or played his songs in concert, including the Grateful Dead, Bob Dylan, John Fogerty, Dr. John, Van Morrison, John
Mellencamp, and others. "It's a shame in a way that people think of Jimmie
Rodgers as the root of just one thing, when he was a root for so many things,"
Phil Everly, half of the famous Everly Brothers once said. "People will talk
about how rock 'n' roll is just a black thing—but here's your story of how it's
more than that. There's so much of that country in it." There have certainly
been threads of country music in rock and roll from the beginning. Elvis Presley, Jerry Lee Lewis, and the rest of the Sun Records rockabilly pioneers also
recorded country songs. In the 1960s Gram Parsons, first with the Byrds and
later with the Flying Burrito Brothers, helped bring country into rock, and
the Eagles, one of the most powerful bands of the 1970s and beyond, were
obviously familiar with country arrangements. Southern rock icons the Allman Brothers and Lynyrd Skynyrd had country roots with the latter including
a blistering version of "Blue Yodel (T for Texas)" on their popular live album
One More from the Road during the 1970s. Even the Rolling Stones occasionally
recorded a country number during their career.[48]

Like Howlin' Wolf before him, Bob Dylan personifies at least a few threads
of a direct connection between the legacy of Jimmie Rodgers and the legacy
of Charley Patton. Dylan idolized Patton and the blues and folk traditions that
Patton represented. "Please myself," the rock icon once told an interviewer
after being asked about the tunes on a recent album, "If I wanted to do that I
would record some Charley Patton songs." While Dylan spoke of Patton from
time to time during interviews through the years, his respect for the bluesman was apparent during recording sessions for his Time Out of Mind album,
released in 1997. The album included a song titled "Highlands" that featured
Dylan's lyrics over a Charley Patton riff. "I had the guitar run off an old Charley Patton record [in mind] for years and always wanted to do something with

that." Dylan once told an interviewer, "I was sitting around, maybe in the dark Delta or maybe in some unthinkable trench somewhere, with that sound in my mind and the dichotomy of the highlands with that seemed to be a path worth pursuing." Four years later, Dylan released the album *Love and Theft*, which included a song titled "High Water (for Charley Patton)" that was dedicated to the bluesman and obviously recorded as a tribute. The song used the symbolism of the flood and the creeping, destructive floodwaters in much the same manner that Patton did in his 1929 song "High Water Everywhere" to evoke a sense of tragic inevitability. Dylan even included lyrical references to the Mississippi towns of Vicksburg and Clarksdale. At the time of the song's release, author and music critic Greg Kot called it "a kind of homage . . . a sweeping portrait of the South's racial history, with the unsung blues singer as a symbol of the region's cultural richness and ingrained social cruelties." Other commentary about the song also centered on its depth of message. In explaining the overall tone and feel of "High Water (for Charley Patton)," cultural historian Eric Lott wrote that the song was "similar to nineteenth-century minstrel music, which is interesting not only because it's influenced by and dedicated to Delta bluesman Patton, but also because it's a song of high seriousness, as though ultimate truths are rooted in cultural plunder."[49]

Dylan was equally infatuated with Jimmie Rodgers, discovering "America's Blue Yodeler" during the 1950s through his recordings. As an eleven-year-old growing up in Hibbing, Minnesota, Dylan—still known only as Robert Zimmerman—listened to Rodgers records repeatedly and, according to some sources, "wrote" one of his first songs by scribbling the lyrics to Rodgers's "A Drunkard's Child" onto a sheet of paper and signing his own name at the bottom of the page. From that point forward, Dylan was artistically smitten. Reflecting on his early experiences with Rodgers's body of work, he later remarked to an interviewer, "The songs were different than the norm. They had more of an individual nature and an elevated conscience, and I could tell that these songs were from a different period of time. I was drawn to their power." In 1997, the same year that he recorded the Patton-influenced "Highlands" for *Time Out of Mind*, Dylan produced a tribute album to Jimmie Rodgers simply titled *The Songs of Jimmie Rodgers*. The release included cover versions of Rodgers classics performed by a wide range of contemporary artists including Bono, Willie Nelson, Iris Dement, Aaron Neville, Jerry Garcia, Mary Chapin Carpenter, Dwight Yoakam, and John Mellencamp. In addition to producing the record, Dylan contributed a cover of "My Blue-Eyed Jane," a song that Rodgers originally recorded in 1930 during a trip to California. In the liner notes for the album, Dylan wrote, "Jimmie Rodgers of course is one of the guiding lights of the twentieth century, whose way with song has always been an inspiration to those of us who have followed the path. A blazing star whose sound was and remains the raw essence of individuality in a sea of conformity, par excellence with no equal."[50]

Chuck Berry has always been among the handful of artists who began their careers in the 1950s who can lay a significant claim the title "Father of Rock and Roll." He is also another human link between Charley Patton's blues tradition and the country tradition of Jimmie Rodgers. Born in 1926 in St. Louis, Charles Edward Anderson Berry grew up listening to blues music and idolizing jazz and blues guitarists Charlie Christian and T-Bone Walker, as well as Muddy Waters. Berry worked in factories, as a janitor, and at one point went to school to study cosmetology before joining a jazz and blues trio in 1952 that played regularly at the Cosmopolitan Club in St. Louis. Berry's big break came three years later when he visited Chicago and met Waters, who suggested that he go and see Chess Records owner Leonard Chess. Chess recorded Berry's first big hit, "Maybellene," which was a reworking of a traditional country song titled "Ida Red." Berry went on to record a string of enduring hits such as "Johnny B. Goode," "Roll Over Beethoven," and "Sweet Little Sixteen" while gathering devotees from the next generation of rock stars who were coming of age as his career peaked. "If you try to give Rock and Roll another name," John Lennon once said, "you might try Chuck Berry." While Berry's repertoire was influenced by blues, he had many hits that had a country flavor, in part because he wanted to market his music to whites as well as African Americans.

Sometimes Berry's black audiences at the Cosmopolitan Club were confused by his innovations that drew country and blues so close together. "Curiosity provoked me to lay a lot of our country stuff on our predominantly black audience and some of our black audience began whispering 'who is that black hillbilly at the Cosmo?'" Berry once said. "After they laughed at me a few times they began requesting the hillbilly stuff and enjoyed dancing to it." One reason that Berry was able to so easily add a country flavor to his music was because he had grown up listening to Jimmie Rodgers records and routinely tuning in to country radio stations that played Rodgers's songs. Like bluesman Howlin' Wolf, Berry listened to Jimmie Rodgers's music and took at least some of it with him into his own career. Carl Perkins, the rockabilly star who recorded with Sam Phillips at Sun Records, befriended Berry on tour during the 1950s and was surprised that Berry knew so much about Rodgers and the history of country music in general. Perkins often sang Rodgers tunes with Berry on tour buses, with Berry correcting Perkins when he got the lyrics wrong. Later Perkins, still amazed, told an interviewer, "I knew when I first met Chuck that he'd been affected by country music. . . . He knew every blue yodel."[51]

In 1983 several music-industry insiders, including Atlantic Records founder Ahmet Ertegun and *Rolling Stone* magazine founder and publisher Jann Wenner, created the Rock and Roll Hall of Fame to "recognize the contributions of those who have had a significant impact on the evolution, development and perpetuation of rock and roll." In 1986 the Hall of Fame inducted its first class of performers, which naturally included some of the most prominent names in rock history such as Little Richard, Chuck Berry, Elvis Presley, James Brown, Ray Charles, and Buddy Holly. They were each inducted, one by one, at a glamorous ceremony staged in New York City at the Waldorf Astoria Hotel. The first group of inductees also included Jimmie Rodgers as one of the great, early influences who gave rise to rock and roll. According to the Hall of Fame, Rodgers's induction was more than justified because his "combination of blues and hillbilly styles made him a true forebear of rock and roll. . . . [A]mong the most noteworthy of his recordings were his series of 'Blue Yodels,' in which he drew from Appalachian hill ballads, black spirituals, rural blues and white pop music—all elements whose electrified synthesis would serves as the blueprint for rock and roll."[52] It was a fitting accolade for a versatile performer who seemed to possess the magic to make any type of music his own.

Charley Patton and Jimmie Rodgers lived their lives in a segregated society, but on many levels they came from the same place, literally and figuratively. Deep South influences moved both men, as did the constraints of a society where both blacks and whites had a difficult time prospering. Both men drew on the human condition for their subject matter, and both men recorded songs with a wide range of themes from religion and death to hell-raising and sex. Both men played with other musicians on occasion but were in essence solo performers more comfortable with a guitar than with any type of manual labor. Even though both men cavorted with different women, and Rodgers had family, they were basically loners who carried with them inner demons as they moved from place to place between appearances. Both men also had a natural talent for performing. Their brains were somehow designed to take life experiences, the things that they saw and felt, and turn those experiences into songs that evoked a range of emotions and moved people. They could sing a song that made people happy and boisterous, or one that made them sad and reflective. Music also gave both men power in a world where they were otherwise powerless. Without his musical abilities Charley Patton likely would have been just another sharecropper who lived and died in the steamy cotton fields of the Mississippi Delta, and Jimmie Rodgers would probably have been little more than a street kid who spent his adult life grinding out a meager living with the railroad or doing odd jobs. Because they could play music, other people noticed them.

The music of Patton and Rodgers is still vibrant today, but not necessarily in their original forms. Most Patton recordings that survive are scratchy, and his voice is hard to understand. Many of Rodgers's recordings, while of better quality, are also difficult to listen to in an era where modern ears are accustomed to complete clarity and sharpness in their music. The performances of Patton and Rodgers remain alive today in their musical progeny, which includes contemporary artists from all popular genres, many of whom have never heard of the two men. Blues and country music, once considered primitive music for the great unwashed, niche music unworthy of sophisticated notice, has become mainstream, generating new generations of talent each decade and billions of dollars in music sales. If blues and country music, through mutual interaction, helped integrate southern culture long before legal integration took hold, then the process that Patton and Rodgers helped start has almost worked too well with regard to the music itself. While individuality certainly remains the foundational element of any successful modern musical act, there is a certain amount of modern music that has been homogenized to the point where it is difficult to categorize. The mainstream has taken in some elements of country, pop, and even blues and made them almost indistinguishable from one another. Conversely, there are still many musicians who stick to purer strains of country and blues despite the great irony that the purer strains do not usually sell as well, are not played as regularly on mainstream radio, and are not frequently featured on television.

Charley Patton and Jimmie Rodgers were not the only entertainers who performed in the blues or country genres during the early twentieth century. They were not even the very first. Both men drew on other players for inspiration just as they drew on their own experiences and surroundings for material. In the end, however, their talent stood out and stood the test of time. They possessed the indefinable quality of all great musicians, an ability to observe, interpret, and articulate the many complicated facets of human existence in a way that was unique and in a way that touched others. During their lifetimes Patton and Rodgers had no idea that their musical influence would span generations. On the surface they seemed to be simple performers, but in truth they were complex, astute, attentive, and ambitious men with natural gifts that would weigh heavily on the future of popular music in America. Be it blues, country, rock, pop, or anything in between, the ghosts of Charley Patton and Jimmie Rodgers are still among us. The echoes of their songs still resonate and, after almost a century, audiences are still in tune with the musical world that both men helped create.

APPENDIX I
Chronology

1891   (April) Charley Patton is born in Hinds County, Mississippi, near the towns of Edwards and Bolton.

1895   Will Dockery establishes Dockery Farms in Sunflower County, Mississippi. The 10,000-acre cotton plantation would be home to Charley Patton and a host of other blues artists in the first decades of the twentieth century.

1897   (Sept. 8) Jimmie Rodgers is born in Lauderdale County, Mississippi, in the Pine Springs Community near Meridian.

1900–1901   Bill Patton moves his family to Dockery Plantation in Sunflower County, where his son Charley will begin his musical career.

1903   Jimmie Rodgers's mother dies of complications related to tuberculosis.

1905   Charley Patton "takes up with" Roxie Gibson, the first of his reported eight "wives," most of whom he did not legally wed.

1910   Patton writes "Pony Blues," "Banty Rooster Blues," "Down the Dirt Road Blues," and several other songs that will be considered his classics.

1911   (April) Rodgers wins an amateur talent contest in Meridian, runs away to tour briefly with a traveling medicine show.

1917   (May 1) Rodgers marries Stella Kelly. The short-lived union produced a daughter, Kathryn, but the couple separated and eventually divorced.

1917   Patton reportedly diagnosed with a heart problem that left him unfit for military service in World War I.

1920   (April 7) Rodgers marries Carrie Cecil Williamson in Meridian. The union would produce two daughters, only one of whom would survive to adulthood.

1923   Rodgers tours briefly with Billy Terrell's Comedians, a traveling show.

1924   Rodgers is diagnosed with tuberculosis, the disease that will eventually take his life.

1925   Entrepreneur and talent scout Henry C. Speir opens his furniture store on Farish Street in Jackson, Mississippi. There he will record Patton and other blues greats.

1927   Rodgers moves to Ashville, North Carolina, where in April and May he performs at least three times on the WWNC radio. Later in the year (August 4) Rodgers records for the first time at Ralph Peer's makeshift studio in Bristol, Tennessee. On November 30 Rodgers records "Blue Yodel (T for Texas)" at Victor Studios in Camden, New Jersey. The song is his first major hit.

1928   Rodgers begins touring as a headliner on Loew's "Southern Time" circuit. He records more songs, with two recording sessions at Victor's Camden studios and one session in Atlanta. Late in the year Rodgers begins broadcasting a weekly radio program in Washington, DC.

1929   (June) Patton travels by train to Richmond, Indiana, where he records for Paramount Records for the first time. Later in the year (October) Patton and Henry "Son" Sims travel to Grafton, Wisconsin, to record for Paramount.

1929   Rodgers tours with the Paul English Players later on a tour sponsored by the Radio-Keith-Orpheum (RKO) theater chain. He also records a movie short titled *The Singing Brakeman*. Later in the year he moves with his family to a mansion he built in Kerville, Texas, and christened "The Blue Yodeler's Paradise." During the year he takes part in recording sessions in New York (February), Dallas (August, October), New Orleans (November), and Atlanta (November).

1930   Patton travels to Grafton, Wisconsin, with Henry "Son" House, Willie Brown, and Louise Johnson for his final recording session for Paramount. During this period Patton moves in with Bertha Lee Pate, a part-time performing partner who was his last "wife."

1930   On July 12, Rodgers records "Blue Yodel No. 9 (Standin' on the Corner)" with accompaniment by Louis Armstrong on trumpet and Armstrong's wife on piano. Although his health continues to deteriorate, Rodgers tours during the summer with Swain's Follies. He records in June and July at Victor's studios in Hollywood, California.

1931   In February, Rodgers's first wife, Stella Kelly, files a paternity suit on behalf of their daughter Kathryn. Later in the year he is sworn in as an honorary Texas Ranger and takes part in a benefit tour with Will Rogers. Rodgers records in Dallas (January), Louisville (June), and at the Victor studios in Camden (October).

1932   Rodgers begins making fewer personal appearances because of his health. In August he takes part in two recording sessions at the Victor studios in Camden and New York City.

1933   Patton receives a serious wound when his throat is cut, reportedly by a jealous husband. The wound affects Patton's singing somewhat.

1933   In March, Rodgers sells the Blue Yodeler's Paradise in Kerrville. He appears twice a week on a radio program on KMAC in San Antonio, Texas. In May, Rodgers travels to New York for recording sessions at the Victor studios in New York City. On May 24 he makes his final recordings. On May 26 Rodgers dies in New York at his room in the Taft Hotel of complications related to tuberculosis.

1934   In January, Patton and Bertha Lee Pate travel to New York City where Patton records for the American Recording Company (ARC). These are his final recordings. On April 28 Patton dies in the Mississippi Delta, reportedly in a house in Indianola, Mississippi. His death certificate lists the cause of death as a "mitral valve disorder."

APPENDIX II
The Songs

Between them, Charley Patton and Jimmie Rodgers left behind a legacy that changed the course of musical history in America. Below are listed all of the recordings by Patton and Rodgers under headings relating to where and when each song was recorded.

Charley Patton's Recorded Work

Recorded on June 14, 1929, in the Gennett Studio, Richmond, Indiana for Paramount Records

"Pony Blues"
"Mississippi Boweavil Blues"
"Screamin' and Hollerin' the Blues"
"Down the Dirt Road Blues"
"Banty Rooster Blues"
"Pea Vine Blues"
"It Won't Be Long"
"Tom Rushen Blues"
"A Spoonful Blues"
"Shake It And Break It (But Don't Let It Fall Mama)"
"Prayer Of Death Part 1 & 2"
"Lord I'm Discouraged"
"I'm Goin' Home"

Recorded in October 1929 at the Paramount studio in Grafton, Wisconsin

"Going To Move To Alabama"
"Elder Greene Blues"
"Circle Round The Moon"
"Devil Sent The Rain Blues"
"Mean Black Cat Blues"

"Frankie And Albert"
"Some These Days I'll Be Gone"
"Green River Blues"
"Hammer Blues"
"Magnolia Blues"
"When Your Way Gets Dark"
"Heart Like Railroad Steel"
"Some Happy Day"
"You're Gonna Need Somebody When You Die"
"Jim Lee Blues Part 1"
"Jim Lee Blues Part 2"
"High Water Everywhere Part 1"
"High Water Everywhere Part 2"
"Jesus Is A Dying-Bed Maker"
"I Shall Not Be Moved"
"Rattlesnake Blues"
"Running Wild Blues"
"Joe Kirby"
"Mean Black Moan"
"Farrell Blues"
"Come Back Corrina"
"Tell Me Man Blues"
"Be True Be True Blues"

Recorded in 1930 at the Paramount studio in Grafton, Wisconsin

"Dry Well Blues"
"Some Summer Day"
"Moon Going Down"
"Bird Nest Bound"

Recorded January 31, 1934, the American Record Corporation (ARC) studio in New York City

"Jersey Bull Blues"
"High Sheriff Blues"
"Stone Pony Blues"
"34 Blues"
"Love My Stuff"

"Revenue Man Blues"
"Oh Death"
"Troubled 'Bout My Mother"
"Poor Me"
"Hang It On The Wall"
"Yellow Bee"
"Mind Reader Blues"

Jimmie Rodgers's Recorded Work

Recorded On August 4, 1927, by Ralph Peer in Bristol, Tennessee

"The Soldiers Sweetheart"
"Sleep Baby Sleep"

Recorded on November 30, 1927, at Victor Studio 1, Camden, New Jersey

"Ben Dewberry's Final Run"
"Mother Was a Lady"
"Blue Yodel (T for Texas)"
"Away Out on the Mountain"

Recorded on February 14–15, 1928, at Victor Studio 1, Camden, New Jersey

"Dear Old Sunny South by the Sea"
"Treasures Untold"
"The Brakeman's Blues"
"The Sailor's Plea"
"In the Jailhouse Now"
"Blue Yodel No. 2 (My Lovin' Gal, Lucille)"*
"Memphis Yodel"
"Blue Yodel No. 3 (Evening Sun Yodel)"

Recorded on June 12, 1928, at Victor Studio 1, Camden, New Jersey

"My Old Pal"
"Mississippi Moon"

* Though released in sequence, Rodgers's "Blue Yodel" songs that were numbered were not recorded in sequence.

"My Little Old Home Down in New Orleans"
"You and My Old Guitar"
"Daddy and Home"
"My Little Lady"
"I'm Lonely and Blue" (unissued—re-recorded at a later date)
"Lullaby Yodel"
"Never No Mo' Blues"

Recorded on October 20–22, 1928, in Atlanta, Georgia

"My Carolina Sunshine Girl"
"Blue Yodel No. 4 (California Blues)"
"Waiting for a Train"
"I'm Lonely and Blue"

Recorded February 21–23, 1929, at Victor Studios in New York City

"Desert Blues"
"Any Old Time"
"Blue Yodel No. 5 (It's Raining Here)"
"High Powered Mama"
"I'm Sorry We Met"

Recorded on August 8–12, 1929, at the Jefferson Hotel in Dallas, Texas

"Everybody Does It in Hawaii"
"Tuck Away My Lonesome Blues"
"Train Whistle Blues"
"Jimmie's Texas Blues"
"Frankie and Johnny"
"Frankie and Johnny" (unissued)
"Home Call"

Recorded on October 22, 1929, at the Jefferson Hotel in Dallas, Texas

"Whisper Your Mother's Name"
"The Land of My Boyhood Dreams"
"Blue Yodel No. 6 (She Left Me This Mornin')"
"Yodeling Cowboy"

"My Rough and Rowdy Ways"
"I've Ranged, I've Roamed, and I've Traveled"

Recorded on November 13, 1929, in New Orleans

"Hobo Bill's Last Ride"

Recorded on November 25–28, 1929, in Atlanta,

"Mississippi River Blues"
"Nobody Knows But Me"
"Anniversary Blue Yodel"
"She Was Happy Till She Met You"
"Blue Yodel No. 11 (I've Got a Gal)"
"A Drunkard's Child"
"That's Why I'm Blue"
"Why Did You Give Me Your Love?"

Recorded between June 30 and July 17, 1930, at Victor Studios in Hollywood, California

"My Blue-Eyed Jane"
"Why Should I Be Lonely"
"Moonlight and Skies"
"Pistol Packin' Papa"
"Take Me Back Again"
"Those Gambler's Blues"
"I'm Lonesome Too"
"The One Rose"
"For The Sake of Days Gone By" (unissued)
"For The Sake of Days Gone By"
"Jimmie's Mean Mama Blues"
"The Mystery of Number Five"
"Blue Yodel No. 8 (Muleskinner Blues)"
"In The Jailhouse Now No. 2"
"Blue Yodel No. 9 (Standin' on the Corner)"
"The Pullman Porters"

Recorded January 31, 1931, at the Texas Hotel in San Antonio, Texas

"T.B. Blues"
"Travellin' Blues"
"Jimmie The Kid"

Recorded June 10–17, 1931, in Louisville, Kentucky

"Why There's a Tear In My Eye"
"The Wonderful City"
"Let Me Be Your Sidetrack"
"Jimmie Rodgers Visits the Carter Family" (unissued)
"The Carter Family and Jimmie Rodgers in Texas" (unissued)
"Jimmie Rodgers Visits the Carter Family"
"The Carter Family and Jimmie Rodgers in Texas"
"When the Cactus Is in Bloom"
"Gamblin Polka Dot Blues"
"Looking For A New Mama"
"What's It?"
"My Good Gal's Gone Blues"
"Southern Cannon-Ball"

Recorded on October 27, 1931, at Victor Studios, Camden, New Jersey

"Rodger's Puzzle Record

Recorded on February 2–6, 1932, at the Jefferson Hotel in Dallas

"Roll Along, Kentucky Moon"
"Hobo's Meditation"
"My Time Ain't Long"
"Ninety-nine Year Blues"
"Mississippi Moon"
"Down the Old Road to Home"
"Blue Yodel No. 10 (Ground Hog Rootin' in My Back Yard)"
"Home Call"

Recorded August 10–16, 1932, at Victor Studio 2, Camden, New Jersey

"In the Hills of Tennessee" (unissued, remade at a later date)
"Mother, the Queen of My Heart"
"Prohibition Has Done Me Wrong" (unissued)
"Rock All Our Babies to Sleep"
"Whippin' That Old T.B."
"No Hard Times"
"Long Tall Mama Blues"
"Peach Pickin' Time Down in Georgia"
"Gambling Bar Room Blues"
"I've Only Loved Three Women"

Recorded August 29, 1932, at Victor Studio 1, New York City

"In the Hills of Tennessee"
"Prairie Lullaby"
"Miss the Mississippi and You"
"Sweet Mama Hurry Home"

Recorded May 17–24, 1933, at Victor Studio 1, New York City

"Blue Yodel No. 12 (Barefoot Blues)"
"Dreaming with Tears in My Eyes"
"The Cowhand's Last Ride"
"I'm Free (from the Chain Gang Now)"
"Dreaming with Tears in My Eyes" (second take)
"Yodeling My Way Back Home"
"Jimmie Rodgers' Last Blue Yodel"
"The Yodeling Ranger"
"Old Pal of My Heart"
"Old Love Letters"
"Mississippi Delta Blues"
"Somewhere Down below the Dixon Line"
"Years Ago"

NOTES

Introduction

Epigraph: Richard Kostelanetz, *The B.B. King Reader: 6 Decades of Commentary* (Milwaukee: Hal Leonard Corporation, 2005), 158.

1. For an account of Rodgers's death, see Nolan Porterfield, *Jimmie Rodgers: The Life and Times of America's Blue Yodeler* (Urbana: University of Illinois Press, 1992), 351–55. This is an outstanding biography of Jimmie Rodgers, a definitive account.

2. For an account of Patton's death, see Stephen Calt and Gayle Dean Wardlow, *King of the Delta Blues: The Life and Music of Charley Patton* (Newton, NJ: Rock Chapel Press, 1988), 247–49.

3. Bill C. Malone, *Don't Get Above Your Raisin': Country Music and the Southern Working Class* (Champaign: University of Illinois Press, 2002), 13; David Evans, *Big Road Blues: Tradition and Creativity in Folk Blues* (New York: Da Capo Press, 1987), 20.

4. John A. Burrison, ed., *Storytellers: Folktales and Legends from the South* (Athens: University of Georgia Press, 1989), 1.

5. For very good general treatments of post–Civil War southern history, see Edward Ayers, *The Promise of the New South: Life After Reconstruction* (New York: Oxford University Press); James C. Cobb, *Redefining Southern Culture: Mind and Identity in the Modern South* (Athens: University of Georgia Press, 1999); Howard Rabinowitz, *The First New South, 1865–1920* (Arlington Heights, IL: Harlan Davidson, 1992); Gavin Wright, *Old South, New South: Revolutions in the Southern Economy since the Civil War* (Baton Rouge: Louisiana State University Press, 1996). For the quote from Howlin' Wolf, see Jesse R. Steinberg and Abrol Fairweather, eds., *Blues-Philosophy for Everyone: Thinking Deep About Feeling Low* (West Sussex, UK: John Wiley and Sons, 2012), 168.

6. James P. Kraft, *Stage to Studio: Musicians and the Sound Revolution, 1890–1950* (Baltimore: Johns Hopkins University Press, 1996), 8.

7. Ayers, *The Promise of the New South*, 195–97. For more detailed discussions of sharecropping, see Edward Royce, *The Origins of Southern Sharecropping* (Philadelphia: Temple University Press, 1994), and Harold D. Woodman, *New South—New Law: Legal Foundations of Credit and Labor Relations in the Postbellum Agricultural South* (Baton Rouge: Louisiana State University Press, 1995).

8. Ayers, *The Promise of the New South*, 195–97; Porterfield, *Jimmie Rodgers*, 24–27. "Waiting on a Train," words and music by Jimmie Rodgers. Copyright 1928 by Peer International Cor-

poration. Copyright renewed. International copyright secured. Used by permission. All rights reserved.

9. "Train Whistle Blues," words and music by Jimmie Rodgers. Copyright 1930 by Peer International Corporation. Copyright renewed. International copyright secured. Used by permission. All rights reserved.

10. Paul Henry Lang, *Music in Western Civilization* (New York: W. W. Norton and Co., 1941), 109–11; Andrea L. Stanton, ed., *Cultural Sociology of the Middle East, Asia, and Africa: An Encyclopedia* (Thousand Oaks, CA: SAGE, 2012), vol. 4: 150–51.

11. Dora Lowenstein, Philip Dodd, and Charlie Watts, eds., *According to the Rolling Stones* (San Francisco: Chronicle Books, 2003), 16.

Chapter One

Epigraph: Johnny Cash with Patrick Carr. *Johnny Cash: The Autobiography.* New York: HarperCollins, 1997, 16.

1. Darden Asbury Pyron, *Southern Daughter: The Life of Margaret Mitchell* (New York: Oxford University Press, 1991), 34; Ayers, *The Promise of the New South*, 373–75; James McBride Dabbs, *The Southern Heritage* (New York: Knopf, 1958), 72, 260–64.

2. Frank E. Grizzard and Daniel Boyd Smith, *Jamestown Colony: A Political, Social, and Cultural History* (Santa Barbara, CA: ABC-CLIO, 2007), 198, 395; Tim Hashaw, *Children of Perdition: Melungeons and the Struggle of Mixed America* (Macon, GA: Mercer University Press, 2006), 18–19.

3. John Boles, *Black Southerners, 1619–1869* (Lexington: University of Kentucky Press, 1984), 18–19.

4. For treatments of the origins of slavery, see Winthrop D. Jordan, *White over Black: American Attitudes toward the Negro, 1550–1812* (Chapel Hill: University of North Carolina Press, 1968), and Ira Berlin, *Many Thousands Gone: The First Two Centuries of Slavery in North America* (Cambridge, MA: Harvard University Press, 2003).

5. 1860 U.S. Census, Hinds County, Mississippi; Mississippi Commission on the War Between the States, *Journal of the State Convention and Ordinances and Resolutions Adopted in 1861* (Jackson, MS: By the Commission, 1962), 86; Ben Wynne, *Mississippi's Civil War: A Narrative History* (Macon, GA: Mercer University Press, 2006), 205–6.

6. John Dollard, *Cast and Class in a Southern Town* (New Haven, CT: Yale University Press, 1937), 186; Philip D. Morgan, *Slave Counterpoint: Black Culture in the Eighteenth-Century Chesapeake and Lowcountry* (Chapel Hill: University of North Carolina Press, 1998), 261.

7. John Michael Giggie, *After Redemption: Jim Crow and the Transformation of African American Religion in the Delta, 1875–1915* (New York: Oxford University Press), 77–81.

8. Houston A. Baker Jr., *Turning South Again* (Durham, NC: Duke University Press, 2001), 90–92.

9. Neil R. McMillen, *Dark Journey: Black Mississippians in the Age of Jim Crow* (Chicago: University of Illinois Press, 1990), 286–87; Jennifer Lynn Ritterhouse, *Growing Up Jim Crow: How*

Black and White Southern Children Learned Race (Chapel Hill: University of North Carolina Press, 2006), 23–25.

10. Gayle Graham Yates, *Life and Death in a Small Southern Town: Memories of Shubuta, Mississippi* (Baton Rouge: Louisiana State University Press, 2004), 62; Grace Elizabeth Hale, *Making Whiteness: The Culture of Segregation in the South, 1890–1940* (New York: Vintage Books, 1998), 9–19.

11. James P. Coleman, "The Mississippi Constitution of 1890 and the Final Decade of the Nineteenth Century," in Richard Aubrey McLemore, ed., *A History of Mississippi* (Hattiesburg: University and College Press of Mississippi, 1973), 8.

12. This flag is the current (2013) state flag of Mississippi.

13. Jerrold M. Packard, *American Nightmare: The History of Jim Crow* (New York: St. Martin's Press, 2002), 69.

14. Stewart Emory Tolnay and E. M. Beck, *A Festival of Violence: An Analysis of Southern Lynchings, 1882–1930* (Champaign: University of Illinois Press, 1995), 18–19.

15. Joseph A. Ranney, *In the Wake of Slavery: Civil War, Civil Rights, and the Reconstruction of Southern Law* (Westport, CT: Praeger Publishing, 2006), 46–49; Dollard, *Cast and Class in a Southern Town*, 173–74; J. Wayne Flynt, *Poor But Proud: Alabama's Poor Whites* (Tuscaloosa: University of Alabama Press, 2001), 48; Richard K. Scher, *Politics in the New South: Republicanism, Race, and Leadership in the Twentieth Century* (Armonk, NY: M. E. Sharp, 1997), 56; Bradley G. Bond, *Political Culture in the Nineteenth-Century South: Mississippi 1830–1900* (Baton Rouge: Louisiana State University Press, 1995), 180–82.

16. Bill C. Malone, *Country Music, U.S.A.* (Austin: University of Texas Press, 1991), 129–31.

17. James C. Cobb, *The Most Southern Place on Earth: The Mississippi Delta and the Roots of Regional Identity* (New York: Oxford University Press, 1992), 97–100. Cobb's book is an outstanding treatment of the history of the Mississippi Delta; R. Douglas Hurt, *American Agriculture: A Brief History* (West Lafayette, IN: Purdue University Press, 2002), 167–70. Also, for more on the origins of sharecropping see Royce, *The Origins of Southern Sharecropping.*

18. John Hope Franklin, *Reconstruction After the Civil War*, 2nd ed. (Chicago: University of Chicago Press, 1994), 212; Eric Foner, *Nothing But Freedom: Emancipation and Its Legacy* (Baton Rouge: Louisiana State University Press, 1983), 45; B.B. King with David Ritz, *Blues All Around Me: The Autobiography of B.B. King* (New York: Avon Books, 1996), 36.

19. Gerhard Kubik, *Africa and the Blues* (Jackson: University Press of Mississippi, 1999), 26.

20. Barbara Wilcots, "African-American Folk Culture," in Joseph M. Flora, Lucinda H. MacKethan, Todd W. Taylor, eds., *The Companion to Southern Literature: Themes, Genres, Places, People, Movements and Motifs* (Baton Rouge: Louisiana State University Press, 2002), 8; Robert Palmer, *Deep Blues* (New York: Penguin Books, 1981), 33.

21. Giles Oakley, *The Devil's Music: A History of the Blues* (De Capo Press, Inc., 1997), 35.

22. James Oliver Horton and Lois E. Horton, *Slavery and the Making of America* (New York: Oxford University Press, 2005), 125; King with Ritz, *Blues All Around Me*, 8–9; John W. Blassingame, *The Slave Community: Plantation Life in the Antebellum South* (New York: Oxford University Press, 1979) 122–25; Frederick Douglass, *Narrative of the Life of Frederick Douglas, an American Slave, Written by Himself*, 6th ed. (London: H. G. Collins, 1851), 20.

23. Sandra L. Beckett, *Transcending Boundaries: Writing for a Dual Audience of Children and Adults* (New York: Garland Publishing, 1999), 152–56; Kellie Jones and Imamu Amiri Baraka, *EyeMinded: Living and Writing Contemporary Art* (Durham, NC: Duke University Press, 2011), 90–92; Lawrence W. Levine, *Black Culture and Black Consciousness: Afro-American Folk Thought from Slavery to Freedom* (New York: Oxford University Press, 1977), 296–98.

24. Catherine Silk and John Silk, *Racism and Anti-Racism in American Popular Culture: Portrayals of African-Americans in Fiction and Film* (Manchester, UK: Manchester University Press, 1990), 8–9; Andrew E. Taslitz, *Reconstructing the Fourth Amendment: A History of Search and Seizure, 1789–1868* (New York: New York University Press, 2006), 92, 98; William W. Freehling, *The Road to Disunion: Secessionists at Bay, 1776–1854* (New York: Oxford University Press, 1990), 84–86; R. A. Lawson, *Jim Crow's Counterculture: The Blues and Black Southerners, 1890–1945* (Baton Rouge: Louisiana State University Press, 2010), ix–xi.

25. Eugene D. Genovese, *Roll Jordan Roll: The World the Slaves Made* (New York: Vintage Books 1976), 183–94; for discussions of the passage from Ephesians (6:5) and others related to the slavery issue, see: Molly Oshatz, *Slavery and Sin: The Fight Against Slavery and the Rise of Liberal Protestantism* (New York: Oxford University Press, 2012), 8–11, and Emmanuel L. McCall, *When All God's Children Get Together: A Memoir of Baptists and Race* (Macon, GA: Mercer University Press, 2007), 22–24.

26. Albert J. Raboteau, *Slave Religion: The Invisible Institution in the South* (New York: Oxford University Press, 2004), 311–12; Blassingame, *The Slave Community*, 137–47; Houston A. Baker Jr. *Long Black Song: Essays in Black American Literature and Culture* (Charlottesville: University Press of Virginia, 1972), 12–13.

27. Raboteau, *Slave Religion*, 65.

28. Dena J. Epstein, *Sinful Tunes and Spirituals: Black Folk Music to the Civil War* (Champaign: University of Illinois Press, 2003), 130.

29. Eric Foner, *Reconstruction: America's Unfinished Revolution, 1863–1877* (New York: Harper and Row Publishers, 1988), 93.

30. Charles Reagan Wilson, *Judgment & Grace in Dixie: Southern Faiths from Faulkner to Elvis* (Athens: University of Georgia Press, 1995), 11.

31. James H. Cone. *The Spirituals and the Blues: an Interpretation* (New York: Seabury Press, 1971), 5.

32. Thomas Wentworth Higginson, *The Writings of Thomas Wentworth Higginson: Army Life in a Black Regiment* (Cambridge, MA: Riverside Press, 1900), 298; A. E. Perkins, "Negro Spirituals from the Far South," *Journal of American Folklore* 35, no. 137 (July–Sept. 1922): 223–49; Blassingame, *The Slave Community*, 138–40; Charles Joiner, "A Single Southern Culture: Cultural Interaction in the Old South" in Ted Ownby, ed., *Black and White Cultural Interaction in the Antebellum South* (Jackson: University Press of Mississippi, 1993), 17.

33. William Ferris, *Blues from the Delta* (New York: Da Capo Press, 1984), 28; Jeff Todd Titon, *Early Downhome Blues: A Musical and Cultural Analysis* (Chapel Hill: University of North Carolina Press, 1994), 17–18.

34. Michael W. Harris, *The Rise of Gospel Blues: The Music of Thomas Andrew Dorsey in the Urban Church* (New York: Oxford University Press, 1992), 154–56; Paul Harvey, *Freedom's Coming:*

Religious Culture and the Shaping of the South from the Civil War through the Civil Rights Era (Chapel Hill: University of North Carolina Press, 2005), 159–60; Albert Murray, *Stomping the Blues* (New York: De Capo Press, 2000), 230; King with Ritz, *Blues All Around Me*, 75.

35. Kubik, *Africa and the Blues*, 24; Francis Davis, *The History of the Blues: The Roots, the Music, the People from Charley Patton to Robert Cray* (New York: Hyperion, 1995), 112; Samuel Charters, *The Legacy of the Blues: Art and Lives of Twelve Great Bluesmen* (New York: Da Capo Press, 1977), 62. Lang, *Music in Western Civilization*, 109–11; Stanton, ed., *Cultural Sociology of the Middle East, Asia, and Africa*, 150–51.

36. Peter Kolchin, *American Slavery, 1619–1877* (New York: Hill and Wang, 1993), 101–3; Jeff Forret, *Race Relations at the Margins: Slaves and Poor Whites in the Antebellum Countryside* (Baton Rouge: Louisiana State University Press, 2006), 15–17; Genovese, *Roll Jordan Roll*, 3; Michael Angelo Gomez, *Exchanging Our Country Marks: The Transformation of African Identities in the Colonial and Antebellum South* (Chapel Hill: University of North Carolina Press, 1998), 176–78; Cash with Carr, *Johnny Cash*.

37. James H. Webb, *Born Fighting: How the Scots-Irish Shaped America* (New York: Broadway Books, 2004), 5, 88; Grady McWhiney, *Cracker Culture: Celtic Ways in the Old South* (Tuscaloosa: University of Alabama Press, 1988), xiv–xv.

38. McWhiney, *Cracker Culture*, 12–14; Wynne, *Mississippi's Civil War*, 4–5; John R. Commons, Ulrich B. Phillips, Eugene Gilmore, Helen L. Sumner, and John B. Andrews, eds., *A Documentary History of American Industrial Society* (Cleveland: Arthur H. Clark Co., 1910), vol. 2: 256.

39. Malone, *Country Music, U.S.A.*, 14–15.

40. Ibid., 4; Norm Cohen, *Long Steel Rail: The Railroad in American Folksong*, 2nd ed. (Champaign: University of Illinois Press, 2000), 26.

41. Joseph Harris, *The Ballad and Oral Literature* (Cambridge, MA: Harvard University Press, 1991), 46–47; Evans, *Big Road Blues*, 44–45.

42. Gary Scott Smith, *Heaven in the American Imagination* (New York: Oxford University Press, 2011), 68–69; Samuel S. Hill Jr., *The South and the North in American Religion* (Macon, GA: Mercer University Press, 2007), 21–22

43. Psalms 98:4.

44. Malone, *Country Music, U.S.A.*, 12; William G. Roy, *Reds, Whites, and Blues: Social Movements, Folk Music, and Race in the United States* (Princeton, NJ: Princeton University Press, 2010), 184–85.

45. J. Wayne Flynt, "Alabama," in Samuel S. Hill, ed., *Religion in the Southern States: A Historical Study* (Macon, GA: Mercer University Press, 1983), 8.

46. Baker, *Long Black Song*, 12–13; Maxine L. Grossman, "Jesus, Mama, and the Constraints of Salvific Love in Contemporary Country Music," in Michael J. Gilmour, ed., *Call Me the Seeker: Listening to Religion in Popular Music* (New York: Continuum International, 2005), 269; Robert Baylor Semple and George William Beale, *A History of the Rise and Progress of the Baptists in Virginia* (Richmond, VA: Pitt & Dickinson, 1894), 57–58; J. Wayne Flynt, *Dixie's Forgotten People, New Edition: The South's Poor Whites* (Bloomington: Indiana University Press, 2004), 121.

47. "A Drunkard's Child," words and music by Jimmie Rodgers and Andrew Jenkins. Copyright 1930 by Peer International Corporation. Copyright renewed. International copyright secured. Used by permission. All rights reserved.

48. Michael P. Graves and David Fillingim, eds., *More Than Precious Memories: The Rhetoric of Southern Gospel Music* (Macon, GA: Mercer University Press, 2004), 10; Don Cusic, *The Sound of Light: A History of Gospel and Christian Music* (Milwaukee: Hal Leonard Corporation), 154–56. James R. Goff, *Close Harmony: A History of Southern Gospel* (Chapel Hill: University of North Carolina Press, 2002), 198–200.

49. Oakley, *The Devil's Music*, 15; For a good treatment of the history of the violin, see David Schoenbaum, *The Violin: A Social History of the World's Most Versatile Instrument* (New York: W. W. Norton & Co., 2012); Chris Goertzen, *Southern Fiddlers and Fiddle Contests* (Jackson: University Press of Mississippi, 2008), 7.

50. Karen Linn, *That Half-Barbaric Twang: The Banjo in American Popular Culture* (Champaign: University of Illinois Press, 1991), 1, 75–76; Thomas Jefferson, *Notes on the State of Virginia by Thomas Jefferson* (Richmond, VA: J. W. Randolph, 1853), 15; Kubik, *Africa and the Blues*, 8.

51. Ken Vose, *Blue Guitar* (San Francisco: Chronicle Books, 1994), 14–16; for a full treatment of the history of the guitar and the Martin Company, see Philip F. Gura, *C. F. Martin and His Guitars, 1796–1873* (Chapel Hill: University of North Carolina Press, 2003).

52. Henry Louis Gates Jr., *The Signifying Monkey: A Theory of African American Literary Criticism* (New York: Oxford University Press, 1988), 1–12, 110–12; Eric Lott, *Love and Theft: Blackface Minstrelsy and the American Working Class* (New York: Oxford University Press, 1993), 4–5; Margaret McKee and Fred Chisenhall, *Beale Black & Blue: Life and Music on Black America's Main Street* (Baton Rouge: Louisiana State University Press, 1993), 195; Ayers, *The Promise of the New South*, 376–77; Ted Gioia, *Delta Blues: The Life and Times of Mississippi Masters Who Revolutionized American Music* (New York: W. W. Norton & Co., 2008), 26.

53. W. T. Lhamon, ed., *Jim Crow, American: Selected Songs and Plays* (Cambridge, MA: Harvard University Press, 2003), xxx; Lott, *Love and Theft*, 5, 94; Davis, *The History of the Blues*, 37; Nick Tosches, *Country: The Twisted Roots of Rock and Roll* (New York: Da Capo Press, 1985), 109–10.

54. Fred J. Hay, ed., *Goin' Back to Sweet Memphis: Conversations with the Blues* (Athens: University of Georgia Press, 2001), 86; Peter C. Muir, *Long Lost Blues: Popular Blues in America, 1850–1920* (Champaign: University of Illinois Press, 2010), 25–27; Davis, *The History of the Blues*, 88; Jaqui Malone, *Steppin' on the Blues: The Visible Rhythms of African American Dance* (Champaign: University of Illinois Press, 1996), 67; Elizabeth Schlappi, *Roy Acuff: The Smoky Mountain Boy* (Gretna, LA: Pelican Publishing, 1993), 20–22.

55. Daniel J. Levitin, *This Is Your Brain on Music: The Science of Human Expression* (New York: Penguin Group, 2006), 261.

56. Tony Russell, *Blacks, Whites, and Blues* (New York: Stein and Day, 1970), 10.

Chapter Two

1. For information on the Vicksburg campaign, see William L. Shea and Terrence J. Winschel, *Vicksburg Is the Key: The Struggle for the Mississippi River* (Lincoln: University of Nebraska Press, 2003), or Edwin Cole Bearss, *The Vicksburg Campaign*, 3 vols. (Dayton, OH: Morningside

Press, 1986). These are just two of a number of works on the campaign that are in print.; U.S. Census, 1900, Hinds County, Mississippi.

2. Calt and Wardlow, *King of the Delta Blues*, 48; U.S. Census, 1900, Hinds County, Mississippi.

3. David Honeyboy Edwards, Janis Martinson, and Michael Robert Frank, *The World Don't Owe Me Nothing: The Life and Times of Delta Bluesman Honeyboy Edwards* (Chicago: Chicago Review Press, 1997), 92; James Segrest and Mark Hoffman, *"Moanin' After Midnight": The Life and Times of Howlin' Wolf* (New York: Pantheon Books, 2004), 20; Paul Oliver, *Blues Fell This Morning: Meaning in the Blues* (Cambridge, UK: Cambridge University Press, 1991), 76–77; Levine, *Black Culture and Black Consciousness*, 291.

4. U.S. Census, 1870, DeSoto County, Mississippi; U.S. Census, 1880, Coahoma County, Mississippi; U.S. Census, DeSoto County, 1860; U.S. Census, 1850, DeSoto County, Mississippi.

5. Calt and Wardlow, *King of the Delta Blues*, 44–46; U.S. Census, 1850, Desoto County, Mississippi; David Evans, Charley Patton Biography, Part 1, Paramountshome.org (accessed April 22, 2013).

6. Evans, Charley Patton Biography, Part 1.

7. Jim O'Neal, Amy Van Singel, eds., *The Voice of the Blues: Classic Interviews from Living Blues Magazine* (New York: Routledge, 2003), 81; Evans, *Big Road Blues*, 175.

8. Christopher A. Waterman, "Race Music: Bo Chatmon, 'Corrina, Corrina,' and the Excluded Middle," in Ronald Michael Radano and Philip Vilas Bohlman, eds., *Music and the Racial Imagination* (Chicago: University of Chicago Press, 2000), 174.

9. Adam Gussow, *Journeyman's Road: Modern Blues Lives from Faulkner's Mississippi to Post-9/11 New York* (Knoxville: University of Tennessee Press, 2007), 137; Gioia, *Delta Blues*, 49–52.

10. Waterman, "Race Music," 174; Ben Sidran, *Black Talk* (New York: Da Capo Press, 1981), 24.

11. U.S. Census 1900, Hinds County, Mississippi.

12. Cobb, *The Most Southern Place on Earth*, 3.

13. Qtd. from William Faulkner, *The Mansion* (New York: Knopf Doubleday, 1965), 53.

14. James C. Cobb, ed., *The Mississippi Delta and the World: The Memoirs of David L. Cohn* (Baton Rouge: Louisiana State University Press, 1995), 3; U.S. Census, 1840, Washington County, Mississippi.

15. James T. Currie, *Enclave: Vicksburg and Her Plantations, 1863–1870* (Jackson: University Press of Mississippi, 1980), 172–74; Cobb, *The Most Southern Place on Earth*, 97.

16. Cobb, *The Most Southern Place on Earth*, 97.

17. This figure comes from census data for the following Mississippi Delta counties in 1900: Bolivar, Carroll, Coahoma, Desoto, Holmes, Humphreys, Issaquena, Leflore, Panola, Quitman, Sharkey, Sunflower, Tallahatchie, Tunica, Warren, Washington, and Yazoo.

18. Cobb, *The Most Southern Place on Earth*, 98; Ward H. Rodgers, "Sharecroppers Drop Color Line," *The Crisis* 24, no. 6 (June 1935): 168–69, 178; Nicholas Lemann, *The Promised Land: The Great Black Migration and How It Changed America* (New York: Vintage Books, 1991), 30–31; J. William Harris, *Deep Souths: Delta, Piedmont and Sea Island Society in the Age of Segregation* (Baltimore: Johns Hopkins University Press, 2001), 79–80.

19. Charles Sallis and James W. Loewen, *Mississippi: Conflict and Change* (New York: Pantheon Books, 1974), 204.

20. Leon F. Litwack, *Trouble in Mind: Southerners in the Age of Jim Crow* (New York: Alfred A. Knopf, Inc., 1998), 123; McMillen, *Dark Journey,* 245–47.

21. William Cohen, *At Freedom's Edge: Black Mobility and the Southern White Quest for Racial Control, 1861–1915* (Baton Rouge: Louisiana State University Press, 1991), 271–72.

22. U.S. Census, Desoto County, Mississippi, 1860, 1870, 1880, 1900; Chi Si Fraternity, *The Sixth Decennial Catalogue of the Chi Si Fraternity* (Auburn, NY: Knapp, Peck and Thomson, 1902), 383; University of Mississippi, *Historical Catalogue of the University of Mississippi, 1849–1909* (Nashville: Marshall & Bruce Co., 1910), 207. Some sources claim that Dockery graduated from the University of Mississippi in either 1885, 1886, or 1889. In the *Historical Catalogue of the University of Mississippi* he is listed as a "new student" in 1885.

23. Calt and Wardlow, *King of the Delta Blues,* 70–71.

24. Davis, *The History of the Blues,* 101; Rand McNally & Co., *The Rand-McNally Official Railway Guide and Hand Book* (Chicago: American Railway Guide Co., 1902), 413; Nick Salvatore, *Singing in a Strange Land: C. L. Franklin, the Black Church, and the Transformation of America* (New York: Little, Brown and Co., 2005), 10.

25. Harris, *Deep Souths,* 188; James C. Giesen, *Boll Weevil Blues: Cotton, Myth, and Power in the American South* (Chicago: University of Chicago Press, 2011), 95–96.

26. Giggie, *After Redemption,* 10; J. Todd Moye, *Let the People Decide: Black Freedom and White Resistance in Sunflower County, Mississippi, 1945–1986* (Chapel Hill: University of North Carolina Press, 2004), 13–18.

27. Charles K. Wolfe and Kip Lornell, *The Life and Legend of Leadbelly* (New York: Da Capo Press, 1992), 85–87; Daniel E. Beaumont, *Preachin' the Blues: The Life and Times of Son House* (New York: Oxford University Press, 2011), 76.

28. Roger Stolle, *Hidden History of Blues in Mississippi* (Charleston, SC: History Press, 2011), 64–66; Calt and Wardlow, *King of the Delta Blues,* 82.

29. Gioia, *Delta Blues,* 112; Beaumont, *Preachin' the Blues,* 50; Nigel Williamson, *The Rough Guide to the Blues* (London: Rough Guides, Ltd., 2007), 120; Samuel Charters, *The Blues Makers* (New York: Da Capo Press, 1991); 36.

30. William Christopher Handy, *Father of the Blues: An Autobiography* (New York: Da Capo Press, 1969), 77.

31. In the song, "Sunflower" is a reference to Sunflower Avenue, a street in Clarksdale.

32. Handy, *Father of the Blues,* 74; Samuel Charters, *The Poetry of the Blues* (New York: Oak Publications, 1963), 12.

33. Beaumont, *Preachin' the Blues,* 35; Calt and Wardlow, *King of the Delta Blues,* 110.

34. Ayers, *The Promise of the New South,* 392; Stephen Calt, *Barrelhouse Words: A Blues Dialect Dictionary* (Champaign: University of Illinois Press, 2009), 12.

35. Edwards, Martinson, and Frank, *The World Don't Owe Me Nothing,* 91–92.

36. Calt and Wardlow, *King of the Delta Blues,* 27, 36–37.

37. Evans, Charley Patton Biography, Part 2, Paramountshome.org (accessed March 26, 2013).

38. Calt and Wardlow, *King of the Delta Blues*, 38, 83, 149.

39. "Blue Yodel No. 3 (Evening Sun Yodel)," words and music by Jimmie Rodgers. Copyright 1928 by Peer International Corporation. Copyright renewed. International copyright secured. Used by permission. All rights reserved.

40. Paul Oliver, *Screening the Blues: Aspects of the Blues Tradition* (New York: Da Capo Press, 1968), 249.

41. The term "rider" in blues parlance is a reference to a female companion and/or sexual partner.

42. "Pistol Packin' Papa," words and music by Jimmie Rodgers and Waldo O'Neal. Copyright 1931 by Peer International Corporation. Copyright renewed. International copyright secured. Used by permission. All rights reserved.

43. Robert Gordon, *Can't Be Satisfied: The Life and Times of Muddy Waters* (Boston: Back Bay Books, 2003), 22; William Ferris, *Give My Poor Heart Ease: Voices of the Mississippi Blues* (Chapel Hill: University of North Carolina Press, 2009), 113.

44. Qtd. in Palmer, *Deep Blues*, 61–62.

45. Qtd. in Wynne, *Mississippi's Civil War*, 153.

46. Dunbar Rowland, *Encyclopedia of Mississippi History, Comprising Sketches of Counties, Towns, Events, Institutions, and Persons* (Madison WI: Selwyn A. Brant, 1907), vol. 2: 221.

47. Porterfield, *Jimmie Rodgers*, 10–11.

48. Ibid., 7–8.

49. For a history of the Mobile and Ohio Railroad, and Meridian's role as a southern railroad center, see J. Parker Lamb, *Railroads of Meridian* (Bloomington: University of Indiana Press, 2012); Jim Cox, *Rails Across Dixie: A History of Passenger Trains in the American South* (Jefferson, NC: McFarland and Co., 2011); and James H. Lemly, *The Gulf, Mobile and Ohio: A Railroad That Had to Expand or Expire* (Homewood, IL: Richard D. Irwin, Inc., 1953).

50. U.S. Census, 1880, Choctaw County, Alabama; U.S. Census, 1900, Lauderdale County, Mississippi; Porterfield, *Jimmie Rodgers*, 7–11.

51. Porterfield, *Jimmie Rodgers*, 11–15.

52. Frank Ryan, *Tuberculosis: The Greatest Story Never Told* (Bromsgrove, Worcestershire, UK: Swift Publishers, 1992), 21.

53. "My Rough and Rowdy Ways," words by Elsie McWilliams, music by Jimmie Rodgers. Copyright 1930 by Peer International Corporation. Copyright renewed. International copyright secured. Used by permission. All rights reserved.

54. Nancy R. Hooyman and Betty J. Kramer, *Living Through Loss: Interventions Across the Life Span* (New York: Columbia University Press, 2006), 94–95.

55. "T. B. Blues," words and music by Jimmie Rodgers and Raymond Hall. Copyright 1931 by Peer International Corporation. Copyright renewed. International copyright secured. Used by permission. All rights reserved. This particular couplet is similar to lyrics in Mamie Smith's "Crazy Blues," where she complains that she cannot "sleep at night" or "eat a bite" because her man has treated her badly.

56. "Whippin' That Old T. B.," words and music by Jimmie Rodgers. Copyright 1933 by Peer International Corporation. Copyright renewed. International copyright secured. Used by permission. All rights reserved.

57. Archie P. McDonald and Mark Daniel Barringer, "Jimmie Rodgers: The Singing Brakeman," in Donald W. Whisenhunt, ed., *The Human Tradition in America Between the Wars, 1920–1945* (Wilmington, DE: Scholarly Resources, Inc., 2002), 35.

58. Porterfield, *Jimmie Rodgers,* 14–15.

59. McDonald and Barringer, "Jimmie Rodgers," 35.

60. Richelle Putnam, *Lauderdale County, Mississippi: A Brief History* (Charleston, SC: History Press, 2011), 75–79; Porterfield, *Jimmie Rodgers,* 17.

61. Carrie Rodgers, *My Husband Jimmie Rodgers* (Nashville: Country Music Foundation Press, 1995), 7.

62. Porterfield, *Jimmie Rodgers,* 22; Barry Mazor, *Meeting Jimmie Rodgers: How America's Original Roots Music Hero Changed the Pop Sounds of a Century* (New York: Oxford University Press, 2009), 13.

63. Paul Hemphill, *The Nashville Sound: Bright Lights and Country Music* (New York: Simon and Schuster, 1970), 132; Cohen, *Long Steel Rail,* 427; William Dillon Piersen, *Black Legacy: America's Hidden Heritage* (Amherst: University of Massachusetts Press, 1993), 183.

64. "Brakeman's Blues," words and music by Jimmie Rodgers. Copyright 1928 by Peer International Corporation. Copyright renewed. International copyright secured. Used by permission. All rights reserved.

65. Max Decharne, *A Rocket in My Pocket: The Hipster's Guide to Rockabilly Music* (London: Profile Books, 2010), 61; Oakley, *The Devil's Music,* 56; Mark Twain, *Life on the Mississippi* (Paris: Leipzig, Bernhard, Tauchnitz, 1883), vol. 1: 269; Palmer, *Deep Blues,* 120; Harris, *Deep Souths,* 191.

66. Levine, *Black Culture and Black Consciousness,* 283.

67. Cobb, *Redefining Southern Culture,* 118; Howard W. Odum and Guy B. Johnson, *The Negro and His Songs: A Study of Typical Negro Songs in the South* (Chapel Hill: University of North Carolina Press, 1925), 158.

68. "Train Whistle Blues," words and music by Jimmie Rodgers. Copyright 1930 by Peer International Corporation. Copyright renewed. International copyright secured. Used by permission. All rights reserved.

69. Lawson, *Jim Crow's Counterculture,* 105–7.

70. "Miss the Mississippi and You," words and music by Bill Halley. Copyright 1932 by Peer International Corporation. Copyright renewed. International copyright secured. Used by permission. All rights reserved.

71. Nolan Porterfield qtd. in Curtis W. Ellison, *Country Music Culture: From Hard Times to Heaven* (Jackson: University Press of Mississippi, 1995), 40. "My Rough and Rowdy Ways," words by Elsie McWilliams, music by Jimmie Rodgers. Copyright 1930 by Peer International Corporation. Copyright renewed. International copyright secured. Used by permission. All rights reserved. "Sleep, Baby, Sleep," words and music by Jimmie Rodgers. Copyright 1953 by Peer International Corporation. Copyright renewed. International copyright secured. Used by permission. All rights reserved.

72. McDonald and Barringer, "Jimmie Rodgers," 35; Richard A. Petersen, *Creating Country Music: Fabricating Authenticity* (Chicago: University of Chicago Press, 1997), 43, 245.

73. "Brakeman's Blues," words and music by Jimmie Rodgers. Copyright 1928 by Peer Inter-

national Corporation. Copyright renewed. International copyright secured. Used by permission. All rights reserved.

74. Nicholas Dawidoff, *In the Country of Country: People and Places in American Music* (New York: Pantheon Books), 4; Petersen, *Creating Country Music*, 43, 245.

75. Pete Daniel, *Standing at the Crossroads: Southern Life in the Twentieth Century* (Baltimore: John Hopkins University Press, 1996), 101. For a detailed account of Rodgers's first marriage, see Porterfield, *Jimmie Rodgers*, 29–34. The book contains excerpts from Porterfield's 1975 interview with Rodgers's first wife.

76. Rodgers, *My Husband Jimmie Rodgers*, 14.

77. Porterfield, *Jimmie Rodgers*, 35–39; Rodgers, *My Husband Jimmie Rodgers*, 14; Mazor, *Meeting Jimmie Rodgers*, 13–15.

78. Malone, *Country Music U.S.A.*, 79.

79. Mary C. Henderson, *Theater in America: 200 Years of Players, Plays, and Productions* (New York: Harry N. Abrams, 1991), 281; Clifford Ashby and Suzanne DePauw May, *Trouping Through Texas: Harley Sadler and His Tent Show* (Bowling Green, KY: Bowling Green University Popular Press, 1982), 1–2.

80. Porterfield, *Jimmie Rodgers*, 49.

81. Jocelyn R. Neal, *The Songs of Jimmie Rodgers: A Legacy in Country Music* (Bloomington: Indiana University Press, 2009), 19–20.

82. Bart Plantenga, *Yodel-ay-ee-oooo: The Secret History of Yodeling Around the World* (New York: Routledge, 2004), 186; Colin Escott, *Lost Highway: The True Story of Country Music* (Washington, DC: Smithsonian Books, 2003), 26; Ashenafi Kebede, *The Roots of Black Music: The Vocal, Instrumental, and Dance Heritage of Africa and Black America* (Trenton, NJ: Africa World Press, 1995), 130; Joseph E. Holloway, *Africanisms in American Culture*, 2nd ed. (Bloomington: Indiana University Press, 2005), 380; Tosches, *Country*, 109–10.

83. Porterfield, *Jimmie Rodgers*, 50–51.

84. *Billboard*, April 3, 1971; Mazor, *Meeting Jimmie Rodgers*, 14.

85. Rodgers, *My Husband Jimmie Rodgers*, 32; Porterfield, *Jimmie Rodgers*, 52–54; Mazor, *Meeting Jimmie Rodgers*, 110–11.

86. Marcus P. Hatfield, M.D., and George Thomas Palmer, M.D., "American Springs," *The Chicago Clinic and Pure Water Journal* 19 (1906): 56; Chas Smith, *Rumble in the Jungle: The Soul of Indigenous Music in America* (Atlanta: Kendall Hunt Publishing, 2007), 277.

87. Porterfield, *Jimmie Rodgers*, 143; Putnam, *Lauderdale County, Mississippi*, 146.

Chapter Three

First epigraph: McKee and Chisenhall, *Beale Black & Blue*, 239. *Second epigraph:* Mazor, *Meeting Jimmie Rodgers*, 248.

1. Andre Millard, *America on Record: A History of Recorded Sound* (Cambridge, UK: Cambridge University Press, 2005), 8–9

2. Jonathan Sterne, *The Audible Past: Cultural Origins of Sound Reproduction* (Durham, NC: Duke University Press, 2003), 185–87; Neil Baldwin, *Edison: Inventing the Century* (Chicago: University of Chicago Press, 2001), 187–88.

3. Carney, *Cuttin' Up: How Early Jazz got America's Ear* (Lawrence: University of Kansas Press, 2009), 3, 13; this is an excellent book on the early development of Jazz in America. William Howland Kenney, *Recorded Music in American Life: The Phonograph and Popular Memory, 1890–1945* (New York: Oxford University Press, 1999), 24–44.

4. Millard, *America on Record*, 244–45; Eric Morritt, "Early Sound Recording Technology and the Bristol Sessions," in Charles K. Wolfe and Ted Olson, eds., *The Bristol Sessions: Writing About the Big Bang of Country Music* (Jefferson, NC: McFarland & Co., Inc., 2005), 8–11.

5. Nelson George, *The Death of Rhythm and Blues* (New York: Penguin Books, 1988), 8; Kenney, *Recorded Music in American Life*, 182–83.

6. W. Fitzhugh Brundage, "African Americans in American Popular Culture, 1890–1930," in W. Fitzhugh Brundage, ed., *Beyond Blackface: African Americans and the Creation of American Popular Culture, 1890–1930* (Chapel Hill: University of North Carolina Press, 2011), 22–23. For a treatment of George W. Johnson's life, see Tim Brooks, *Lost Sounds: Blacks and the Birth of the Recording Industry, 1890–1919* (Champaign: University of Illinois Press, 2004), 1–73.

7. Carney, *Cuttin' Up*, 16; Susan Curtis, *Dancing to a Black Man's Tune: A Life of Scott Joplin* (Columbia: University of Missouri Press, 1994), 68–71; Emily Epstein Landau, *Spectacular Wickedness: Sex, Race, and Memory in Storyville, New Orleans* (Baton Rouge: Louisiana State University Press, 2013), 19–29.

8. Handy, *Father of the Blues*, 93–94; Ellis Cashmore, *The Black Culture Industry* (New York: Routledge, 1997), 37.

9. John Strausbaugh, *Black Like You: Blackface, Whiteface, Insult & Imitation in American Popular Culture* (New York: Penguin Group, 2006), 138–39; Christine Acham, *Revolution Televised: Prime Time and the Struggle for Black Power* (Minneapolis: University of Minnesota Press, 2004), xii–xiv; Lynn Abbot and Doug Seroff, "'They Cert'ly Sound Good to Me': Sheet Music, Southern Vaudeville, and the Commercial Ascendancy of the Blues," in David Evans, ed., *Ramblin' on My Mind: New Perspectives of the Blues* (Champaign: University of Illinois Press, 2008), 49–50.

10. Russell Sanjek, *American Popular Music and Its Business: The First Four Hundred Years* (New York: Oxford University Press, 1988), vol. 2: 31; Scott Yanow, *Jazz on Record: The First Sixty Years* (San Francisco: Backbeat Books, 2003), 14–15.

11. Linda Dahl, *Stormy Weather: The Music and Lives of a Century of Jazzwomen* (New York: Pantheon Books, 1984), 111–18; Chip Deffaa, *Voices of the Jazz Age: Profiles of Eight Vintage Jazzmen* (Champaign: University of Illinois Press, 1992), 6–12. For further information on "Ma" Rainey, see Sandra R. Lieb, *Mother of the Blues: A Study of Ma Rainey* (Amherst: University of Massachusetts Press, 1981).

12. Paul Oliver et al., *Yonder Comes the Blues: The Evolution of a Genre* (Cambridge, UK: Cambridge University Press, 2001), 257; Kenney, *Recorded Music in American Life*, 114–15.

13. Rick Kennedy and Randy MacNutt, *Little Labels—Big Sound: Small Record Companies and the Rise of American Music* (Bloomington: University of Indiana Press, 1999), 24–27; *The Crisis* 27, no. 2 (December, 1923): 95.

14. Oakley, *The Devil's Music*, 120.

15. Ibid., 55.

16. Evans, *Big Road Blues,* 76–78.

17. Edwards, Martinson, and Frank, *The World Don't Owe Me Nothing,* 92; Oakley, *The Devil's Music,* 55.

18. Calt and Wardlow, *King of the Delta Blues,* 28.

19. Ibid., 144.

20. Davis, *The History of the Blues,* 97; Ayers, *The Promise of the New South,* 392.

21. Calt and Wardlow, *King of the Delta Blues,* 146–48; James Obrecht, "Deep Down in the Delta: The Adventures of Son House, Willie Brown & Friends," *Guitar Player,* August 1992, 72.

22. Adam Gussow, *Seems Like Murder Here: Southern Violence and the Blues Tradition* (Chicago: University of Chicago Press, 2002), 196.

23. Tom Rushing to Ben Wynne, correspondence dated August 9, 2010, in the possession of the author; Robin Rushing to Ben Wynne, August 10, 2010, in the possession of the author.

24. Rushing to Wynne, August 9, 2010.

25. "Gambling Bar Room Blues," words and music by Jimmie Rodgers and Shelly Lee Alley. Copyright 1933 by Peer International Corporation. Copyright renewed. International copyright secured. Used by permission. All rights reserved.

26. Palmer, *Deep Blues,* 58–59; Calt and Wardlow, *King of the Delta Blues,* 166–68.

27. Giesen, *Boll Weevil Blues,* 95–96; Elijah Wald, *Escaping the Delta: Robert Johnson and the Invention of the Blues* (New York: HaperCollins, 2004), 65, 119–20.

28. Gayle Dean Wardlow, *Chasin' That Devil Music: Searching for the Blues* (San Francisco: Backbeat Books, 1998), 131–49; a pioneer in the field of blues research, Wardlow interviewed Speir in the 1960s. Titon, *Early Downhome Blues,* 213.

29. Calt and Wardlow, *King of the Delta Blues,* 16.

30. Evans, *Big Road Blues,* 46; Titon, *Early Downhome Blues,* 63–65; Kennedy and MacNutt, *Little Labels—Big Sound,* 32–34.

31. Gioia, *Delta Blues,* 71.

32. Ibid., 67; estimate of Charley Patton's record sales found in Palmer, *Deep Blues,* 77.

33. Oliver et al., *Yonder Comes the Blues,* 290; Alan Young, *Woke Me Up This Morning: Black Gospel Singers and the Gospel Life* (Jackson: University Press of Mississippi, 1997), 9; *Chicago Defender,* September 7 and 14, 1929.

34. Paul Oliver, *The Story of the Blues* (Boston: Northeastern University Press, 1997), 174; Tosches, *Country,* 172.

35. Wardlow, *Chasin' That Devil Music,* 29.

36. Beaumont, *Preachin' the Blues,* 60–63; Edward Komara, "Blues in the Round, *Black Music Research Journal,* vol. 17, no. 1 (Spring, 1997), 3–17; Calt and Wardlow, *King of the Delta Blues,* 215–17.

37. Calt and Wardlow, *King of the Delta Blues,* 240–41; Tosches, *Country,* 141; Wardlow, *Chasin' That Devil Music,* 147–48.

38. Calt and Wardlow, *King of the Delta Blues,* 248–49; Davis, *The History of the Blues,* 104; Wardlow, *Chasin' That Devil Music,* 95–100; David Dacaire, *Blues Singers: Biographies of 50 Legendary Artists of the Early 20th Century* (Jefferson, NC: McFarland & Co., 1999), 8.

39. Porterfield, *Jimmie Rodgers,* 63.

40. Ibid., 66–67; U.S. Bureau of the Census, *Fifteenth Census of the United States: 1930: Population* (Washington, DC: U.S. Government Printing Office, 1933), 212.

41. Gerald Leinwand, *1927: High Tide of the 1920s, a Year in Detail, a Distant Mirror of the Present* (New York: Four Walls and Eight Windows, 2001), 256; Alan B. Albarran and Gregory G. Pitts, *The Radio Broadcasting Industry* (Boston: Allyn and Bacon, 2001), 17–28.

42. McDonald and Barringer, "Jimmie Rodgers," 38; Malone, *Country Music, U.S.A.*, 80.

43. Richard Blaustein, "Before the Myth was Born: Claude Grant of the Tenneva Ramblers Remembers Jimmie Rodgers," in Wolfe and Olson, eds., *The Bristol Sessions*, 169.

44. Porterfield, *Jimmie Rodgers*, 70–71; Kip Lornell, *Virginia's Blues, Country, and Gospel Records, 1902–1943: An Annotated Discography* (Lexington: University Press of Kentucky, 1989), 74.

45. Greil Marcus, *The Old, Weird America: The World of Bob Dylan's Basement Tapes* (New York: Picador, 1997), 120.

46. David Hatch and Stephen Millward, *From Blues to Rock: An Analytical History of Pop Music* (Wolfeboro, NH: Manchester University Press, 1987), 29–30; Tony Russell, *Country Music Originals: The Legends and the Lost* (New York: Oxford University Press, 2007), 72–73; Richard Carlin, *Country Music: A Biographical Dictionary* (New York: Routledge, 2003), 3–4.

47. Oliver, *Screening the Blues*, 249.

48. "Blue Yodel No. 11," words and music by Jimmie Rodgers. Copyright 1933 by Peer International Corporation. Copyright renewed. International copyright secured. Used by permission. All rights reserved.

49. Benjamin Filene, *Romancing the Folk: Public Memory and American Roots Music* (Chapel Hill: University of North Carolina Press, 2000), 35; Nigel Parker, *Music Business: Infrastructure, Practice and Law* (London: Sweet and Maxwell Ltd., 2004), 66.

50. Charles K. Wolfe, *Tennessee Strings: The Story of Country Music in Tennessee* (Knoxville: University of Tennessee Press, 1977), 44.

51. Charles K. Wolfe, "Music," in Carroll Van West, ed., *The Tennessee Encyclopedia of History and Culture* (Nashville: Rutledge Hill Press, 1998), 659; *Billboard*, December 28, 2002.

52. Patrick Carr, *The Illustrated History of Country Music* (New York: Doubleday, 1979), 53; Porterfield, *Jimmie Rodgers*, 107–8.

53. Richard Koszarski, *Hollywood on the Hudson: Film and Television in New York from Griffith to Sarnoff* (New Brunswick, NJ: Rutgers University Press, 2008), 169.

54. "Blue Yodel No. 1 ('T' for Texas)," words and music by Jimmie Rodgers. Copyright 1928 by Peer International Corporation. Copyright renewed. International copyright secured. Used by permission. All rights reserved.

55. Gerard Herzhaft, *Encyclopedia of the Blues* (Fayetteville: University of Arkansas Press, 1992), 365.

56. Bill Wyman and Richard Havers, *Bill Wyman's Blues Odyssey* (New York: DK Publishing, 2001), 182.

57. Qtd. in Oliver et al., *Yonder Comes the Blues*, 193.

58. Mark Zwonitzer with Charles Hirshberg, *Will You Miss Me When I'm Gone? The Carter Family & Their Legacy in American Music* (New York: Simon and Schuster, 2002), 141.

59. "Blue Yodel No. 11," words and music by Jimmie Rodgers. Copyright 1933 by Peer Inter-

national Corporation. Copyright renewed. International copyright secured. Used by permission. All rights reserved.

60. "Looking For a New Mama," words and music by Jimmie Rodgers. Copyright 1931 by Peer International Corporation. Copyright renewed. International copyright secured. Used by permission. All rights reserved.

61. Karl Hagstrom Miller, *Segregating Sound: Inventing Folk and Pop Music in the Age of Jim Crow* (Durham, NC: Duke University Press, 2010), 238.

62. Kostelanetz, *The B.B. King Reader*, 158; Miller, *Segregating Sound*, 57, 238; Mazor, *Meeting Jimmie Rodgers*, 38–39.

63. Larry Birnbaum, *Before Elvis: The Pre-History of Rock and Roll* (Lanham, MD: Scarecrow Press, 2013), 200; Oliver et al., *Yonder Comes the Blues*, 192–93.

64. "Memphis Yodel," words and music by Jimmie Rodgers. Copyright 1928 by Peer International Corporation. Copyright renewed. International copyright secured. Used by permission. All rights reserved.

65. Mazor, *Meeting Jimmie Rodgers*, 59–62.

66. *Billboard*, May 16, 1953.

67. "Blue Yodel No. 9 (Standin' on the Corner)," words and music by Jimmie Rodgers. Copyright 1931 by Peer International Corporation. Copyright renewed. International copyright secured. Used by permission. All rights reserved.

68. Robert Coltman, "Roots of the Country Yodel: Notes Toward a Life History," in Nolan Porterfield, ed., *Exploring Roots Music: Twenty Years of the JEMF Quarterly* (Oxford, UK: Scarecrow Press, 2004), 139.

69. Dawidoff, *In the Country of Country*, 12.

70. Chris Comber and Mike Paris, "Jimmie Rodgers," in Bill C. Malone and Judith McCulloh, eds., *Stars of Country Music: From Uncle Dave Mason to Johnny Rodriguez* (Champaign: University of Illinois Press, 1975), 130.

71. "Jimmie Rodgers: Hillbilly World to Honor his Memory," *Billboard*, May 16, 1953; Holly George-Warren, *Public Cowboy No. 1: The Life and Times of Gene Autry* (New York: Oxford University Press, 2007), 28.

72. "Blues Singer to Head New Bill at Loew's," *Atlanta Constitution*, November 11, 1928, 21A. For more on Marcus Loew, see chapter 7 in Robert Sobel, *The Entrepreneurs: Explorations Within the American Business Tradition* (New York: Weybright and Talley, 1974).

73. Malone, *Country Music, U.S.A.*, 89; Putnam, *Lauderdale County, Mississippi*, 75–79; Petersen, *Creating Country Music*, 44–46.

74. "Honors Captured at Loew's Capitol by 'Blues' Singer," *Atlanta Constitution*, November 13, 1928, 19; "Jimmie Rodgers: Founding Father," *Billboard*, April 3, 1971.

75. Terry Teachout, *Pops: A Life of Louis Armstrong* (New York: Houghton Mifflin Harcourt Publishing Co., 2009), 150; Donald Clarke, *The Rise and Fall of Popular Music: A Narrative History from the Renaissance to Rock 'n' Roll* (New York: St. Martin's Press, 1996), 146–48; Malone, *Country Music, U.S.A.*, 127–28; Max Jones and John Chilton, *Louis: The Louis Armstrong Story* (Boston: Little, Brown, 1971), 236.

76. Ben Yagoda, *Will Rogers: A Biography* (Norman: University of Oklahoma Press, 1993),

277–78; Ray Robinson, *An American Original: A Life of Will Rogers* (New York: Oxford University Press, 1996), 204–5.

77. "T. B. Blues," words and music by Jimmie Rodgers and Raymond Hall. Copyright 1931 by Peer International Corporation. Copyright renewed. International copyright secured. Used by permission. All rights reserved.

78. Zwonitzer with Hirshberg, *Will You Miss Me When I'm Gone?* 141.

79. Daniel, *Standing at the Crossroads*, 100–101; Petersen, *Creating Country Music*, 245; Porterfield, *Jimmie Rodgers*, 285.

80. "William W. Sterling," Austin (TX) *American*, April 27, 1960, August 28, 1969; *Billboard*, March 14, 1931; "The Yodeling Texas Ranger," *Kerrville (TX) Mountain Sun*, February 26, 1931.

81. "The Yodeling Ranger," words and music by Jimmie Rodgers. Copyright 1933 by Peer International Corporation. Copyright renewed. International copyright secured. Used by permission. All rights reserved.

82. Ronnie Pugh, *Ernest Tubb: The Texas Troubadour* (Durham, NC: Duke University Press, 1996), 12; Rick Koster, *Texas Music* (New York: St. Martin's Press, 2000), 11; "Jimmie Rodgers: Hillbilly World to Honor his Memory."

83. "Jimmie Rodgers: Hillbilly World to Honor his Memory."

84. Carrie Rodgers, *My Husband, Jimmie Rodgers*, 207; Ellison, *Country Music Culture*, 40–43; Mazor, *Meeting Jimmie Rodgers*, 119–20; Comber and Paris, "Jimmie Rodgers," 134–36.

Chapter Four

First epigraph: Paul Williams, *Bob Dylan, Performing Artist 1986–1990 and Beyond: Mind Out of Time* (London: Omnibus Press, 2004), 330. *Second epigraph:* Keith Richards to Ben Wynne, undated correspondence ca. 1990, in the author's possession.

1. For reference to James W. Silver, see James W. Silver, *Mississippi: A Closed Society* (rpt., Jackson: University Press of Mississippi, 2012); W. E. B. Dubois, *The Souls of Black Folk* (Rockville, MD: Arc Manor, 2008), 16.

2. "Mississippi Blues Trail Unveiled," *Stone County (MS) Enterprise*, December 27, 2006.

3. Glenn C. Altschuler, *All Shook Up: How Rock 'n' Roll Changed America* (New York: Oxford University Press, 2003), 35.

4. Lawson, *Jim Crow's Counterculture*, 14–16; Dick Weissman, *Talkin' 'bout a Revolution: Music and Social Change in America* (Milwaukee: Hal Leonard Corporation, 2010), 84–85; Dick Weissman, *Blues: The Basics* (New York: Routledge, 2005), 105–6.

5. Evans, *Big Road Blues*, 16.

6. William Grimes, "Jerry Leiber, Prolific Writer of 1950s Hits, Dies at 78," *New York Times*, August 22, 2011; David Fricke, "Leiber and Stoller," *Rolling Stone*, April 19, 1990; Jerry Leiber and Mike Stoller with David Ritz, *Hound Dog: The Leiber and Stoller Autobiography* (New York: Simon and Schuster, 2009), 34; "Willie Mae Thornton: Hound Dog," *Billboard*, March 14, 1953.

7. Wyman and Havers, *Bill Wyman's Blues Odyssey*, 73; Gioia, *Delta Blues*, 109.

8. Segrest and Hoffman, *"Moanin' After Midnight,"* 20.

9. Palmer, *Deep Blues,* 57.

10. For information on the Great Migration, see Isabel Wilkerson, *The Warmth of Other Suns: The Epic Story of America's Great Migration* (New York: Random House, 2010), and James N. Gregory, *The Southern Diaspora: How the Great Migrations of Black and White Southerners Transformed America* (Chapel Hill: University of North Carolina Press, 2005).

11. Rich Cohen, *Machers and Rockers: Chess Records and the Business of Rock & Roll* (New York: W. W. Norton and Co., Inc., 2004), 71; William Bearden, *Memphis Blues: Birthplace of a Musical Tradition* (Charleston, SC: Arcadia Press, 2006), 6.

12. Palmer, *Deep Blues,* 255; James T. Patterson, *Grand Expectations: The United States, 1945–1975* (New York: Oxford University Press, 1996), 373; Jay Stevens, *Storming Heaven: LSD and the American Dream* (New York: Grove Press, 1987), 97–98.

13. A number of good studies on the folk music revival and roots music are available, including Robert Cantwell, *When We Were Good: The Folk Revival* (Cambridge, MA: Harvard University Press, 1996), Ronald D. Cohen, *Rainbow Quest: The Folk Music Revival and American Society, 1940–1970* (Amherst: University of Massachusetts Press, 2002), and Filene, *Romancing the Folk.*

14. James E. Perone, *Mods, Rockers, and the Music of the British Invasion* (Westport, CT: Greenwood Publishing Group, Inc., 2009), 8–12; Roberta Freund Schwartz, *How Britain Got the Blues: The Transition and Reception of American Blues Style in the United Kingdom* (Burlington, VT: Ashgate Publishing Co., 2007), 49–119.

15. For more on Broonzy, see Bob Riesman, *I Feel So Good: The Life and Times of Big Bill Broonzy* (Chicago: University of Chicago Press, 2011). For more on Waters, see Gordon, *Can't Be Satisfied*; Jas Obrecht, ed., *Rollin' and Tumblin': The Post-War Blues Guitarists* (San Francisco: Miller Freeman, Inc., 2000), 108–9.

16. Colin Harper, *Dazzling Stranger: Bert Jansch and the British Folk and Blues Revival* (London: Bloomsbury Publishing, 2006), 1–83; Perone, *Mods, Rockers, and the Music of the British Invasion,* 120–21; Brad Tolinski, *Light and Shade: Conversations with Jimmy Page* (Toronto: McClelland & Stewart, 2012), 67.

17. Wald, *Escaping the Delta,* 245; Bruce Cook, *Listen to the Blues* (New York: Charles Scribner's Sons, 1973), 181–82.

18. Davis, *The History of the Blues,* 237.

19. Palmer, *Deep Blues,* 261.

20. Gordon, *Can't Be Satisfied,* 24. Sandra B. Tooze, *Muddy Waters: The Mojo Man* (Ontario: ECW Press, 1997), 30–33; Obrecht, ed., *Rollin' and Tumblin',* 95–97.

21. Davis, *The History of the Blues,* 99–100.

22. Wald, *Escaping the Delta,* xv. The Blues Foundation: International Home of the Blues, www.blues.org (accessed April 2013).

23. Palmer, *Deep Blues,* 263; Edwards, Martinson, and Frank, *The World Don't Owe Me Nothing,* 91–92.

24. Segrest and Hoffman, *"Moanin' After Midnight,"* 19–20.

25. Brian Jones made his remarks about Howlin' Wolf on the episode of "Shindig!" that aired May 26, 1965.

26. Lowenstein, Dodd, and Watts, eds., *According to the Rolling Stones,* 92; Theodore Gracyk, *I Wanna Be Me: Rock Music and Political Identity* (Philadelphia: Temple University Press, 2001), 59–61; Will Romano, *Incurable Blues: The Troubles and Triumph of Blues Legend Hubert Sumlin* (San Francisco: Backbeat Books, 2005), 74–75.

27. Cobb, *The Most Southern Place on Earth,* 280; Evans, Charley Patton Biography, Part 1; Harris, *Deep Souths,* 189.

28. American Folklife Center, www.loc.gov/folklife/index.html (accessed January 2013); Everett True, *The White Stripes and the Sound of Mutant Blues* (London: Omnibus Press, 2004), 58; "Lord Have Mercy," *Billboard,* September 13, 2003; "Prized Black Recordings Picked for the Library of Congress," *Jet,* March 26, 2007, 20–22.

29. Hank Bordowitz, *Bad Moon Rising: The Unauthorized History of Creedence Clearwater Revival* (Chicago: Chicago Review Press, 1998), 246.

30. Don Cusic, *Discovering Country Music* (Westport, CT: Greenwood Publishing, 2008), 21; Filene, *Romancing the Folk,* 222.

31. Pugh, *Ernest Tubb,* 13–14.

32. Barry Shank, *Dissonant Identities: The Rock and Roll Scene in Austin, Texas* (Hanover, NH: University Press of New England, 1994), 145–47.

33. Loretta Lynn, Patsi Bale Box, *Loretta Lynn: Still Woman Enough* (New York: Hyperion, 2002), 89; Loretta Lynn and George Vecsey, *Loretta Lynn: Coalminer's Daughter* (New York: Da Capo Press, 1976), 94; Lawrence Clayton and Joe W. Specht, eds., *The Roots of Texas Music* (College Station: Texas A&M University Press, 2003), 83.

34. Don Cusic, *Gene Autry: His Life and Career* (Jefferson, NC: McFarland and Co., 2007), 20–25; George-Warren, *Public Cowboy No. 1,* 57–66.

35. Tom Ewing, ed., *The Bill Monroe Reader* (Champaign: University of Illinois Press, 2000), 34–35.

36. For more on Snow, see Hank Snow, Jack Ownbey, and Bob Burris, *The Hank Snow Story* (Campaign: University of Illinois Press, 1994).

37. Mazor, *Meeting Jimmie Rodgers,* 51; Wald, *Escaping the Delta,* 56; Kostelanetz, *The B.B. King Reader,* 210; Segrest and Hoffman, "Moanin' After Midnight," 21–23.

38. Mazor, *Meeting Jimmie Rodgers,* 202; Colin Escott, *Hank Williams: The Biography* (New York: Little Brown and Co., 2004), 13, 254.

39. "Jimmie Rodgers: Hillbilly World to Honor his Memory"; Diane Pecknold, *The Selling Sound: The Rise of the Country Music Industry* (Durham, NC: Duke University Press, 2007), 71–74; Bobbie Ann Mason, *Elvis Presley* (New York: Penguin Books, 2007), 17.

40. Nick Tosches, *Hellfire* (New York: Grove Press, 1989), 21, 242; Joe Bonomo, *Jerry Lee Lewis: Lost and Found* (New York: Continuum International Publishing Group, Inc., 2009), 36–38.

41. Stephen Miller, *Johnny Cash: The Life of an American Icon* (London: Omnibus Press, 2003), 74. Quote from Louis Armstrong taken from season 2, episode 6, of "The Johnny Cash Show," originally aired October 28, 1970.

42. Beatles, *The Beatles Anthology* (San Francisco: Chronicle Books, 2000), 27.

43. Reference to Ellison, *Country Music Culture.*

44. Malone, *Country Music U.S.A.*, 84; Porterfield, *Jimmie Rodgers*, 361–62; Hemphill, *The Nashville Sound*, 134.

45. "Four Eligible to CMA's 'Fame' Under New Voting," *Billboard*, August 14, 1965; Ellison, *Country Music Culture*, 119.

46. "Jimmie Rodgers: Founding Father," *Billboard*, April 3, 1971; "Mainstream Pop Displays Its Punch at the Grammys," *Billboard*, March 9, 1985; Wolfe and Olson, eds., *The Bristol Sessions*, 3.

47. Putnam, *Lauderdale County, Mississippi*, 146–47; Mazor, *Meeting Jimmie Rodgers*, 59.

48. Mazor, *Meeting Jimmie Rodgers*, 253.

49. Williams, *Bob Dylan, Performing Artist 1986–1990 and Beyond*, 330; "Love and Theft," *Chicago Tribune*, September 11, 2001; "Reborn Again," *Los Angeles Times*, December 14, 1997; Eric Lott, "Love and Theft," in James J. H. Dettmer, *The Cambridge Companion to Bob Dylan* (Cambridge, UK: Cambridge University Press, 2009), 167–68.

50. Clinton Heylin, *Bob Dylan: Behind the Shades Revisited* (New York: HarperCollins, 2000), 11; Clinton Heylin, *Revolution in the Air: The Songs of Bob Dylan, 1957–1973* (Chicago: Chicago Review Press, 2012), 25–27; Larry David Smith, *Writing Dylan: The Songs of a Lonesome Traveler* (Westport, CT: Praeger Publishing, 2005), 7–9.

51. Carl Perkins and David McGee, *Go Cat, Go! The Life and Times of Carl Perkins, the King of Rockabilly* (New York: Hyperion Books, 1997), 215–16; Birnbaum, *Before Elvis*, 151; Gerald Lyn Early, *Ain't But a Place: An Anthology of African American Writing About St. Louis* (St. Louis: Missouri Historical Society Press, 1998), 181–82; quote by John Lennon from the February 15, 1972, episode of *The Mike Douglas Show*, featuring Lennon and Yoko Ono with a guest appearance by Chuck Berry.

52. Holly George-Warren, *The Rock and Roll Hall of Fame: The First 25 Years* (New York; HarperCollins Publishers, 2009), 14–16.

BIBLIOGRAPHY

Books and Articles

Acham, Christine. *Revolution Televised: Prime Time and the Struggle for Black Power.* Minneapolis: University of Minnesota Press, 2004.

Albarran, Alan B., and Gregory G. Pitts. *The Radio Broadcasting Industry.* Boston: Allyn and Bacon, 2001.

Altschuler, Glenn C. *All Shook Up: How Rock 'n' Roll Changed America.* New York: Oxford University Press, 2003.

Ashby, Clifford, and Suzanne DePauw May. *Trouping Through Texas: Harley Sadler and His Tent Show.* Bowling Green, KY: Bowling Green University Popular Press, 1982.

Ayers, Edward L. *The Promise of the New South: Life After Reconstruction.* New York: Oxford University Press, 1992.

Baker, Houston A., Jr. *Long Black Song: Essays in Black American Literature and Culture.* Charlottesville: University Press of Virginia, 1990.

———. *Turning South Again.* Durham, NC: Duke University Press, 2001.

Baldwin, Neil. *Edison: Inventing the Century.* Chicago: University of Chicago Press, 2001.

Bearden, William. *Memphis Blues: Birthplace of a Musical Tradition.* Charleston, SC: Arcadia Press, 2006.

Bearss, Edwin C. *The Campaign for Vicksburg.* 3 vols. Dayton, OH: Morningside House, Inc., 1986.

Beatles. *The Beatles Anthology.* San Francisco: Chronicle Books, 2000.

Beaumont, Daniel E. *Preachin' the Blues: The Life and Times of Son House.* New York: Oxford University Press, 2011.

Berlin, Ira. *Many Thousands Gone: The First Two Centuries of Slavery in North America.* Cambridge, MA: Harvard University Press, 2003.

Birnbaum, Larry. *Before Elvis: The Pre-History of Rock and Roll.* Lanham, MD: Scarecrow Press, 2013.

Blassingame, John W. *The Slave Community: Plantation Life in the Antebellum South.* New York: Oxford University Press, 1979.

Blaustein, Richard. "Before the Myth was Born: Claude Grant of the Tenneva Ramblers Remembers Jimmie Rodgers." In Wolfe and Olson, eds., *The Bristol Sessions*.

Boles, John. *Black Southerners, 1619–1869*. Lexington: University of Kentucky Press, 1984.

Bonomo, Joe. *Jerry Lee Lewis: Lost and Found*. New York: Continuum International Publishing Group, Inc., 2009.

Bordowitz, Hank. *Bad Moon Rising: The Unauthorized History of Creedence Clearwater Revival*. Chicago: Chicago Review Press, 1998.

Boyer, Paul S. Clifford Clark, Sandra Hawley, Joseph F. Kett, Andrew Rieser. *The Enduring Vision: A History of the American People from 1865*. Boston: Wadsworth, Cengage Learning, 2010.

Brooks, Tim. *Lost Sounds: Blacks and the Birth of the Recording Industry, 1890–1919*. Champaign: University of Illinois Press, 2004.

Brundage, W. Fitzhugh, ed. *Beyond Blackface: African Americans and the Creation of American Popular Culture, 1890–1930*. Chapel Hill: University of North Carolina Press, 2011.

Burrison, John A., ed., *Storytellers: Folktales and Legends from the South*. Athens: University of Georgia Press, 1989.

Calt, Stephen. *Barrelhouse Words: A Blues Dialect Dictionary*. Champaign: University of Illinois Press, 2009.

———, and Gayle Dean Wardlow. *King of the Delta Blues: The Life and Music of Charley Patton*. Newton, NJ: Rock Chapel Press, 1988.

Cantwell, Robert. *When We Were Good: The Folk Revival*. Cambridge, MA: Harvard University Press, 1996.

Carlin, Richard. *Country Music: A Biographical Dictionary*. New York: Routledge, 2003.

Carney, Court. *Cuttin' Up: How Early Jazz got America's Ear*. Lawrence: University of Kansas Press, 2009.

Carr, Patrick. *The Illustrated History of Country Music*. New York: Doubleday, 1979.

Cash, Johnny, with Patrick Carr. *Johnny Cash: The Autobiography*. New York: HarperCollins, 1997.

Cashmore, Ellis *The Black Culture Industry*. New York: Routledge, 1997.

Charters, Samuel. *The Blues Makers*. New York: Da Capo Press, 1991.

Chi Si Fraternity. *The Sixth Decennial Catalogue of the Chi Si Fraternity*. Auburn, NY: Knapp, Peck and Thomson, 1902.

Clarke, Donald. *The Rise and Fall of Popular Music: A Narrative History from the Renaissance to Rock 'n' Roll*. New York: St. Martin's Press, 1996.

Clayton, Lawrence, and Joe W. Specht, eds. *The Roots of Texas Music*. College Station: Texas A&M University Press, 2003.

Cobb, James C. *The Most Southern Place on Earth: The Mississippi Delta and the Roots of Regional Identity*. New York: Oxford University Press, 1992.

———. *Redefining Southern Culture: Mind and Identity in the Modern South.* Athens: University of Georgia Press, 1999.

———, ed. *The Mississippi Delta and the World: The Memoirs of David L. Cohn.* Baton Rouge: Louisiana State University Press, 1995.

Cohen, Norm. *Long Steel Rail: The Railroad in American Folksong.* 2nd ed. Champaign: University of Illinois Press, 2000.

Cohen, Rich. *Machers and Rockers: Chess Records and the Business of Rock & Roll.* New York: W. W. Norton and Co., Inc., 2004.

Cohen, Ronald D. *Rainbow Quest: The Folk Music Revival and American Society, 1940–1970.* Amherst, MA: University of Massachusetts Press, 2002.

Cohen, William. *At Freedom's Edge: Black Mobility and the Southern White Quest for Racial Control, 1861–1915.* Baton Rouge: Louisiana State University Press, 1991.

Coleman, James P. "The Mississippi Constitution of 1890 and the Final Decade of the Nineteenth Century." In Richard Aubrey McLemore, ed., *A History of Mississippi.* Hattiesburg: University and College Press of Mississippi, 1973.

Coltman, Robert. "Roots of the Country Yodel: Notes Toward a Life History." In Nolan Porterfield, ed., *Exploring Roots Music: Twenty Years of the JEMF Quarterly.* Oxford, UK: Scarecrow Press, 2004.

Comber, Chris, and Mike Paris. "Jimmie Rodgers." In Bill C. Malone and Judith McCulloh, eds., *Stars of Country Music: From Uncle Dave Mason to Johnny Rodriguez.* Champaign: University of Illinois Press, 1975.

Cone, James H. *The Spirituals and the Blues: an Interpretation.* New York: Seabury Press, 1971.

Cook, Bruce. *Listen to the Blues.* New York: Charles Scribner's Sons, 1973.

Cooper, William J., Jr. and Thomas E. Terrill. *The American South: A History,* second edition, vol. 1. New York: McGraw Hill, 1991.

Cox, Jim. *Rails Across Dixie: A History of Passenger Trains in the American South.* Jefferson, NC: McFarland and Co., 2011.

Currie, James T. *Enclave: Vicksburg and Her Plantations, 1863–1870.* Jackson: University Press of Mississippi, 1980.

Curtis, Susan. *Dancing to a Black Man's Tune: A Life of Scott Joplin.* Columbia: University of Missouri Press, 1994.

Cusic, Don. *Discovering Country Music.* Westport, CT: Greenwood Publishing, 2008.

———. *Gene Autry: His Life and Career.* Jefferson, NC: McFarland and Co., 2007.

———. *The Sound of Light: A History of Gospel and Christian Music.* Milwaukee: Hal Leonard Corporation, 2002.

Dabbs, James McBride. *The Southern Heritage.* New York: Knopf, 1958.

Dacaire, David. *Blues Singers: Biographies of 50 Legendary Artists of the Early 20th Century.* Jefferson, NC: McFarland & Co., 1999.

Dahl, Linda. *Stormy Weather: The Music and Lives of a Century of Jazzwomen*. New York: Pantheon Books, 1984.

Daniel, Pete. *Standing at the Crossroads: Southern Life in the Twentieth Century*. Baltimore: John Hopkins University Press, 1996.

Davis, Francis. *The History of the Blues: The Roots, the Music, the People from Charley Patton to Robert Cray*. New York: Hyperion, 1995.

Dawidoff, Nicholas. *In the Country of Country: People and Places in American Music*. New York: Pantheon Books, 1997.

Decharne, Max. *A Rocket in My Pocket: The Hipster's Guide to Rockabilly Music*. London: Profile Books, 2010.

Deffaa, Chip. *Voices of the Jazz Age: Profiles of Eight Vintage Jazzmen*. Champaign: University of Illinois Press, 1992.

Dettmer, James J. H. *The Cambridge Companion to Bob Dylan*. Cambridge, UK: Cambridge University Press, 2007.

Dixon, Willie, and Don Snowden, *I Am the Blues: The Willie Dixon Story*. New York: Da Capo Press, 1989.

Dollard, John. *Cast and Class in a Southern Town*. New Haven, CT: Yale University Press, 1937.

Dubois, W. E. B. *The Souls of Black Folk*. Rockville, MD: Arc Manor, 2008.

Early, Gerald Lyn. *Ain't But a Place: An Anthology of African American Writing About St. Louis*. St. Louis: Missouri Historical Society Press, 1998.

Edwards, David Honeyboy, Janis Martinson, and Michael Robert Frank. *The World Don't Owe Me Nothing: The Life and Times of Delta Bluesman Honeyboy Edwards*. Chicago: Chicago Review Press, 1997.

Ellison, Curtis W. *Country Music Culture: From Hard Times to Heaven*. Jackson: University Press of Mississippi, 1995.

Epstein, Dena J. *Sinful Tunes and Spirituals: Black Folk Music to the Civil War*. Champaign: University of Illinois Press, 2003.

Escott, Colin. *Hank Williams: The Biography*. New York: Little Brown and Co., 2004.

———. *Lost Highway: The True Story of Country Music*. Washington, DC: Smithsonian Books, 2003.

Evans, David. *Big Road Blues: Tradition and Creativity in the Folk Blues*. New York: Da Capo Press, 1987.

———, ed. *Ramblin' on My Mind: New Perspectives of the Blues*. Champaign: University of Illinois Press, 2008.

Ewing, Tom, ed., *The Bill Monroe Reader*. Champaign: University of Illinois Press, 2000.

Fahey, John. *Charley Patton*. Worthing, UK: Littlehampton Book Services, Ltd., 1970.

Faulkner, William. *The Mansion*. New York: Knopf Doubleday, 1965.

Ferris, William. *Blues from the Delta*. New York: Da Capo Press, 1984.

———. *Give My Poor Heart Ease: Voices of the Mississippi Blues.* Chapel Hill: University of North Carolina Press, 2009.

Filene, Benjamin. *Romancing the Folk: Public Memory and American Roots Music.* Chapel Hill: University of North Carolina Press, 2000.

Flynt, J. Wayne. *Dixie's Forgotten People, New Edition: The South's Poor Whites.* Bloomington: Indiana University Press, 2004.

———. *Poor But Proud: Alabama's Poor Whites.* Tuscaloosa: University of Alabama Press, 2001.

Foner, Eric. *Nothing But Freedom: Emancipation and Its Legacy.* Baton Rouge: Louisiana State University Press, 1983.

———. *Reconstruction: America's Unfinished Revolution, 1863–1877.* New York: Harper and Row Publishers, 1988.

Forret, Jeff. *Race Relations at the Margins: Slaves And Poor Whites in the Antebellum Countryside.* Baton Rouge: Louisiana State University Press, 2006.

Franklin, John Hope. *Reconstruction After the Civil War.* 2nd ed. Chicago: University of Chicago Press, 1994.

Freehling, William W. *The Road to Disunion: Secessionists at Bay, 1776–1854.* New York: Oxford University Press, 1990.

Gates, Henry Louis, Jr., *The Signifying Monkey: A Theory of African American Literary Criticism.* New York: Oxford University Press, 1988.

Genovese, Eugene D. *Roll Jordan Roll: The World the Slaves Made.* New York: Vintage Books 1976.

George-Warren, Holly. *Public Cowboy No. 1: The Life and Times of Gene Autry.* New York: Oxford University Press, 2007.

———. *The Rock and Roll Hall of Fame: The First 25 Years* (New York; HarperCollins Publishers, 2009.

Giesen, James C. *Boll Weevil Blues: Cotton, Myth, and Power in the American South.* Chicago: University of Chicago Press, 2011.

Giggie, John Michael. *After Redemption: Jim Crow and the Transformation of African American Religion in the Delta, 1875–1915.* New York: Oxford University Press.

Gilmour, Michael J., ed. *Call Me the Seeker: Listening to Religion in Popular Music.* New York: Continuum International, 2005.

Gioia, Ted. *Delta Blues: The Life and Times of Mississippi Masters Who Revolutionized American Music.* New York: W.W. Norton & Co., 2008.

Goertzen, Chris. *Southern Fiddlers and Fiddle Contests.* Jackson: University Press of Mississippi, 2008.

Goff, James R. *Close Harmony: A History of Southern Gospel.* Chapel Hill: University of North Carolina Press, 2002.

Gomez, Michael Angelo. *Exchanging Our Country Marks: The Transformation of African*

Identities in the Colonial and Antebellum South. Chapel Hill: University of North Carolina Press, 1998.

Gordon, Robert. *Can't Be Satisfied: The Life and Times of Muddy Waters.* Boston: Back Bay Books, 2003.

Gracyk, Theodore. *I Wanna Be Me: Rock Music and Political Identity.* Philadelphia: Temple University Press, 2001.

Graves, Michael P., and David Fillingim, eds., *More Than Precious Memories: The Rhetoric of Southern Gospel Music.* Macon, GA: Mercer University Press, 2004.

Gregory, James N. *The Southern Diaspora: How the Great Migrations of Black and White Southerners Transformed America.* Chapel Hill: University of North Carolina Press, 2005.

Grizzard, Frank E., and Daniel Boyd Smith. *Jamestown Colony: A Political, Social, and Cultural History.* Santa Barbara, CA: ABC-CLIO, 2007.

Gura, Philip F., *C. F. Martin and His Guitars, 1796–1873.* Chapel Hill: University of North Carolina Press, 2003.

Gussow, Adam. *Journeyman's Road: Modern Blues Lives from Faulkner's Mississippi to Post-9/11 New York.* Knoxville: University of Tennessee Press, 2007.

———. *Seems Like Murder Here: Southern Violence and the Blues Tradition.* Chicago: University of Chicago Press, 2002.

Hale, Grace Elizabeth. *Making Whiteness: The Culture of Segregation in the South, 1890–1940.* New York: Vintage Books, 1998.

Hammond, James Henry. "Speech on the Admission of Kansas, under the LeCompton Constitution." *Selections from the Speeches and Writings of the Hon. James H. Hammond.* Spartanburg, SC: Reprint Co., 1978.

Handy, William Christopher. *Father of the Blues: An Autobiography.* New York: Da Capo Press, 1969.

Harper, Colin. *Dazzling Stranger: Bert Jansch and the British Folk and Blues Revival.* London: Bloomsbury Publishing, 2006.

Harris, J. William. *Deep Souths: Delta, Piedmont and Sea Island Society in the Age of Segregation.* Baltimore: Johns Hopkins University Press, 2001.

Harris, Michael W. *The Rise of Gospel Blues: The Music of Thomas Andrew Dorsey in the Urban Church.* New York: Oxford University Press, 1992.

Harvey, Paul. *Freedom's Coming: Religious Culture and the Shaping of the South from the Civil War through the Civil Rights Era.* Chapel Hill: University of North Carolina Press, 2005.

Hashaw, Tim. *Children of Perdition: Melungeons and the Struggle of Mixed America.* Macon, GA: Mercer University Press, 2006.

Hatch, David, and Stephen Millward. *From Blues to Rock: An Analytical History of Pop Music.* Wolfeboro, NH: Manchester University Press, 1987.

Hatfield, Marcus P., M.D., and George Thomas Palmer, M.D. "American Springs," *The Chicago Clinic and Pure Water Journal* 19 (1906): 56.

Hay, Fred J., ed. *Goin' Back to Sweet Memphis: Conversations with the Blues.* Athens: University of Georgia Press, 2001.

Hemphill, Paul. *The Nashville Sound: Bright Lights and Country Music.* New York: Simon and Schuster, 1970.

Henderson, Mary C. *Theater in America: 200 Years of Players, Plays, and Productions.* New York: Harry N. Abrams, 1991.

Herzhaft, Gerard. *Encyclopedia of the Blues.* Fayetteville: University of Arkansas Press, 1992.

Heylin, Clinton. *Bob Dylan: Behind the Shades Revisited.* New York: HarperCollins, 2000.

———. *Revolution in the Air: The Songs of Bob Dylan, 1957–1973.* Chicago: Chicago Review Press, 2012.

Higginson, Thomas Wentworth, *The Writings of Thomas Wentworth Higginson: Army Life in a Black Regiment.* Cambridge, MA: Riverside Press, 1900.

Holloway, Joseph E. *Africanisms in American Culture,* 2nd ed. Bloomington: Indiana University Press, 2005.

Hooyman, Nancy R., and Betty J. Kramer. *Living Through Loss: Interventions Across the Life Span.* New York: Columbia University Press, 2006.

Horton, James Oliver, and Lois E. Horton. *Slavery and the Making of America.* New York: Oxford University Press, 2005.

Hurt, R. Douglas. *American Agriculture: A Brief History.* West Lafayette, IN: Purdue University Press, 2002.

Jefferson, Thomas. *Notes on the State of Virginia by Thomas Jefferson.* Richmond, VA: J. W. Randolph, 1853.

Jones, Max, and John Chilton. *Louis: The Louis Armstrong Story.* Boston: Little, Brown, 1971.

Jordan, Winthrop D. *White over Black: American Attitudes toward the Negro, 1550–1812.* Chapel Hill: University of North Carolina Press, 1968.

Kebede, Ashenafi. *The Roots of Black Music: The Vocal, Instrumental, and Dance Heritage of Africa and Black America.* Trenton, NJ: Africa World Press.

Kennedy, Rick, and Randy MacNutt. *Little Labels—Big Sound: Small Record Companies and the Rise of American Music.* Bloomington: University of Indiana Press, 1999.

Kenney, William Howland. *Recorded Music in American Life: The Phonograph and Popular Memory, 1890–1945.* New York: Oxford University Press, 1999.

King, B.B., with David Ritz. *Blues All Around Me: The Autobiography of B. B. King.* New York: Avon Books, 1996.

Kolchin, Peter. *American Slavery, 1619–1877.* New York: Hill and Wang, 1993.

Komara, Edward. "Blues in the Round." *Black Music Research Journal*, vol. 17, no. 1 (Spring, 1997), 3–17.

Kostelanetz, Richard. *The B.B. King Reader: 6 Decades of Commentary*. Milwaukee: Hal Leonard Corporation, 2005.

Koster, Rick. *Texas Music*. New York: St. Martin's Press, 2000.

Koszarski, Richard. *Hollywood on the Hudson: Film and Television in New York from Griffith to Sarnoff*. New Brunswick, NJ: Rutgers University Press, 2008.

Kraft, James P. *Stage to Studio: Musicians and the Sound Revolution, 1890–1950*. Baltimore: Johns Hopkins University Press, 1996.

Kubik, Gerhard. *Africa and the Blues*. Jackson: University Press of Mississippi, 1999.

Lamb, J. Parker. *Railroads of Meridian*. Bloomington: University of Indiana Press, 2012.

Landau, Emily Epstein. *Spectacular Wickedness: Sex, Race, and Memory in Storyville, New Orleans*. Baton Rouge: Louisiana State University Press, 2013.

Lang, Paul Henry. *Music in Western Civilization*. New York: W. W. Norton and Co., 1941.

Lawson, R. A. *Jim Crow's Counterculture: The Blues and Black Southerners, 1890–1945*. Baton Rouge: Louisiana State University Press, 2010.

Leiber, Jerry, and Mike Stoller with David Ritz. *Hound Dog: The Leiber and Stoller Autobiography*. New York: Simon and Schuster, 2009.

Leinwand, Gerald. *1927: High Tide of the 1920s, a Year in Detail, a Distant Mirror of the Present*. New York: Four Walls and Eight Windows, 2001.

Lemann, Nicholas. *The Promised Land: The Great Black Migration and How It Changed America*. New York: Vintage Books, 1991.

Lemly, James H. *The Gulf, Mobile and Ohio: A Railroad That Had to Expand or Expire*. Homewood, IL: Richard D. Irwin, Inc., 1953).

Levine, Lawrence W. *Black Culture and Black Consciousness: Afro-American Folk Thought from Slavery to Freedom*. New York: Oxford University Press, 1977.

Levitin, Daniel J. *This Is Your Brain on Music: The Science of Human Expression* (New York: Penguin Group, 2006.

Lhamon, W. T., ed., *Jim Crow, American: Selected Songs and Plays*. Cambridge, MA: Harvard University press, 2003.

Lieb, Sandra R. *Mother of the Blues: A Study of Ma Rainey*. Amherst: University of Massachusetts Press, 1981.

Linn, Karen. *That Half-Barbaric Twang: The Banjo in American Popular Culture*. Champaign: University of Illinois Press, 1991.

Litwack, Leon F. *Trouble in Mind: Southerners in the Age of Jim Crow*. New York: Alfred A. Knopf, Inc., 1998.

Lornell, Kip. *Virginia's Blues, Country, and Gospel Records, 1902–1943: An Annotated Discography*. Lexington: University Press of Kentucky, 1989.

Lott, Eric. *Love and Theft: Blackface Minstrelsy and the American Working Class*. New York: Oxford University Press, 1993.

Lowenstein, Dora, Philip Dodd, and Charlie Watts, eds. *According to the Rolling Stones.* San Francisco: Chronicle Books, 2003.

Lynn, Loretta, and Patsi Bale Box. *Loretta Lynn: Still Woman Enough.* New York: Hyperion, 2002.

———, and George Vecsey. *Loretta Lynn: Coalminer's Daughter.* New York: Da Capo Press, 1976.

Malone, Bill C. *Country Music, U.S.A.* Austin: University of Texas Press, 1991.

———. *Don't Get Above Your Raisin': Country Music and the Southern Working Class.* Champaign: University of Illinois Press, 2002.

Malone, Jaqui. *Steppin' on the Blues: The Visible Rhythms of African American Dance.* Champaign: University of Illinois Press, 1996.

Marcus, Greil. *The Old, Weird America: The World of Bob Dylan's Basement Tapes.* New York: Picador, 1997.

Mason, Bobbie Ann. *Elvis Presley.* New York: Penguin Books, 2007.

Mazor, Barry. *Meeting Jimmie Rodgers: How America's Original Roots Music Hero Changed the Pop Sounds of a Century.* New York: Oxford University Press, 2009.

McCall, Emmanuel L. *When All God's Children Get Together: A Memoir of Baptists and Race.* Macon, GA: Mercer University Press, 2007.

McDonald, Archie P., and Mark David Barringer. "Jimmie Rodgers: The Singing Brakeman." In Donald W. Whisenhunt, ed., *The Human Tradition in America Between the Wars, 1920–1945.* Wilmington, DE: Scholarly Resources, Inc., 2002.

McKee, Margaret, and Fred Chisenhall. *Beale Black & Blue: Life and Music on Black America's Main Street.* Baton Rouge: Louisiana State University Press, 1993.

McMillen, Neil R. *Dark Journey: Black Mississippians in the Age of Jim Crow.* Chicago: University of Illinois Press, 1990.

McWhiney, Grady. *Cracker Culture: Celtic Ways in the Old South.* Tuscaloosa: University of Alabama Press, 1988.

Millard, Andre. *America on Record: A History of Recorded Sound.* Cambridge, UK: Cambridge University Press, 2005.

Miller, Karl Hagstrom. *Segregating Sound: Inventing Folk and Pop Music in the Age of Jim Crow.* Durham, NC: Duke University Press, 2010.

Miller, Stephen. *Johnny Cash: The Life of an American Icon.* London: Omnibus Press, 2003.

Mississippi Commission on the War Between the States. *Journal of the State Convention and Ordinances and Resolutions Adopted in 1861.* Jackson, MS: By the Commission, 1962.

Morritt, Eric. "Early Sound Recording Technology and the Bristol Sessions." In Wolfe and Olson, eds., *The Bristol Sessions.*

Moye, J. Todd. *Let the People Decide: Black Freedom and White Resistance in Sunflower County, Mississippi, 1945–1986.* Chapel Hill: University of North Carolina Press, 2004.

Muir, Peter C. *Long Lost Blues: Popular Blues in America, 1850–1920.* Champaign: University of Illinois Press, 2010.

Murray, Albert. *Stomping the Blues.* New York: De Capo Press, 2000.

Neal, Jocelyn R. *The Songs of Jimmie Rodgers: A Legacy in Country Music.* Bloomington: Indiana University Press, 2009.

Norrell, Robert J. *Up From History: The Life of Booker T. Washington.* Cambridge, MA: Harvard University Press, 2009.

Oakley, Giles. *The Devil's Music: A History of the Blues.* De Capo Press, Inc., 1997.

Obrecht, James. "Deep Down in the Delta: The Adventures of Son House, Willie Brown & Friends." *Guitar Player,* August 1992.

———, ed. *Rollin' and Tumblin': The Post-War Blues Guitarists.* San Francisco: Miller Freeman, Inc., 2000.

Odum, Howard W., and Guy B. Johnson. *The Negro and His Songs: A Study of Typical Negro Songs in the South.* Chapel Hill: University of North Carolina Press, 1925.

Oliver, Paul. *Screening the Blues: Aspects of the Blues Tradition.* New York: Da Capo Press, 1968.

———. *The Story of the Blues.* Boston: Northeastern University Press, 1997.

Oliver, Paul, et al. *Yonder Comes the Blues: The Evolution of a Genre.* Cambridge, UK: Cambridge University Press, 2001.

O'Neal, Jim, and Amy Van Singel, eds., *The Voice of the Blues: Classic Interviews from Living Blues Magazine.* New York: Routledge, 2003.

Oshatz, Molly. *Slavery and Sin: The Fight Against Slavery and the Rise of Liberal Protestantism.* New York: Oxford University Press, 2012.

Ownby, Ted, ed. *Black and White Cultural Interaction in the Antebellum South.* Jackson: University Press of Mississippi, 1993.

Packard, Jerrold M. *American Nightmare: The History of Jim Crow.* New York: St. Martin's Press, 2002.

Palmer, Robert. *Deep Blues.* New York: Penguin Books, 1981.

Parker, Nigel. *Music Business: Infrastructure, Practice and Law.* London: Sweet and Maxwell, Ltd., 2004.

Pecknold, Diane. *The Selling Sound: The Rise of the Country Music Industry.* Durham, NC: Duke University Press.

Perkins, A. E. "Negro Spirituals from the Far South." *Journal of American Folklore* 35, no. 137 (July–Sept. 1922): 223–49.

Perkins, Carl, and David McGee. *Go Cat, Go! The Life and Times of Carl Perkins, the King of Rockabilly.* New York: Hyperion Books, 1997.

Perone, James E. *Mods, Rockers, and the Music of the British Invasion.* Westport, CT: Greenwood Publishing Group, Inc., 2009.

Petersen, Richard A. *Creating Country Music: Fabricating Authenticity.* Chicago: University of Chicago Press, 1997.

Pfeifer, James Michael. *Rough Justice: Lynching and American Society, 1874–1947.* Champaign: University of Illinois Press, 2006.

Plantenga, Bart. *Yodel-ay-ee-oooo: The Secret History of Yodeling Around the World.* New York: Routledge, 2004.

Porterfield, Nolan. *Jimmie Rodgers: The Life and Times of America's Blue Yodeler.* Urbana: University of Illinois Press, 1992.

Pugh, Ronnie. *Ernest Tubb: The Texas Troubadour.* Durham, NC: Duke University Press, 1996.

Putnam, Richelle. *Lauderdale County, Mississippi: A Brief History.* Charleston, SC: History Press, 2011.

Pyron, Darden Asbury. *Southern Daughter: The Life of Margaret Mitchell.* New York: Oxford University Press, 1991.

Raboteau, Albert J. *Slave Religion: The Invisible Institution in the South.* New York: Oxford University Press, 2004.

Rand McNally & Co. *The Rand-McNally Official Railway Guide and Hand Book.* Chicago: American Railway Guide Co., 1902.

Riesman, Bob. *I Feel So Good: The Life and Times of Big Bill Broonzy.* Chicago: University of Chicago Press, 2011.

Ritterhouse, Jennifer Lynn. *Growing Up Jim Crow: How Black and White Southern Children Learned Race.* Chapel Hill: University of North Carolina Press, 2006.

Robinson, Ray. *An American Original: A Life of Will Rogers.* New York: Oxford University Press, 1996.

Rodgers, Carrie. *My Husband Jimmie Rodgers.* Nashville: Country Music Foundation Press, 1995.

Rodgers, Ward H. "Sharecroppers Drop Color Line." *The Crisis* 24, no. 6 (June 1935): 168–69, 178.

Romano, Will. *Incurable Blues: The Troubles and Triumph of Blues Legend Hubert Sumlin.* San Francisco: Backbeat Books, 2005.

Rowland, Dunbar. *Encyclopedia of Mississippi History, Comprising Sketches of Counties, Towns, Events, Institutions, and Persons.* Vol. 2. Madison WI: Selwyn A. Brant, 1907.

Roy, William G. *Reds, Whites, and Blues: Social Movements, Folk Music, and Race in the United States.* Princeton, NJ: Princeton University Press, 2010.

Royce, Edward. *The Origins of Southern Sharecropping.* Philadelphia: Temple University Press.

Russell, Tony. *Blacks, Whites, and Blues.* New York: Stein and Day, 1970.

———. *Country Music Originals: The Legends and the Lost.* New York: Oxford University Press, 2007.

Ryan, Frank. *Tuberculosis: The Greatest Story Never Told.* Bromsgrove, Worcestershire, UK: Swift Publishers, 1992.

Sallis, Charles, and James W. Loewen. *Mississippi: Conflict and Change.* New York: Pantheon Books, 1974.

Salvatore, Nick, *Singing in a Strange Land: C. L. Franklin, the Black Church, and the Transformation of America.* New York: Little, Brown and Co., 2005.

Sanjek, Russell. *American Popular Music and Its Business: The First Four Hundred Years.* Vol. 2. New York: Oxford University Press, 1988.

Scher, Richard K. *Politics in the New South: Republicanism, Race, and Leadership in the Twentieth Century.* Armonk, NY: M. E. Sharp, 1997.

Schoenbaum, David. *The Violin: A Social History of the World's Most Versatile Instrument.* New York: W. W. Norton & Co., 2012.

Schwartz, Roberta Freund. *How Britain Got the Blues: The Transition and Reception of American Blues Style in the United Kingdom.* Burlington, VT: Ashgate Publishing Co., 2007.

Segrest, James, and Mark Hoffman. *"Moanin' After Midnight": The Life and Times of Howlin' Wolf.* New York: Pantheon Books, 2004.

Shank, Barry. *Dissonant Identities: The Rock and Roll Scene in Austin, Texas.* Hanover, NH: University Press of New England, 1994.

Shapiro, Harry, and Caesar Glebbeek. *Jimi Hendrix: Electric Gypsy.* New York: St. Martin's Press, 1995.

Shea, William L., and Terrence J. Winschel. *Vicksburg Is the Key: The Struggle for the Mississippi River.* Lincoln: University of Nebraska Press, 2003.

Sidran, Ben. *Black Talk.* New York: Da Capo Press, 1981.

Silk, Catherine, and John Silk. *Racism and Anti-Racism in American Popular Culture: Portrayals of African-Americans in Fiction and Film.* Manchester, UK: Manchester University Press, 1990.

Silver, James W. *Mississippi: A Closed Society.* Rpt. Jackson: University Press of Mississippi, 2012.

Smith, Chas. *Rumble in the Jungle: The Soul of Indigenous Music in America.* Atlanta: Kendall Hunt Publishing, 2007.

Smith, Gary Scott. *Heaven in the American Imagination,* New York: Oxford University Press, 2011.

Smith, Larry David. *Writing Dylan: The Songs of a Lonesome Traveler.* Westport, CT: Praeger Publishing, 2005.

Snow, Hank, Jack Ownbey, and Bob Burris. *The Hank Snow Story.* Campaign: University of Illinois Press, 1994.

Sobel, Robert. *The Entrepreneurs: Explorations Within the American Business Tradition.* New York: Weybright and Talley, 1974.

Stanton, Andrea L. ed. *Cultural Sociology of the Middle East, Asia, and Africa: An Encyclopedia.* Vol. 4. Thousand Oaks, CA: SAGE, 2012.

Sterne, Jonathan. *The Audible Past: Cultural Origins of Sound Reproduction.* Durham, NC: Duke University Press, 2003.

Stevens, Jay. *Storming Heaven: LSD and the American Dream.* New York: Grove Press, 1987.

Stolle, Roger. *Hidden History of Blues in Mississippi.* Charleston, SC: History Press, 2011.

Strausbaugh, John. *Black Like You: Blackface, Whiteface, Insult & Imitation in American Popular Culture.* New York: Penguin Group, 2006.

Taslitz, Andrew E. *Reconstructing the Fourth Amendment: A History of Search and Seizure, 1789–1868.* New York: New York University Press, 2006.

Teachout, Terry. *Pops: A Life of Louis Armstrong.* New York: Houghton Mifflin Harcourt Publishing Co., 2009.

Titon, Jeff Todd. *Early Downhome Blues: A Musical and Cultural Analysis.* Chapel Hill: University of North Carolina Press, 1994.

Tolinski, Brad. *Light and Shade: Conversations with Jimmy Page.* Toronto: McClelland & Stewart, 2012.

Tolnay, Stewart Emory, and E. M. Beck. *A Festival of Violence: An Analysis of Southern Lynchings, 1882–1930.* Champaign: University of Illinois Press, 1995.

Tooze, Sandra B. *Muddy Waters: The Mojo Man.* Ontario: ECW Press, 1997.

Tosches, Nick. *Country: The Twisted Roots of Rock and Roll.* New York: Da Capo Press, 1985.

———. *Hellfire.* New York: Grove Press, 1989.

True, Everett. *The White Stripes and the Sound of Mutant Blues.* London: Omnibus Press, 2004.

Twain, Mark. *Life on the Mississippi.* Paris: Leipzig, Bernhard, Tauchnitz, 1883.

United States. Bureau of the Census. *Fifteenth Census of the United States: 1930. Population.* Washington, DC: Government Printing Office, 1933.

University of Mississippi. *Historical Catalogue of the University of Mississippi, 1849–1909.* Nashville: Marshall & Bruce Co., 1910.

Vose, Ken. *Blue Guitar.* San Francisco: Chronicle Books, 1994.

Wald, Elijah. *Blues: A Very Short Introduction.* New York: Oxford University Press, 2010.

———. *Escaping the Delta: Robert Johnson and the Invention of the Blues.* New York: HaperCollins, 2004.

Wardlow, Gayle Dean. *Chasin' That Devil Music: Searching for the Blues.* San Francisco: Backbeat Books, 1998.

Waterman, Christopher A. "Race Music: Bo Chatmon, 'Corrina, Corrina,' and the Excluded Middle." In Ronald Michael Radano and Philip Vilas Bohlman, eds., *Music and the Racial Imagination.* Chicago: University of Chicago Press, 2000.

Webb, James H. *Born Fighting: How the Scots-Irish Shaped America.* New York: Broadway Books, 2004.

Weissman, Dick. *Blues: The Basics.* New York: Routledge, 2005.

———. *Talkin' 'bout a Revolution: Music and Social Change in America.* Milwaukee: Hal Leonard Corporation, 2010.

Whisenhunt, Daniel W., ed. *The Human Tradition in America Between the Wars, 1920–1945.* Wilmington, DE: Scholarly Resources, Inc., 2002.

Williams, Paul. *Bob Dylan, Performing Artist 1986–1990 and Beyond: Mind Out of Time.* London: Omnibus Press, 2004.

Williamson, Nigel. *The Rough Guide to the Blues.* London: Rough Guides, Ltd., 2007.

Wilkerson, Isabel. *The Warmth of Other Suns: The Epic Story of America's Great Migration.* New York: Random House, 2010.

Wilson, Charles Reagan. *Judgment & Grace in Dixie: Southern Faiths from Faulkner to Elvis.* Athens: University of Georgia Press, 1995.

Wolfe, Charles K. "Music." In Carroll Van West, ed., *The Tennessee Encyclopedia of History and Culture.* Nashville: Rutledge Hill Press, 1998.

———. *Tennessee Strings: The Story of Country Music in Tennessee.* Knoxville: University of Tennessee Press, 1977.

———, and Kip Lornell. *The Life and Legend of Leadbelly.* New York: Da Capo Press, 1992.

———, and Ted Olson, eds., *The Bristol Sessions: Writing about the Big Bang of Country Music.* Jefferson, NC: Mcfarland & Co., Inc., 2005.

Wyman, Bill, and Richard Havers. *Bill Wyman's Blues Odyssey.* New York: DK Publishing, 2001.

Wynne, Ben. *Mississippi's Civil War: A Narrative History.* Macon, GA: Mercer University Press, 2006.

Yagoda, Ben. *Will Rogers: A Biography.* Norman: University of Oklahoma Press, 1993.

Yanow, Scott. *Jazz on Record: The First Sixty Years.* San Francisco: Backbeat Books, 2003.

Yates, Gayle Graham. *Life and Death in a Small Southern Town: Memories of Shubuta, Mississippi.* Baton Rouge: Louisiana State University Press, 2004.

Young, Alan. *Woke Me Up This Morning: Black Gospel Singers and the Gospel Life.* Jackson: University Press of Mississippi, 1997.

Zwonitzer, Mark, with Charles Hirshberg. *Will You Miss Me When I'm Gone? The Carter Family & Their Legacy in American Music.* New York: Simon and Schuster, 2002.

Newspapers and Magazines

Atlanta Constitution.
Austin (Texas) American.
Billboard.

Chicago Defender.
Chicago Tribune.
Clarion-Ledger (Jackson, Mississippi).
Guitar Player.
Kerrville (Texas) Mountain Sun.
Los Angeles Times.
Meridian (Mississippi) Star.
New York Times.
Rolling Stone.
Stone County (Mississippi) Enterprise.

Federal Government Records

U.S. Census, 1850, DeSoto County, Mississippi.
U.S. Census, 1860. DeSoto County, Mississippi.
U.S. Census, 1870. DeSoto County, Mississippi.
U.S. Census, 1880, Choctaw County, Alabama.
U.S. Census, 1880. Coahoma County, Mississippi.
U.S. Census, 1880. DeSoto County, Mississippi.
U.S. Census, 1900. DeSoto County, Mississippi.
U.S. Census, 1900. Hinds County Mississippi.
U.S. Census, 1900, Lauderdale County, Mississippi.

Web Sites

Blues Foundation: International Home of the Blues. www.blues.org.
Country Music Hall of Fame and Museum. countrymusichalloffame.org.
Mississippi Blues Trail. www.msbluestrail.org.
Paramountshome.org. www.paramountshome.org.
Rock and Roll Hall of Fame. rockhall.com.

Television Programs

Shindig! Date aired: May 26, 1965.
The Johnny Cash Show. Date aired: October 28, 1970.
The Mike Douglas Show. Date aired: February 15, 1972.

Miscellaneous Correspondence

Richards, Keith, to Ben Wynne. Undated correspondence circa 1990 in the author's possession.

Rushing, Ottis W., Jr. to Ben Wynne. Correspondence dated August 10, 2010, in the possession of the author.

Rushing, Robin, to Ben Wynne. Correspondence dated August 10, 2010, in the possession of the author.

Rushing, Tom, to Ben Wynne. Correspondence dated August 9 and August 10, 2010, in the possession of the author.

CREDITS

My Rough and Rowdy Ways
Words by Elsie McWilliams
Music by Jimmie Rodgers
Copyright © 1930 by Peer International Corporation
Copyright Renewed
International Copyright Secured. All Rights Reserved

Blue Yodel No. 9 (Standin' on the Corner)
Looking for a New Mama
Words and Music by Jimmie Rodgers
Copyright © 1931 by Peer International Corporation
Copyright Renewed
International Copyright Secured. All Rights Reserved

T. B. Blues
Words and Music by Jimmie Rodgers and Raymond Hall
Copyright © 1931 by Peer International Corporation
Copyright Renewed
International Copyright Secured. All Rights Reserved

Pistol Packin' Papa
Words and Music by Jimmie Rodgers and Waldo O'Neal
Copyright © 1931 by Peer International Corporation
Copyright Renewed
International Copyright Secured. All Rights Reserved

Miss the Mississippi and You
Words and Music by Bill Halley
Copyright © 1932 by Peer International Corporation
Copyright Renewed
International Copyright Secured. All Rights Reserved

Blue Yodel No. 12
Blue Yodel #11 (I've Got a Gal)
Whippin' That Old T.B.
The Yodeling Ranger
Words and Music by Jimmie Rodgers
Copyright © 1933 by Peer International Corporation

INDEX

influence, 4, 9, 10, 12, 13, 14, 152, 155, 156, 160, 167, 187–95, 201–3, 204, 205; music as reflection of popular tastes, 4, 6; as performer, 10, 11, 98, 99, 101, 115, 132, 147, 157–58, 161, 163, 164, 190, 193, 197–98, 204; photograph with custom-made guitar, *following p. 115*; popularity of, 150, 194, 195, 197; posthumous honors of, 198–99; poverty of, 3, 7–8; as product of times and environment, 60, 61, 167, 203; publicity photographs of, *following p. 115*, 157; and race relation, 153–54; and radio, 144–45, 159, 164, 188, 197; as railroad man, 8, 95, 98, 99–102, 104, 105–6, 108, 112–13, 115, 143, 154, 166; recorded work of, 212–16; as recording artist, 1, 5, 9, 10, 13, 86–87, 96, 102, 105, 110, 116, 117, 123, 150, 151, 152, 157, 158, 159, 160, 161–63, 165–66, 167, 187, 193, 194, 195, 204; record sales, 152, 158, 159, 160, 163, 193, 194; relationships with women, 9, 95, 99, 106, 108, 158, 162, 163, 203; religious overtones in music of, 49, 101; and Rock and Roll Hall of Fame, 203; and roots music, 14, 177, 194, 197; songwriting of, 8, 84–85, 86, 87–88, 100, 114, 132, 147–48, 153, 155, 157, 159, 164, 195, 197, 201; and tent-repertoire shows, 109–10, 111, 112; tribute albums to, 194, 201–2; tuberculosis of, 95–96, 112–13, 115, 128, 142, 143, 158, 161–62, 163, 164–66; vocal style of, 4, 96, 115, 151, 152, 156, 157, 160, 189, 191; as white bluesman, 152–54, 156–57; yodeling of, 57, 110–11, 112, 151–52, 156, 190, 191, 192–93, 197, 198, 203. *See also specific song titles*
Rodgers, June Rebecca (daughter), 111–12
Rodgers, Kathryn (daughter), 107, 163
Rodgers, Stella Kelly (wife), 106–7, 108, 163, 227n75
Rodgers, Talmadge, 93, 96, 98
Rodgers, Walter, 93, 96
Rogers, Martha Woodberry, 92
Rogers, Roy, 190–91
Rogers, Will, 161

Rogers, Will, Jr., 161
Rogers, Zachary, 91–92, 98
Rolling Stone, 203
Rolling Stones, 13, 173, 178–80, 183–85, 200
roots music, 10, 14, 177, 194, 197
Ruebush-Keiffer publishing company, 50
"Running Wild Blues" (Patton), 129
Rushing, Tom, 131–32

Schmidt, Oscar, 54–55
Schmidt, Otto, 54–55
"Screamin' and Hollerin' the Blues" (Patton), 86, *following p. 115*
segregation: and African American musicians, 66–67; and American popular music, 2–3; and black-white musical exchange, 59, 60, 100, 166, 204; in churches, 33, 36; and education, 21, 22, 23; effect on black and white communities, 5, 15–16, 26; effect on musical development, 5–6; and landowners, 70; laws governing, 2–3, 21–22, 23, 24, 26, 32, 59, 60, 61, 166; multi-layered system of, 24; racial inferiority defined by, 20; and recording business, 146–47; and social control, 23–24, 31; and white identity, 22–23
"Shake It And Break It (But Don't Let It Fall Mama)" (Patton), 89, 129
sharecropping system: and African American musicians, 66–67; and debt, 6–7, 27–28, 72, 74, 76; and economic dependence of African Americans, 6–7, 28–29; legislation supporting, 7, 28; living conditions of sharecroppers, 72–73; as means of social control, 7, 28, 72, 73; in Mississippi Delta, 6–7, 28, 72–74, 76; and John Patton, 64; and poor whites, 7, 28; as replacement for slavery, 28, 63; tenant farming compared to, 27
sheet music, 10, 118, 120, 121, 125
"Shindig!" (television show), 184–85
Shines, Johnny, 102, 173, 192
The Singing Brakeman (film), *following p. 115*, 160